A Guide to
Better Teaching

A Guide to Better Teaching

Skills, Advice, and Evaluation for College and University Professors

Leila Jahangiri and Tom Mucciolo

ROWMAN & LITTLEFIELD PUBLISHERS, INC.
Lanham • Boulder • New York • Toronto • Plymouth, UK

Published by Rowman & Littlefield Publishers, Inc.
A wholly owned subsidiary of The Rowman & Littlefield Publishing Group, Inc.
4501 Forbes Boulevard, Suite 200, Lanham, Maryland 20706
http://www.rowmanlittlefield.com

Estover Road, Plymouth PL6 7PY, United Kingdom

British Library Cataloguing in Publication Information Available

Library of Congress Cataloging-in-Publication Data

Jahangiri, Leila.
    A guide to better teaching : skills, advice, and evaluation for college and university professors / Leila Jahangiri and Tom Mucciolo.
        p.   cm.
    Includes bibliographical references and index.
    ISBN 978-1-4422-0892-6 (cloth : alk. paper)
    ISBN 978-1-4422-0894-0 (electronic : alk. paper)
    1. College teaching—United States.   2. College teachers—United States.
I. Mucciolo, Tom.   II. Title.
LB2331.J34   2011
378.1′250973—dc23   2011026506

∞ ™ The paper used in this publication meets the minimum requirements of American National Standard for Information Sciences—Permanence of Paper for Printed Library Materials, ANSI/NISO Z39.48-1992.

Printed in the United States of America

To our families who encourage us
our colleagues who challenge us
and our teachers who inspire us . . .

Contents

List of Figures and Tables

Introduction

You must learn from the mistakes of others. You can't possibly live long
enough to make them all yourself.

—Sam Levenson

A university professor is sitting at his desk, staring at a brief e-mail message
from the department chair: "Bill, your assessments came in and I noticed you
averaged 7.4 out of 10 in student evaluation. I think you are doing well, but I
would love to see you be an 8 or higher for next semester. I am confident that
this will not be a problem for you." Although Bill does have a *measurement*
of his effectiveness, unfortunately, he has no idea what must be done to
improve that level, other than try to just "be an 8." But if he knew which
specific skills to target, he would be able to better plan a self-improvement
path. *A Guide to Better Teaching* is about describing effective teaching, determining which skills to target in order to be more effective, and measuring
your effectiveness.

For many years, we have been observing the presentation and teaching
skills of a number of different groups of people from a variety of fields and
disciplines. Tom has the advantage of more than twenty-five years of interacting with industry leaders, corporate executives, and government clients. Leila
has nearly twenty years in academia, with a focus on education and faculty
development, as well as being an experienced clinician in the health care profession. From a chance meeting, we discovered that although we operated in
seemingly diverse environments, we shared a common interest in effective
presentations and effective teaching. As a department chair at New York University (NYU), Leila was hiring numerous full-time faculty members and

developing a large department. Her goal was to see growth and enhancement of the teaching in a systematic manner. Having observed Tom training major industry leaders in corporate environments, Leila asked "Why can't faculty go through the same rigor as industry leaders?" After a lengthy discussion, we noted that teaching, leadership training, and public speaking are not dissimilar and that there are many overlapping skills. We realized that an opportunity existed to merge our experiences for creating a unique faculty development program. Later that year, Tom joined NYU as an adjunct faculty. What makes this collaboration effective is that although our individual experiences are widely different, we share a common goal of finding ways to help teachers teach better and leaders lead better, and in the process, allow teachers to become leaders.

It was in the early fall of 2005 when we first collaborated to observe select groups of instructors at New York University. The whole idea behind the faculty development effort was to collectively evaluate the effectiveness of each faculty member in the pilot group, in order to improve the overall quality of teaching, and then discuss our observations. We each had a unique viewpoint on how to develop the skills in a person so that he or she could be a more effective communicator. We agreed that through observation and feedback, one could continually improve. However, we realized that this time- and resource-intensive observation process may not be practical and not a model that could be easily duplicated in other institutions or departments. It was clear that not every teacher had access to an expert or peer observer. Even if that were possible, not every instructor was comfortable being evaluated by another person on a continual basis. But beyond having a "subjective evaluator," many instructors wanted clarity on the evaluation *criteria* itself. The question became "What am I being judged on, exactly?"

The challenge for us was in finding an "agreed-upon" set of criteria that could be used to judge or evaluate a faculty. We believed that reaching such a consensus would require a student or *learner's perspective* based on preferences. In other words, we wanted to know what learners most desired from teachers. This was the start of our series of studies, interviews and analyses. Later, we examined and confirmed these learner preferences with those of experts and peers.

The research to uncover learner preferences is described in detail in this book, but to sum it up, a two-question, open-ended survey, asking what qualities students liked most and least in a teacher/presenter, was given to learners. Responses were coded and grouped according to similar relationships, resulting in the emergence of twenty-one skills or "preferred characteristics," which later led to developing a form of assessment or measurement.

The chapters and sections in this book provide a comprehensive explanation of what makes a teacher effective. However, constructing exams and evaluating students are also key components of an effective teacher. It is not within the scope of this book to provide an explanation of techniques, strategies, or procedures in the design of exams or methods for continual assessment of students. You will find that the educational literature is rich with textbooks on principles and fundamentals of student assessments.

On the other hand, our students evaluate us too! There are a number of instruments available for students to evaluate teachers, and this book identifies the most preferred characteristics of effective instructors. You can be a much better teacher when you understand the most important needs of your learners and know what elements of your skill you should improve. For the new teacher, the numerous challenges and opportunities discussed in this book offer insight into understanding how you can meet the expectations of those you teach. For the adjunct faculty, the supporting research allows you to target the specific needs of your learners while bringing your real-world experiences into your academic approach to teaching. For the seasoned professor who may have an additional mentoring role, the offered suggestions and the skills assessment tools can be used to improve the efforts of peers or junior faculty as you bring them up to the same level of effectiveness that you may expect from yourself. For those who have switched careers and entered a new world of academics, there is much to learn and this book shows you how to use your past experience to offer different perspectives that energize the group, helping learners make human connections between theory and real-world practice. What is described here is based on our findings and further substantiated by a thorough review of the educational literature in each of the skill categories. Ultimately, it is our goal to provide you with critical perspectives, suggestions, and techniques for improvement.

A Guide to Better Teaching is arranged into three sections: Perspectives, Skills, and Assessments. The Perspectives section discusses overall and generalized concepts from a learner's perspective along with our findings. The Skills section focuses on three core areas: *personality, process*, and *performance*. The personality skills help to create logical and emotional *impressions*, while the process and performance skills are *expressions* of organization and delivery. Your ability to weave these impressions and expressions into a seamlessly cohesive set of skills will enhance your overall effectiveness. As you examine each of the skills in these sections you will also notice a number of references that provide a more in-depth understanding. In addition, there are numerous tables that summarize, as well as visually oriented short stories that clarify concepts and outline ideas to help you become a more effective teacher. To recap the highlights of each of the three chapters in the Skills section, a *summary and strategy table* is provided. The Assessments section helps you determine your baseline and a means to identify and measure your specific strengths and weaknesses. For your convenience, our assessment tools are accessible online (for a free download, visit: www.rowmanlittlefield.com/isbn/1442208929). *A Guide to Better Teaching*, along with the assessment tools, aims to improve your deficient areas. Therefore, from here on, we refrain from using the word "weaknesses" and instead use "challenges" implying that you will overcome these. Eliminating challenges and further leveraging your strengths, which we call "opportunities," will ultimately lead to greater effectiveness.

SUGGESTED METHOD OF READING THIS BOOK

As you navigate through the book, you will note that the skills are discussed individually, but grouped according to functional areas. There are several cross-references, although the majority of the writing focuses on one particular skill at a time. The advantage to this format is that you can actually skip around as you read and still get the essence of every skill. This flexible arrangement of the content allows you to use this book as a reference tool, where you can randomly review a particular skill multiple times in order to develop proficiency in a desired area.

As you use this book along with the assessment tools to continually self-improve, you will enhance your abilities. You will not only be able to measure your level of effectiveness, or measure the effectiveness of others, you will understand what it takes to be an effective teacher.

PERSPECTIVES

Experience is not what happens to a man. It is what a man does with what happens to him.

—Aldous Huxley

1

From a Learner's Perspective

Retire into yourself as much as possible.
Associate with people who are likely to improve you.
Welcome those whom you are capable of improving.
The process is a mutual one.
People learn as they teach.

—Seneca

The great philosophers Socrates, Plato, and Aristotle were more than think-ers, more than teachers, they were *learners*. Their collective sage wisdom has shaped many of our current educational precepts and principles. They offered profound insights into self-knowledge and critical thinking, emphasizing that knowledge serves a practical, moral, and ethical purpose in society. What made these men such great philosophers is that they viewed the world from a learner's perspective, that is, they learned from observing life, and taught from a totality of experiences. They promoted the notion of a man as a "whole being," the sum of those parts that are moral, ethical, scholarly, and practiced. Their collective philosophy was revived into the reflection of the "Renaissance Man," someone who was more complete by excelling in a wide variety of subjects or skills such as the arts, sciences, and religion. In other words, the essence of a "complete person" was not defined by a single talent or skill, but by a total picture of a personal expression of life that had a pro-found impact on society.

Effective teachers often embrace the notion of the "complete person" by going *beyond teaching* so that learners are inspired. While the vision of hav-ing such a profound impact on a society of learners is desirable, you may be wondering how you can accomplish this. If you observe teaching from a learner's perspective, you can begin to create the *complete picture* of your teaching effectiveness.

3

The Effective Teacher

There are numerous books, articles, papers, and reports that attempt to define the essence of teaching effectiveness. The subjective nature of the term *effectiveness* opens the door to debate as to which definition is *the* definition to use. Of course, there is no single choice. In light of the myriad explanations, we believe that effectiveness can be described as *the extent to which teaching advances learning*, that is, the level at which the expertise contributes to the attainment of knowledge or skill. It may be said that from a learner's perspective, a teacher's effectiveness stems from the ability to be useful, helpful, and valuable in facilitating learning.[1] Thus, while the *act of teaching* involves skills, unless the teaching activity is tied to a learning outcome, it is not considered effective from a learner's perspective. After all, a person can teach *efficiently* by managing the environment, organizing lessons, and covering the curriculum. But if learning objectives are not met, the person is not teaching *effectively*. This distinguishes "good" teaching from "successful" teaching. It appears that good teaching is judged by standards of practice, measured against institutional norms, and focused on the task of teaching whereas successful teaching is about the longer-term achievement of learning outcomes.[2]

If good teaching is a process of communication, then successful teaching is a measurement of that process in terms of learning. However, to become a successful teacher, one must first be *good enough* to be effective. This clearly suggests that skills or abilities can be developed or enhanced to the point where a teacher can be successful in *advancing learning* toward established outcomes, thereby creating a complete picture of teaching effectiveness.

Who Should Assess?

In any educational setting the evaluation of teaching is required in order to continually improve the learning process. In fact, when dealing with a review process it is best if observations are made from different perspectives. The good news is that when a teacher is being reviewed, those observing are learners in some capacity, whether evaluating content, performance, or effectiveness. Thus, the evaluation of a teacher is done from a learner's perspective. There are many evaluative formats used to assess the level of effectiveness of instructors.[3] These mechanisms can be categorized into three major types of observations including *student* ratings, *peer* reviews, and *self*-evaluations.[4]

Student Evaluations

The most common format for measuring teaching effectiveness has been from a traditional learner's perspective in the form of a *student evaluation*, although such rating of instruction has been debated in the educational litera-ture.[5-23] However, it is generally believed that student evaluations are reliable and therefore they are considered an effective method for measuring teaching quality.[24] In most cases, students evaluate instructors across a variety of *pre-defined* skill areas and the quantifiable ratings are generally meant to help improve teaching, although the feedback is also used as part of the criteria for promotion. At times, instructors may "teach to the form" by making sure evaluation criteria are met, and this may hinder the expanded development of teaching expertise. To mitigate that challenge, another form of evaluation offers a different learner's perspective—that of another instructor.

Peer Reviews

Reviews by colleagues are considered to be another valuable method of evaluation and feedback.[25-30] The purpose of the peer review process is to assist in the development of effective teaching skills based on constructive comments from other teachers. If you are a novice instructor, or even a part-time teacher becoming familiar with the academic environment, it can be helpful to have a more seasoned faculty member observe you in front of stu-dents and later discuss with you opportunities for improvement. Peer review can become a mentoring process that allows others in your situation to share a "best practices" perspective for improving your teaching activity. Because of scheduling issues and time restraints, there may be very few opportunities to have one or more of your fellow instructors watch you. However, videos of your "teaching in action" can be recorded and reviewed at a more conve-nient time to allow multiple peers to observe your archived work.[31, 32] In the absence of peer review opportunities, there is yet another method of evalua-tion, where the learner's perspective is *yours*.

Self-Evaluations

In addition to student assessments and peer reviews, a more private method of evaluation, done through self-reflection, is a *self-assessment*. You see through your own eyes before you see through the eyes of others. It is from your personal perspective that you gain a highly realistic interpretation. Expe-rience is your "teacher" and, like a "student," you can evaluate your own learning. But, can a person truly self-assess? There are potential biases in such a scenario. Some might argue that when the judge is the self, there is a tendency to be lenient. Others argue that the self is the most critical judge of all. "I'm my own worst critic," is spoken by many who judge themselves more harshly than others might judge them. A number of studies support the value of self-evaluation as a method of measuring teaching effectiveness in academic settings.[3, 31, 33-36] Those who self-assess gain awareness of different teaching styles through personal observation (a *reflective* approach) for self-development.[33, 37, 38] The evaluation of oneself leads to an understanding of personal style, which can be compared or contrasted to other styles.

Self-assessment is more accurate when the personal review is measured against an accepted standard. How can we arrive at such an agreement? Given the diversity of learners, there surely cannot be one, single, agreed-upon standard student evaluation. When it comes to other teachers, there is not a universally accepted instrument for peer review. Yet, when we describe effectiveness as *"the extent to which teaching advances learning"* the implication is that there *is a standard* from which to measure the level of effectiveness. Yes, there actually is a standard—it's *you*! You are the benchmark from which your efficiency can be measured. You are the point of reference for how your skills can be developed. You are the starting point for assessing *your* level of effectiveness, because from a learner's perspective, in this case, the *learner* is you.

Learner Preferences

This all sounds great, but exactly what is it that you are evaluating in yourself? A self-assessment has little value if there are no checkpoints, no guideposts, or no quantifiable metrics against which self-learning can be measured. It would be helpful to know what is *expected of you*, so that you can have a target or goal to meet such expectations. When you were a college student, you knew the checkpoints (assignments), guideposts (course outlines), and quantifiable metrics (exams) for you to monitor your progress. As a result, you understood which areas needed more work so that you could make adjustments and continually self-improve toward meeting the defined expectations or learning outcomes. Yet, as a teacher, it may appear that there is no established set of guidelines or clearly defined "effectiveness" curriculum for you to follow other than your continual on-the-job experience. So how can you self-improve with few defined parameters and vague expectations of just being "better" at teaching?

Fortunately, there is a set of guidelines, which we call *learner preferences*. These are the skills that learners prefer and expect to experience from effective teachers. In other studies where learner needs were met, students performed better in achieving learning outcomes.[8, 39-45]

Understanding learner preferences helps you to identify those areas that need to be developed in order to maximize your effectiveness, as judged from a learner's perspective. This is the basis of the assessment tools in this book.

A Guide to Better Teaching is designed to help you evaluate your own level of effectiveness so that you can meet the needs and expectations of your learners.

Effective Teachers and the Learning Process

The outcome of teaching is where the students learn the taught material. An effective teacher, by definition, puts the focus on learning. Assessment of the learning process, regarding what is actually absorbed, is far more complicated, and there is an abundance of literature on this topic. In general, a direct correlation between teaching effectiveness and student outcomes is difficult to prove. While our goal in this book is to focus on ways to help instructors be more effective, we cannot claim that a higher or greater learning process has occurred just because the teachers are teaching better. Nonetheless, we can agree that a more effective teacher invariably creates a better environment for the learning process to flourish.

Getting to Know *You*

Whether you are a new teacher, an adjunct faculty, or a seasoned professor, your objective is to use this comprehensive information to analyze your own effectiveness or the effectiveness of others around you. While the book itself serves as a continual reference for understanding effective teaching and skill development, the assessment tools in this book will help you identify your challenges and track your improvement. Additionally, as an instructor, you could perform a series of self-assessments, then check your self-evaluations against a peer's assessment (from a recent observation) to see if there is any correlation.

Before you read the rest of this book, we suggest you jump to chapter 6 ("Assess Yourself," page 263), and complete your own self-evaluation using the assessment form and reflecting back on your most recent teaching experience. (The self-evaluation assessment form is also available as a free download at www.rowmanlittlefield.com/isbn/1442208929.) This will give you an initial perspective of your skills prior to reading anything in this book that may alter your impressions. *After* you read the book, we encourage you to go back and *re-evaluate* to compare with your original observations. It is possible that after reading our discussions of the skill categories you may judge yourself differently with respect to certain areas, or you may validate existing abilities, or discover characteristics about yourself that you had not considered. Your self-assessment is the process of self-reflection toward self-improvement. What are you waiting for? Assess yourself!

2

The Science Behind the Scenes

About the time we think we can make ends meet, somebody moves the ends.

—Herbert Hoover

In the fall of 2005 we embarked on a journey toward evaluating the performance of academicians from the perspective of learners. Our goal was to identify the factors that individuals believe contribute toward a better understanding of the information being communicated. To unearth these issues we decided to conduct a study. Although our initial focus was on academicians and students, we expanded the study to include those in the public domain who communicate content in a variety of learning settings such as continuing education, training, seminars, conferences, as well as distance learning and online webcasts. The purpose of our study was to identify learner preferences of effective classroom teachers or presenters.

While the concept of *classroom teaching effectiveness* semantically suggests an academic setting, the "classroom" can be any group setting, and the word *teaching* can apply to any communication of information intended for the benefit of a listener. Thus, by identifying criteria for teacher quality preferences as perceived by current and past students, the findings also apply to any communication activity involving a speaker (presenter) and one or more listeners (audience). For this reason, the role of *teacher* and *presenter* are interchangeable when it comes to communicating content to a group. Moreover, in the academic setting, the terms *teacher, professor, instructor, lecturer, faculty*, and *educator* are more common; whereas, in the public arena, the words *presenter, speaker, narrator, trainer*, and *facilitator* are most often used. In all cases, the standard view or model of communication is the same: the dynamic interpersonal interaction between a sender and a receiver of information.[1]

9

Preferences of Different Learners

To design our qualitative study, rather than creating a list of traits or characteristics from which a respondent might choose, we elected to ask open-ended questions so that participants could offer unrestricted comments. A two-question survey, asking what qualities learners liked most and least in a teacher/presenter, was given to two groups: *students* and *professionals*. A student learner is defined as one who is *required* to participate in a course. A professional learner is one who *elects* to enhance their existing knowledge by participating in a learning activity. The type of learner can be the same person. For example, an individual may be required to take a course on Microsoft's Excel spreadsheet program. This individual will listen as a student learner. The same individual, at a later date, decides to expand his knowledge base and elects to take an advanced Excel course. He will now listen as a professional learner. In each case, the overall preferences for effective teaching are found to be the same; but the emphasis on the desired characteristics of the teacher, on these separate occasions, is different.

In our initial published study, a total of 300 subjects provided 2,300 written responses to the two-question survey.[2] The original study was limited to the health care profession, using the most readily accessible groups of students, faculty, and health care professionals from the medical and dental communities. However, using indicators from the initial data in the study, we expanded the reach by conducting similar methodology, using the same two-question survey, with a vast number of diverse groups encompassing students and professionals. By expanding the research we gathered data from over 1,800 individuals, who provided more than 15,000 responses. In analyzing the responses from all of these other groups, the results were highly consistent with the published research findings, thereby increasing the confidence that this research has universal applications beyond the original subjects studied. Irrespective of the subject matter, learners are found to have common preferences for effective teachers.

Categorizing Preferences

From the collected data in the study, descriptive words within the responses were coded and grouped according to similar relationships, resulting in the emergence of twenty-one skills (characteristics), grouped into three core categories or major areas of *personality*, *process*, and *performance*, and outlined in Table 2.1. The core categories and related skills are covered in more detail in chapters 3, 4, and 5.

Table 2.1.   The twenty-one skills grouped according to the three "core" categories

Preferred Characteristics of Effective Teachers/Presenters	
Core Category	Skills
PERSONALITY	Caring
	Empathy
	Happiness
	Energy
	Passion
	Motivation
	Expertise
	Inspiration
	Self-Confidence
	Approachable
	Personal Appearance
PROCESS	Content Development
	Content Organization
	Content Design
	Additional Sense Stimulation
	Environment
PERFORMANCE	Body Language Style
	Speaking Style
	Technology
	Focus
	Interaction

The "personality" traits include eleven skills related to individual *behavior* irrespective of course content or delivery of that content. The "process" category includes five skills dealing with the organization and design of the content that is used for instructional purposes. The "performance" area covers five skills inherent in the delivery of the content. Figure 2.1 illustrates the how learner preferences of students and professionals differ in the core categories.

There is considerable discussion in the literature of each of these characteristics as contributing to or influencing teaching effectiveness based on personal traits, instructional content and the manner in which the information is conveyed.[3–11] While the terms used to describe specific attributes varies across different studies, the general reference to particular skills is similar. For example, both faculty and student perceptions of effectiveness included traits such as: encouraging, approachable, respectful, knowledgeable, passionate, enthusiastic, caring, as well as showing a sense of humor.[5, 8, 12] Teachers who develop a concise, organized, easy-to-follow topic are considered

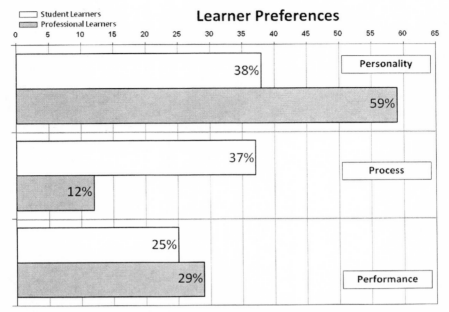

Figure 2.1.   Learner preferences of students and professionals, based on "core category" skills

helpful to learners and enhance the learning experience.[7, 13–17] An instructor who is able to make difficult or challenging topics easily understandable while managing the classroom climate is considered more effective than those teachers who have no control of the group or cannot simplify the materials.[7, 14, 15, 18–22] An educator who speaks clearly, does not drift from the topic, and openly interacts with students establishes a better learning environment.[7, 13, 14, 22–24]

These references clearly indicate that learners can recognize the quality of the teaching in terms of observable characteristics, or when expected attributes are missing. For instance, an instructor's *lack of* respect for a student's opinion, or a teacher's *non*caring attitude negatively affects teaching effectiveness because these learner preferences are *not* met.

While the presence or absence of preferred teacher qualities is significant, a closer look at the results of our research study shows that the two groups of learners, students and professionals, appear to have *different* preferences in teacher/presenter characteristics. For student learners, the skills related to *content design, content organization,* and *content development* were at the forefront of their preferences. Professional learners favored elements of speaker *self-confidence, body language style,* and *energy.* Both groups highly valued *expertise* and *speaking style.* These findings reveal that the same presentation (in both content and delivery) given to different groups of learners will yield different outcomes, based on audience preferences. Table 2.2 compares the top five (of twenty-one) preferred characteristics of teachers from the perspective of student learners and professional learners.

This research offers an opportunity to classify teachers according to the skills that appeal to particular groups for specific purposes. For example, a teacher whose skills are better suited to student learners may not necessarily be as effective delivering similar content to a group of professional learners, who would judge the presentation according to a different set of preferred characteristics.

A Self-Assessment Method

To bring the research to life, we designed an instrument to measure the effectiveness of a teacher.[25] The assessment, which you were encouraged to take earlier, can be used for both self-reflection or peer observation, evaluating up to eighty independent skills in a presenter to arrive at a measurement of a speaker's effectiveness in relation to different audience types or learners (students, professionals and a mix of both). This assessment tool and its derivatives are discussed in greater detail in chapter 6.

To further test the validity of this assessment tool, a sample of 125 volunteers were selected and subjected to our assessment and to that of an existing evaluation tool within their institution. The volunteers were from different countries. This was done intentionally in order to test the assessment tool in a variety of cultures and learning environments. Where these teachers/presenters were speaking at corporate events or meetings, the comparative evaluation criteria was provided by the conference management as the routine method of assessment. These comparative evaluation criteria/forms were

Table 2.2.   The top five characteristics (skills) preferred by student and professional learners

Top Five Preferred Characteristics	
Student Learners	*Professional Learners*
Content Design	Self-Confidence
Content Organization	Expertise
Content Development	Speaking Style
Expertise	Energy
Speaking Style	Body Language Style

diverse and did not follow a standard format. However, when findings were generalized and compared, the correlation was very strong between our assessment and the comparison. The direct analysis of this data proved to be difficult, but the participants provided valuable feedback and reported our instrument as critical in identifying areas for improvement. Our findings together with this sample analysis led directly to our formal design of the evaluation forms offered in this book.

In summary, the effective teacher is one who contributes to a student's acquisition of knowledge by optimizing learner preferred characteristics. The remainder of this book focuses on the details related to each of the core categories of *personality*, *process*, and *performance* and the skills within each area, offering you advice on how to develop each skill in order to become a more effective teacher. The last chapter, "Skills Assessment Tools," provides directions to access the electronic versions of the evaluation forms so that you can measure the level of your effectiveness and receive an automatically calculated index.

SKILLS

I am always ready to learn, although I do not always like being taught.

—Winston Churchill

3

Personality

Setting an example is not the main means of influencing another, it is the only means.

—Albert Einstein

When developing skills for effective teaching, individual qualities make all the difference. An instructor's persona shapes the manner in which content is taught and ultimately learned. As an instructor, you can gain a learner's perspective by being attentive to those attributes that students value most, while being aware of the qualities they desire least. In that regard, a view of learner comments in these specific areas is helpful. Table 3.1 outlines some of the positive or negative keywords, relative to the personality skills, as expressed by different groups of learners.[1]

The personality elements described in this chapter focus on the logical and emotional *impressions* made on learners as information is communicated. While each skill is important, the learner preferences for certain skills vary. Figure 3.1 illustrates the significance that student learners attach to each of the personality skills.

Among an identified group of personality elements, student learners express the highest preference for *expertise*, *caring*, *empathy*, and *approachability*; and, to a lesser degree, they prefer the skills of *self-confidence* and *energy* followed by *happiness*, *motivation*, *personal appearance*, *inspiration*, and *passion*.[1] As you develop your effectiveness using the skills assessment tools, any of your "personality" challenges should be addressed according to the significance noted in figure 3.1 so that you can prioritize your efforts based on learner preferences. For example, if you find that you are challenged in the areas of *expertise* and *empathy*, you should work on "expertise" first, because this is a more highly preferred skill as perceived by student learners.

17

Table 3.1.   Feedback on personality skills from both student and professional learners

Personality Skill	Feedback from Learners	
	Negative	*Positive*
Caring	has an attitude, highly critical, arrogant, sarcastic, gives negative comments	encouraging, helpful, constructive feedback
Empathy	lack of understanding, single viewpoint, no sympathy, disrespectful	shares feelings, offers personal experience, appreciative, sees multiple perspectives
Happiness	shows anger, expresses disappointment, annoyed	smiles, adds humor, fun, entertaining
Energy	looks too serious, tired, deadbeat, not lively	engaging, attentive, engrossing, excited, dynamic, spirited
Passion	apologizes for the topic, detached	likes the subject, speaks from the heart, credible
Motivation	boring, dull, uninteresting	moving, good feeling, energizing, enthusiastic
Expertise	complex, too thorough, knows too much, lightweight, little substance	knowledgeable, simplifies information, relates to the audience, command of material, connects the topics
Inspiration	(no keywords given)	want to learn more, stimulating, relevant, more than just a teacher, take-home value

Table 3.1. (Continued)

Personality Skill	Feedback from Learners	
	Negative	Positive
Self-Confidence	looks nervous, anxious, intimidated, afraid of questions	calm, in control, prepared, practiced, can think on their feet
Approachable	interrupts people, never asks for comments, discourages questions	encourages participation, allows questions, open, friendly
Personal Appearance	sloppy, improper humor, inappropriate comments	polished, professional, dresses appropriately

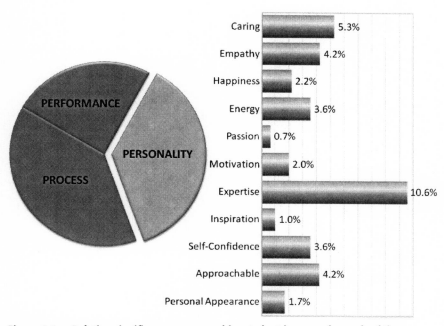

Figure 3.1.   Relative significance expressed by student learners for each of the Personality skills

A person's personality is a collection of traits that are woven together, overlapping and harmonious, blurring the lines between particular areas. We have separated the elements into individual topics for discussion to foster a deeper understanding. This separation will also allow you to work on specific skills. However, you will realize that the personality traits are interrelated. For example, an instructor who *enjoys the topic* is not only expressing a *passion*, but is also exhibiting a form of *happiness*, and is likely to demonstrate enthusiasm or a visible sense of *energy* while delivering the content. While these traits are discussed separately in this chapter, they are closely related. *Caring* and *empathy*, for instance, are about feelings; *happiness, energy, passion*, and *motivation* are forms of expression; *expertise* and *inspiration* involve logic and outcome; and, *self-confidence, approachability*, and *personal appearance* deal with presence. As you peruse the personality elements, keep in mind that the relationships are intertwined among the traits to create a whole persona, shaping the foundation of your style and influencing the skills of content (*process*) and of delivery (*performance*) that are necessary for effective teaching.

CARING

Flatter me, and I may not believe you.
Criticize me, and I may not like you.
Ignore me, and I may not forgive you.
Encourage me, and I will not forget you.

—William Arthur Ward

Caring can be described as a characteristic of one who appears genuine and sincere.[1] When evaluating a teacher, learners look for student-centered or student-oriented behaviors, including caring, friendliness, fairness, compassion, and a willingness to listen as important elements in the interpersonal context of an effective instructor.[2, 3] It is not unusual for a learner to expect this type of behavior from a teacher, especially since the teacher-student relationship is built on trust, where each brings a shared responsibility to the learning process.

The caring professor is one who supervises, guides, and attentively watches over the development of the learners. Effective teachers genuinely *like* their students and sincerely enjoy the teaching. This is the essence of caring. If we subscribe to the adage "Do unto others as you would have them do unto you," then it follows that if teachers seem to care about the students, the students will care about the class. In other words, if teachers clearly demonstrate that they have the best interests of the students at heart, then the students will likely attend class more often and listen more attentively.[4] Therefore, the very perception of a caring teacher will have a positive effect on learning.

Relative to learning, Aristotle postulated the concept of "ethos" or ethical attitude, which includes the elements of intelligence, character, and good will. The last of these is referenced in the modern literature as "perceived caring," that is, the intended good will toward the receiver. From this perception a learner judges a caring teacher as a more *credible* source of knowledge, more *competent* and more *trustworthy*, all of which contribute to a more positive learning environment.[5, 6] While caring is a personality trait and one that is difficult to define equally for every instructor, the presence or lack of caring is evidenced through visible or vocal actions. For example, a teacher who takes extra time to personally help a student understand course material demonstrates a *visible* willingness to help by being more nonverbally *immediate* (closer in proximity, available, and accessible).[7]

Beyond visible presence, an instructor can be verbally *responsive* (communicative or interactive) using other caring actions such as *encouragement* and *positive reinforcement*, the effects of which lead to an increase in a desired behavior. Conversely, non-caring actions such as making *negative comments*, being *sarcastic*, or always *finding fault* may be perceived as punitive, yet are just as visible and will only serve to reduce a teacher's effectiveness.

Encouraging Learners

There is a moment when you have to let go of the bicycle as you teach a child to ride, knowing that falling is quite possible but not necessarily inevitable. The delicate balance may come down to your simple vocal effort, such as "You can do it!" Surely you can reflect on your early school days when you brought home a paper with a gold star representing a teacher's "seal of approval" for a job well done. Be it a sticker, a checkmark, or a handwritten comment, your success story was displayed prominently for the whole family to see. Words of support can be stimulating, reassuring, and often the difference between success and failure. How often do you use encouragement in your teaching? While it is easy to offer encouragement to an already strong student, it is necessary to provide encouragement to a weaker or struggling student.

Encouragement offered by an instructor can be in the form of *praise*. It can be directed to an individual based on *effort* ("that was a good try") or *ability* ("you are very good at this"); or, the praise may be nontargeted and given to the entire group ("excellent," "that's great," etc.). As with any form of feedback, the positive nature of the comments is most preferred by learners, but general praise alone is not effective unless it relates to a specific behavior or targets a particular task.[8] Just saying "that's good" merely tells the learner that *something* is good, but nothing specific. However, the phrase, "your idea of adding an introductory paragraph to that section is a good use of the prose technique we've been discussing" compliments the learner's ability and connects the praise to the topic. When linked to a learner's ability or effort, supportive feedback demonstrates a teacher's caring attitude as being genuine and sincere.

Encouragement should serve a learning purpose and be used appropriately, yet sparingly. In fact, praising *ability* too often may lead to consequences when the learner falls short of expectations, as in the comment, "I'm surprised that you didn't know that formula." However, commending *effort* improves ability because the learner is encouraged to keep trying harder for a specific reason, as in the remark, "I am impressed with how much better you are getting at solving these equations."[9]

⚋⚋ Comparatives Are Better ⚋⚋

Whereas superlatives stand alone, signifying achievement, comparatives give the perception of something that is measured against all others, implying a degree of effort.

In the advertising world, "best" clearly implies "better," but "better" certainly means "best." This may be how truth in advertising can be sustained, as many manufacturers each want to claim to have the best, greatest, highest, lowest, easiest, fastest, and so on. Yet, how can more than one claim superiority? Because the "best" car is better than *at least one* other car, but there is no claim to being better than *every* other car.

Conversely, to claim you have the "better" of something implies a comparison to *all* other similar items, of which yours is better, and, by default, the "best." After all, the "better" one must be best because it's better when compared to all the rest!

This is why one of the advertising slogans for Bounty paper towels includes the words "Quicker Picker Upper," and not "quickest," implying that Bounty's absorbing ability is quicker than *all* other brands. Avis uses the phrase "We Try Harder" but not "hardest," suggesting that their customer service efforts are superior to *all* the other competitors.

—∾⌇∾—

When encouraging learner effort, consider using comparatives in your statements, such as "you are getting *better* at this"; or, "that is a *more* effective approach"; or, "you now have a *stronger* grasp of the concept." Comparatives imply measurement and signify effort or a move toward improvement. Superlatives may be used for specific achievements related to a learner's existing ability, such as "you scored the *highest* grade"; or, "that was the *most* important issue you brought to light"; or, "by far, this is the *best* example of your creativity."

Encouragement also has to do with teacher attention. The very fact that a professor offers supportive feedback to a learner brings focus to the learner and may serve to motivate others to seek similar attention. The sincere display of attention is from the teacher's personal perspective. For example, using lead-in words such as "I like the way that you . . ." or, "What I find interesting about your comment . . ." or "I am really impressed with your . . ." offer a personal connection to the learner. The use of the word "I" supports the genuineness of the comment.

Adding Positive Reinforcement

We often hear teachers say, "I wish my students would care as much as I do." How can you infuse into your learners the same caring attitude that you demonstrate? The perception of caring is enhanced from positive reinforcement. Yet, even though encouraging words may sound *positive*, unless behavior improves, there is no *reinforcement*. A positive reinforcement causes an *increase* in the desired behavior.[10] This book can give positive reinforcement only if you experience an increase in effective teaching.

Giving positive reinforcement is a *skill*. It must be intentionally practiced so that it becomes automatic and second nature to you. It requires a conscious effort on your part and the skill is not developed overnight. Effective teachers remind themselves continuously to foster a positive reinforcement environment. The good news is that the effect on the students is immediate. To reinforce suggests strengthening an already existing condition in a continual fashion; that is, over and over again. Positive reinforcement is a *process*, not a prize. Do not confuse reinforcement with reward. A reinforcement of appropriate behavior would lead to continual efforts to recreate that behavior over and over again. A reward for appropriate behavior can reduce motivation in the sense that once the reward is gained, the behavior (the effort used to seek the reward) may disappear. The reward can be the culmination of an achievement and not necessarily the continuation of effort.

This is not to suggest that honors, incentives, and rewards be discontinued; rather, such recognition should be reserved for individual achievement but should not be expected to contribute to ongoing group efforts. Positive reinforcement is more likely to motivate students toward reaching learning outcomes because the focus is on continual improvement, supported by a caring instructor who has the best interest of the learners at heart. Table 3.2 offers suggestions for incorporating positive reinforcement into teaching.

While encouragement and positive reinforcement give learners the perception of caring, more often than not, teachers use critique and negative feedback in an attempt to help students learn. The challenge is in how learners receive such advice, especially if it appears harsh.

Managing Critical Commentary

In general, learners view criticism as negative, but instructors can balance positive and negative feedback into a form of *constructive criticism*, which is a mix of critical observations and encouraging support.[11] As an instructor, you may prefer to avoid critique, thinking that a student may be discouraged and subsequently uninterested in learning. However, if your critical analysis is genuine and sincere (caring), not targeted with bias or malice, and leads to learner improvement or motivational effort, then the criticism is constructive. Even if the words sound critical, the professor who is able to bring a sense of fairness to educational commentary while keeping the student's best interest at heart will epitomize the perception of caring.

Table 3.2. Strategies and tactics for including positive reinforcement in teaching

	Tips for Giving Positive Reinforcement	
Strategy	Tactic	Example
Recognize RIGHT	Intermittently or occasionally find what learners are doing *right*. Then, acknowledge, commend, or draw attention to the desired behavior.	A student is making mistakes on several stages of a project. Find one stage that is correct and start your feedback with "I like the way this part worked. Can you apply the same strategy to the other stages?"
Seek SMALL	Look for minor improvements and don't expect major changes. The goal is to recognize some degree of improvement, even if the overall performance is still a challenge.	A learner consistently struggles with essay construction. If only a good introductory paragraph is produced, acknowledge it, even if the rest is still challenging.
Plan POSSIBLE	Anticipate undesirable behavior by establishing group rules in advance.	Make an agreement with the learners that a session will end 5 minutes early as long as no one is 5 minutes late. Peer pressure (influence) may increase punctuality.

For example, the following critique may be perceived as negative if openly directed at a student during class. "Based on your prior results, I am surprised at your lack of attention to detail in this project. I believe you are better than this and I expect more from you." While the high achiever may accept the assessment as helpful, other learners may find it difficult to see the constructiveness in this type of criticism, which perhaps should have been reserved for private discussion if possible. A more constructive approach might have been phrased, "It's a bit unlike you to miss some of the details in this project, especially since you outlined the strategy so clearly. I am sure you will be more attentive to these types of situations the next time you face them." The critique is tempered with support. It is in the best interest of the high achiever that the teacher be attentive to constructive improvement, by identifying both a deficiency and a skill, while sounding encouraging at the same time. However, the fine line between constructive criticism and harsh critique is very easy to cross, especially when teachers view learners in a negative light, frequently finding fault and pointing out problems.

Injecting Sarcasm and Negativity

Inappropriate behavior is not limited to learners. At times, you may demonstrate an uncaring "attitude" and your delivery style may bring out the worst in you, causing you to be sarcastic or to elicit negative comments, which in turn may adversely affect learning. Sarcastic remarks and condescending comments that degrade or belittle students are considered rude and offensive. Such negativity contributes to the learner's perception that the instructor is less caring or doesn't care at all.[12]

Learners identify non-caring teachers has having an "attitude" or as being arrogant, especially when instructors use superiority and expertise as a way of putting students down or demeaning them.[3] To justify misbehavior, some teachers think they are being funny with sarcastic comments and snide remarks, but in reality, offensiveness can be biting and harmful, especially when an individual is the butt of the joke. Inappropriate or improper comments also adversely affect your *personal appearance* as a professional educator (see "Appearing Distracting" in the "Personal Appearance" section of this chapter, page 109). Table 3.3 includes several examples of negative

Table 3.3. A collection of offensive comments made by various university instructors as reported by students

Sarcastic and Offensive Faculty Comments in Classrooms
Your comments are not helpful, so please keep them to yourself.
I really don't think you can handle this course.
I am very disappointed in you, and you don't belong here.
I can only imagine how your other instructors feel.
If you knew how to study, you would know how to pass.
I don't really think you'll amount to anything.
What makes this class so effortless—is you.
Well, well, well. Some of you actually decided to show up.
It's called reading. Try it sometime.
Too bad you can't make talking to your friends a career.
You probably use the cafeteria to study, since this classroom seems to be the place to eat.
If that is not the president on the phone, then hang up.
You're wasting my time.
The good news about your lateness is that there's less time for me to deal with your mistakes.
If someone asks what you'll be when you get out of college, tell them "forty-five."

comments that have been spoken by faculty and reported by students as being sarcastic, offensive, or abusive.

At times, negativity may appear in the form of a general tone or pessimistic view, such as a philosophical perspective or a social commentary. For example, a political science professor is leading a group discussion about universal health care and makes the following remark, "Well, this is what happens when you elect officials who are out of touch with reality. The whole system is bad! I think the country is falling apart." While it is not wrong for an instructor to offer an opinion, the negativity in the tone puts the learners into a defensive listening posture, concerned that comments made to the contrary could be rejected by the teacher, who has already made a bold and decisive statement. When negative comments become social commentary, bias becomes the focus, rather than logic. As an instructor, avoid injecting negativity into learning, especially because you are a voice of authority and your biases will bring an unconstructive influence to the environment.

Finding Fault

Are you the type of instructor who focuses mainly on learner mistakes? Do you notice what you *don't* like more often than pointing out what you *do* like? It is so much easier to look for weaknesses, than it is to work from strengths. Many professors spend more time finding fault with learners in the attempt to teach toward some level of perfection. The justification is that by eliminating errors, learners will achieve mastery. But, because perfection is impossible, the probability of failure rises and students may end up getting the impression that they can't do anything right. Feelings of inadequacy and apprehension limit active involvement, causing teachers to find further fault in learners for not participating or understanding.[13] In turn, teachers may actually force participation, selecting students who may be unprepared to provide an adequate response. Those unwilling volunteers then feel "picked on" or singled out, and their desire to be actively involved plunges. The cycle continues and the overall perception of caring disappears when students feel that the teacher is not satisfied with the group's performance.

The fear of a teacher's criticism impacts learner confidence. When receiving a fault-finding comment a learner may feel intimidated, humiliated, embarrassed, rejected or "put-down" in some way.[14] A professor's tone of voice, facial expressions, demeanor, and body language may appear uninviting and further contribute to the negative effect of the remark.[15] At times, a teacher can express dissatisfaction through silence by being completely unresponsive to a comment or suggestion, clearly implying that the learner's contribution is not valued.

⧫⧫ Stare Tactics ⧫⧫

Professor Tully teaches pathology at a large medical school. He is a tall, thin man, who wears reading glasses, which he usually slides to the very tip of his nose in order to see beyond them. But, as he tilts his head downward to stare over the top of his glasses, the appearance is quite intimidating. Typically he walks with his chest pushed forward and his hands locked behind his back, sauntering in a looming manner through the halls.

As part of his course he takes a group of medical students to early-morning ward rounds. Although most students are sleepy, Professor Tully wakes them up with one of his bone-chilling stares. He usually finds a corner where he displays a radiograph or some pathological information to the students. Without a word, he tilts his head down and gestures to each student, staring intently over his glasses, expecting an immediate list of differential diagnoses about the displayed case.

As each student offers a diagnosis, Professor Tully does not comment in any way, other than with his penetrating stare. The students can only wonder if they are on the right track or if they are close to the proper diagnosis. Afraid of saying anything wrong, the students become more focused on their fear of the professor's silent criticism than on thinking about the diagnosis.

⧫⧫⧫

In some cases, instructors who continually find fault with learners may be expressing frustration with their failed attempts at improving student performance. If you are getting aggravated because your learners are not meeting your expectations, then you will likely focus on identifying weaknesses. The better you are at finding fault, the more fault you will find. The more fault you find, the less success you will see. The less success you see, the less effective you will be. To be more effective, consider minimizing your dissatisfaction so that your comments appear constructive rather than derogatory. Table 3.4 offers alternative approaches to otherwise fault-finding statements.

The Darker Side—Uncaring

Do you ever find yourself reprimanding, correcting, or punishing learners for inappropriate behavior or other misdoings? You are not alone. It is not uncommon for teachers to give greater attention to students when they misbehave or when they fail to adhere to established guidelines and then use punitive measures to correct these problems. It is much easier to punish than it is to reinforce, especially because punishment quickly suppresses problem

Table 3.4. Alternative approaches to fault-finding statements

Saying It Another Way . . .	
Finding Fault	*Alternate Approach*
What I don't like about . . .	The part I like about your . . .
You keep missing the point.	Let's re-examine this.
That is not correct.	You may be referring to something else.
Close, but not what I was looking for.	I can see how you could interpret it that way.
Way off.	To clarify the question . . .
You obviously have no idea.	How did you arrive at that?
Maybe you should read the chapter.	Once you review the chapter . . .
This is the third time you made this error.	Perhaps we should try another method.
That part will not work.	Some of this works.
I am disappointed in you.	This work can be very challenging.

behavior. If punishment worked it would be used less frequently. However, when bad behavior recurs, teachers resort to more frequent and sometimes more severe forms of punishment, rather than addressing the underlying cause of the misbehavior.

⚞ The Sound of Trouble ⚟

Sam is a college sophomore taking a course in modern literature. He is making loud, sarcastic, and distracting comments during class. The professor stops for a moment and asks Sam to leave. The punishment suppresses the bad behavior by removing Sam, the distracting student. Yet, if Sam found the class boring and was obnoxious for that reason, then the removal serves as a reward by taking him out of what he perceives to be a bad environment, especially considering that Sam doesn't see removal as such a bad thing in comparison to the class.

In reality, Sam is *negatively reinforced* into repeating the bad behavior in order to avoid staying in a boring class. In turn, the teacher is negatively reinforced to continue using punitive measures that remove such distractions each time they occur. In addition, although the rest of the class may have "learned a lesson" that being a distraction in class is not tolerated, these learners were not problematic to begin with, and needed no coercion or warning to be on good behavior.

Did the punishment solve the problem and ensure that Sam will not misbehave in class again? If it did, Sam would enjoy the class after the first removal, having learned a lesson. But it is more likely that Sam will be bored again and his bad behavior will recur, followed by another punishment. As

Sam misses more classes, the chance of succeeding in the course diminishes. While the punishment continually gets rid of Sam, it does not offer any solution to his boredom. The teacher must find a way to keep Sam's interest in order to stem the tide of his recurring bad behavior. To meet this challenge will require time and energy on the part of the teacher. Such effort is usually not made. This is why it is so much more common to punish bad behavior than to deal with the cause.

—————

Some professors see corrective action as a disciplinary tactic. But do not confuse discipline with punishment. Discipline is training for improvement; punishment suppresses negative behavior but does not teach an alternative.[10] Rather than temporarily dismissing the problem, it is better to address the causes and find ways to manage the issue. Managing difficulty involves effort. When instructors feel overwhelmed with teaching, research, and administrative and other activities, spending additional time trying to work with behaviorally challenged learners becomes impractical. But in the larger picture of education, it is less effective to use punishment to sweep these problems under the rug; they will simply recur, worsen, or multiply if the underlying causes remain. Instructors who make the effort to help misbehaving students improve their attitude and gain a sense of responsibility will minimize recurring bad behavior and thereby reduce classroom disruptions, making the environment more favorable for learning.

Faculty should channel frustration into positive feedback instead of corrective action. This responsibility can be very taxing and time consuming, but the rewards outweigh the cost when students no longer become distracting or disruptive. The caring professor appears genuine and sincere in promoting a learning atmosphere of encouragement and positive reinforcement, cultivating a more trusting teacher-student relationship that is continually focused on the best interest of the learners.

EMPATHY

> If there is any one secret of success, it lies in the ability to get the other person's point of view and see things from his angle as well as your own.

> —Henry Ford

We describe *empathy* as a characteristic of a teacher who sees and understands from the perspective of the audience.[1] The empathetic teacher relates to the learners on an emotional level and, as a result, the learners feel that the teacher cares about them.[4] Although empathy is sometimes associated with sympathy, they are not the same from an emotional perspective. Empathy implies a shared understanding of mutual experiences, whereas sympathy relates to a feeling for someone's suffering. Empathy is akin to "putting oneself into another person's shoes," as if sharing the feeling *with* them.[16] Sympathy is recognizing another person's situation and feeling *for* them. The empathetic person has "been there." The sympathetic person has not.

⟿ Let the Third Person Be First ⟿

Professor Richards teaches a graduate course in managerial psychology. He is trying to get his students to empathize with various business situations, even though they have not had the exact experiences in their limited work lives. He tells the students that many business people make blanket statements of opinion that have little basis or evidence. According to the professor, "Unsupported assertions are usually polarizing and become sources of conflict in the workplace." To practice empathy, the professor continually tests a student's personal commitment to an unsupported assertion.

Each time a student makes an opinion-based statement that assigns blame, fault, responsibility, or accountability to a group identified only by a third-person generic name (such as "they," "them," or "those"), Professor Richards asks the student to restate the assertion using the first person (such as "I," "we," or "us") to include the student in the claim.

The professor argues that if empathy can be described as "putting oneself in another's shoes," then altering a statement about others, to include oneself, invokes a shared feeling of responsibility.

For example, suppose a student says, "They don't know what they are doing!" Professor Richards asks the student to repeat the statement using the first person, as in "I don't know what I am doing!" If the student suddenly feels uncomfortable, then he or she will likely refrain from making such unsupported assertions. A phrase like "people do this all the time" would be changed to "I do this all the time," making the statement more difficult to utter, especially when the professor points out that the person making the statement is part of the greater whole called "people" and hence, must be included. The professor's exercise helps teach the skill of empathy.

—∾∽∽—

From an educational perspective, empathy is an important communication skill because it is represents a shared understanding of feelings, needs, and ideas, even to the extent that one person is able to "imagine" the feelings of another, as if sharing them. Although learners may identify certain attributes of teachers based on the course or program of study (arts, sciences, etc.) the general personality traits (caring, empathy, happiness, etc.) tend to be consistent across disciplines.[17] For example, psychology students may expect to see more relationship-building efforts from psychology teachers, based on the course attributes, but that doesn't mean they desire less interpersonal behavior from math and science teachers.

When talking about teachers in an understanding manner, learners have been known to use phrases such as, "I can relate to him," or "I know where she's coming from," or "The professor and I really see eye-to-eye." In an educational sense, students feel better knowing that a teacher has been in a similar situation and can therefore understand the relative challenges or difficulties of the learning environment. Therefore, it is important for an instructor to recall experiences that match the current feelings of the learners.

Been There, Done That

How often do you recall experiences, or even imagine scenarios that match the current feelings of your learners? For example, if a student is having difficulty understanding a particular procedure, do you put yourself into that student's shoes and share the challenge? Or, do you treat the issue as something that the learner needs to overcome in order to master the procedure. We are not suggesting you do the work for your learners. Nor are we advocating that you let them struggle until they eventually succeed or fail in their attempts. The empathetic approach is to share the journey toward learning, even though you have already been there and done that.

A professor who is sensitive to a learner's needs is perceived as more empathetic, and in turn, more caring.[18] This sensitivity is immediately perceptible from observing an instructor's nonverbal and verbal cues, which is why first impressions are the most critical when establishing a rapport with a group of learners.[19] While body language actions (facial expressions, gestures, etc.) contribute to the overall impression given by a teacher, empathy

Table 3.5. Examples of teacher comments containing empathetic words

Empathy in Language	
Empathetic Words	*Example*
Understand	I *understand* your point.
Feel	What makes you *feel* that way?
Sense, realize, importance	My *sense* is that you do *realize* the *importance* of this.
Experience	That is exactly the *experience* I had when I was a student.
Believe, appreciate	I *believe* you can *appreciate* this to the same extent that I do.
Value	I *value* your opinion.
Perceive	Do you *perceive* this to be true?
Suppose, worth	Do you *suppose* this is *worth* trying?
Recognize, appear	We both *recognize* the predicament but we *appear* to differ in the approach.
Seem, awareness	We *seem* to share the same *awareness* of the issue.
Pleasure	It is a *pleasure* working with you.
Grateful	I am *grateful* that you brought that to my attention.
Grasp, significance	You certainly seem to *grasp* the *significance* of the problem.
Wisdom	That choice shows both *wisdom* and clarity.

is a shared experience and is mostly noticed during interaction, discussion, or other verbal discourse with learners. The actual words you say to your students can bring into play feelings of empathy, so it is important to consider language choices in dialogue. To improve your skills in the area of empathy think about choosing words that evoke *shared emotions*. Table 3.5 lists examples of empathetic phrases you may consider using during interaction with learners.

Feeling Connected

If "history is the best teacher," then it is not surprising that through your experiences you may offer a perspective or view of the world that changes how learners see the world. The perception of empathy in a teacher arises from an *emotional link*. Learners must "feel" that you are *guiding* them, rather than *telling* them. To establish an emotional connection in the current context of learning you must make an effort to see the world through the eyes of your students.

⚛ The Sign ⚛

A struggling young writer takes the same path each day to his place of concentration, the public library. One morning, the very first day of spring, the writer passes a blind man who sits with a cup filled with pencils and holds a weathered cardboard sign that says "Please help me, I am blind." The writer has very little money but manages to drop a coin into the man's cup.

The blind man says to the writer, "Royal Copenhagen?" The writer is puzzled for a moment, but the blind man continues, "You are wearing Royal Copenhagen cologne. I haven't smelled that scent for years."

The writer replies, "It's my dad's stuff. He gave me some of his old bottles of aftershave and told me I would need to smell good when I meet the publishers of my first book. But, I don't even have one chapter done and that's what really stinks!" They both laugh.

As the writer begins to walk away, the blind man says, "Wait! Take a pencil. You gave me something and I want to return the favor."

The writer says, "Oh, no, that's okay, I don't need to take a pencil."

But the blind man insists, saying, "Please, take one, it may help you write a sentence or two. You know, one well-written phrase can change someone's world."

The writer smiles, "Alright, sure," and as he takes a pencil from the cup, he says, "By the way, I noticed your sign is stained a bit from the rain and the words are hard to read now. Would you like me to fix it?"

"That would be wonderful, thank you!" said the blind man.

The writer takes a pencil and turns the cardboard over using the fresh side to make nice block letters that are easier to read.

Later that afternoon, the writer is on his way home from the library and he passes the blind man, who shouts after him, "Royal Copenhagen! Hey! Royal Copenhagen! Is that you?"

The writer stops and walks over to the blind man, "You remembered! Yes it is me. What can I do for you?"

The blind man says, "Ever since you left this morning, my cup has been overflowing with money, and not just coins, I mean dollar bills! I have never had this much attention. What did you write on my sign when you said you would fix it?"

The writer said, "I looked at the world through your eyes and wrote what I felt."

"Well . . . what does it say?" asks the blind man, eagerly.

The writer responds, "Today is spring, but I can't see it."

⌇∿⌇

Share your experiences in such a way that your students apply the lessons that you once learned to something they are currently experiencing. If a learner says to you, "I never thought of doing it that way," you can be confident that the learner has made a *connection* to your advice, as if a light bulb went off or an "aha!" moment transpired. Compare that comment with, "I will do it that way because you told me." Such a statement suggests that your "way" of doing things is perceived as a requirement, making the experience more of an imposition instead of a connection. Your effort should be to let your past experiences filter into the learner's current state without imposing. If you "push" your experiences onto the learners, they may feel that you have less respect for their personal approach to the subject matter.

A Matter of Respect

We have seen comments about teachers on student evaluations such as "doesn't respect my opinion" or "never takes me seriously" or "my way of doing things doesn't count." These statements reflect the thoughts of learners who believe that the instructor does not have a real concern for the opinions and feelings expressed in the classroom. The feeling of disrespect can arise when there is a perceived lack of understanding or empathy in situations where learners challenge the relevancy of content. For instance, suppose a student asks "why do I even have to know this?" The question may stem from a frustration on the part of the learner who may be unable to grasp the material. As an instructor, you may interpret the inquiry as interrogation, feeling as if the student is challenging your reasoning or credibility. If you are offended by the question, you will likely snap back and suddenly the shared understanding between teacher and student is strained, and your response will appear disrespectful.

Even though learning is a shared responsibility, which includes mutual respect, the teacher has the advantage of power, rank, knowledge, expertise, experience, and so many other authoritative elements that can easily make learners feel intimidated. Therefore, it is up to you to initially consider each inquiry as *curiosity* rather than contempt, in order to avoid a defensive stance that results in an offensive response. Imagine learners as novices or beginners who are naively inquisitive about the world they have yet to explore but one you have so often experienced. You can respect students by addressing concerns with logical or current perspective. In the earlier example of "why do I even have to know this?" your respectful response might be to position the information as part of a learning process that enhances knowledge; or, to clearly explain the relevancy in terms of a real-world applications (see chapter 4, "Content Development," page 124). In either case, when learners are satisfied with teacher responses the feeling of mutual respect rises.

At times, a student may be purposely condescending, obnoxious, or distracting. A disruptive learner is disrespectful not only to the instructor but to fellow students, dampening the classroom climate and creating a feeling of uneasiness. In these situations, you must use your authority to manage such misbehavior in order to show respect to the rest of the group. The needs of the group must take precedence over the personal agenda of an individual or even a teacher in order to respectfully share a more complete learning experience. The skill of empathy is enhanced through mutual understanding and respect. Table 3.6 lists several strategies that you can use to enhance empathy with learners.

If you can employ some or all of these empathetic approaches to teaching, you will widen your scope by understanding challenges from a learner's perspective.

Table 3.6. List of some strategies to enhance empathy in a teaching environment

Empathy in Action

Refer to learners on a first-name basis to build interpersonal relationships.
Encourage debate, discussion, and other discourse, allowing learners to openly express personal opinions and ideas; and "agree to disagree" if necessary.
Make the environment "safe" for sharing comments, concerns, and feelings.
Recognize that a student can be "having a bad day" just as much as you.
Treat learner questions as explorations of curiosity.
Consider timely grading of exams, papers, and other performance indicators.
Identify different learning preferences and adjust to individual needs.
Set fair and acceptable rules and guidelines early and honor the system.
Create mutual experiences that allow you to learn with your students.
Promote honesty and accept reasonable excuses for oversights or tardiness.
Allow learners to "get to know" you more personally, but professionally.
Model the behavior you expect from others.
Share responsibility for learner success or failure.
Ask "what would I do if I were a student in this situation?"

HAPPINESS

Happiness cannot come from without. It must come from within. It is not what we see and touch or that which others do for us which makes us happy; it is that which we think and feel and do, first for the other fellow and then for ourselves.

—Helen Keller

We describe the skill of *happiness* as a characteristic of someone who evidently enjoys teaching.[1] Are you noticeably happy when you teach? While learners appreciate your enjoyment of teaching, our research uncovered a number of comments that observed happiness from a *missing* perspective. It's not that learners expect happiness; rather, they detest unhappiness in an instructor. In other words, it is easier for others to see the lack of joy in you than it is for them to expect your excitement. The emphasis is on evidence and there are a number of articles in the educational literature that identify the value, effect, and learner preference for an instructor who genuinely enjoys the teaching and makes an effort to bring that joy into the classroom though happiness, humor, and other nonverbal or tangible actions.[2, 19–24] Because learners prefer your expression of happiness, you owe it to yourself to identify the elements of your teaching that you truly enjoy.

If someone says "I am so happy to be here!" wouldn't you expect to see the expression of that happiness manifest itself in some way? Perhaps the person smiles, raises the eyebrows, laughs, or offers some evidence of the joy. From a distance, the appearance of happiness should be evident. Can people actually perceive the joy in you while you teach, or do they only notice the lack of it?

⟿ The Serious Comic ⟿

Brent is a professor of sociology at a large university in the Midwest of the United States. I met Brent at a social function, a dinner to be exact, the night before I was to observe him teaching to his undergraduate students. At the dinner, he was relaxed, funny, interactive, and he appeared to have a personality that anyone would enjoy.

The next day, while observing him with his class, I noticed a different Brent. He spoke well and had command of his topic, but was quite reserved in his delivery style. He did not use any of the personality traits that I had enjoyed seeing in him the prior evening. I was perplexed.

After his session, I asked him, "Would you say this was typical of the way that you teach?" He listened as I elaborated, hinting at the personality differences in him that I observed from the night before versus the current day's class.

Brent became a bit defensive and said, "Of course there's a difference! Obviously, I can't be myself with the students. This is a serious topic!"

〜〜〜〜

Some may argue that there is no room for levity, humor, or fun in the classroom; rather, it should be strictly business or purely data driven. This is not to imply that education should be taken lightly, but studies suggest that happiness is an *emotional expression* that is conducive to learning. In fact, there is clear neurological evidence that learning is only possible through an emotional investment, because thoughts and emotions are biologically connected.[25, 26] It is not surprising, then, that learners feed off an instructor's happiness by finding an emotionally meaningful connection to the material. If the teacher likes teaching, and that happiness is evident, then the students will like learning.[4] The evidence of joy humanizes an instructor and reveals a wider spectrum of his or her personality.

Certainly, colorful personalities do have an advantage. If someone is witty or humorous, they can use that vibrant personality to enhance learner engagement. However, if someone is not innately funny, they shouldn't try to be. The goal is to be genuine and natural, letting your own version of your happiness appear. In some situations, you may have to work on this skill, especially if your reputation carries a serious tendency. Once a reputation is created, good or bad, it may be difficult to alter it until the next cycle of students. For example, a professor who initially is seen as being very serious and perhaps known to be "distant" will have a harder time in future encounters with the same students to be perceived in any other manner. Such a reputation can eventually change by concentrating on the opportunities associated with this skill of happiness, such as smiling or incorporating humor.

What's Missing Is Quite Obvious

Most people can recognize the degree to which you *are* or *are not* happy. Happiness is one of the easiest personality attributes to read, especially because it is one of the six universal emotions (happiness, sadness, fear, surprise, anger, disgust) that are visibly perceptive in expressions.[21, 27, 28] Similar to other outward expressions, such as energy and enthusiasm, a teacher's happiness can be seen through concrete visible actions, such as body language and vocal tones.[29] Moreover, an instructor's enjoyment of the teaching is linked to student satisfaction, motivation, and learning.[30]

While the presence of personality characteristics can add value to the learning experience, the absence of joy can have an equal but opposite impact. When we looked at trends as to why students didn't attend certain classes, the reasons were more related to the professor's lack of personality, in part due to the perception of some unhappiness in teaching, rather than simply the student's limited interest in the topic itself.[3]

Proximity is important in judging the appearance of happiness. In a larger classroom the students might see just a portion of your body, perhaps only your hands, parts of your face, and possibly your smile. The distance may limit how clearly your expressions of joy can be seen, and your vocal tones or choice of words may be more significant in conveying feelings of happiness. However, in a small classroom setting, where the proximity is closer, it is very easy to perceive whether you are happy about being there. If students sense that you're unhappy about teaching, then it follows that they will be unhappy about learning from you. If you're distracted, upset, disgruntled about giving this class, or bored of making this presentation multiple times, then it's almost impossible to have the same impact as if you were in a better mood.

If you're not having a good time *teaching*, then how can anyone have a good time *learning*? This does not mean that you have to tell jokes. Remember that learners more easily recognize the lack of happiness in an instructor, that is, the *missing* component, supporting the apparent contradiction that when a preferred characteristic is not visible, the students can see it.

Showing Anger or Disappointment

As an instructor, one of the challenges to the happiness factor is when you show anger or disappointment during a lecture or discussion. Keep in mind that showing "anger" does not necessarily mean being angry at anyone in particular. The type of anger we're talking about is more of a frustration than anything else, sometimes referred to as "lecture letdown." In fact, faculty frustration is more obvious in small group settings where the instructor is closer to the learners. The local proximity highlights the nonverbal behavior to the point where the smallest of facial expressions (frowns, squinting, or widening of the eyes, etc.) are clearly visible.

The outward display of anger or disappointment is dictated by temperament, where some professors effectively manage the anger or disappointment better than others. In fact, instructors have differing responses to anger based on the level of *emotional intelligence*.[31] Regardless of how you manage your feelings, the ability to control your emotions is critical in trying to maintain a healthy learning environment, especially when dealing with negative emotions such as anger or disappointment.

There are many classroom situations where one can see evidence of such negativity. For example, based on a reaction to attendance, some professors begin a lecture in a punitive manner. At the outset, the instructor says, "The last time I came to give a lecture nobody showed up! I know I'm preaching to the choir here, so where is everybody else?" The reality of that punishing remark is that "everybody else" represents the group of students who *are not* in the classroom and therefore not hearing that remark. Sadly, it is those who showed up that are penalized and the learner reaction is to perceive the teacher as less empathetic and more non-caring. Instead of expressing happiness toward those who chose to attend, the professor shows disappointment regarding those who are absent. This negative tone immediately resonates with the existing group and the learning environment is compromised.

Even where the topic is very important to learners, if you start a class in a visibly negative manner, students will become defensive, apprehensive, and participate less often. This will prevent them from learning openly about the topic. Avoid ultimatums. Reconsider harsh statements or punitive actions that would upset the students, and be conscious of behavior that would put learners on guard.

At times, you may find yourself dissatisfied with a particular topic. Possibly you've given the same lecture many times and now you're bored with the material. Or, you have been assigned a topic that is of little interest you. Or, perhaps you have a group of students who appear to have no interest in the topic at all. Or, maybe you're just tired. Any of these reasons may cause you to deliver the content in a way that makes you appear angry or disappointed. The frustration may be visible in the phrases you choose. For instance, you might say to a group of learners who appear less than attentive, "Now look! It's bad enough that I have to teach this stuff, the least you people could do is listen!" Or your irritation may be more subtle and closer to personal disappointment in the teaching, saying, "I understand this topic is not really that interesting but it's something we have to learn." While the phrase is empathetic in tone, the implication is a shared feeling of unhappiness.

You may unknowingly place an unrealistic expectation on learning with a comment such as, "This topic is extremely complicated and so difficult to explain, that I really need to have your undivided attention." A learner will immediately think "even if I try my best, I probably will never master these concepts, because here is an expert giving the presentation who is having a hard time making it simple for me to understand." Instead, in anticipation of what you consider to be a challenging or a boring topic, start with a positive statement such as, "I am delighted to see you here and let's see how we can simplify this topic together!" As an instructor, you need to offer opportunities for learning, not set the group up for failure.

Be aware of how you approach student performance on material you've already taught. Your initial reaction can set the tone for anxiety in the students. For example, suppose you begin the lecture by saying "I'm disappointed that none of you did well in your exam." This statement puts the entire class in a defensive posture, especially because many of them will feel responsible in some way for causing the disappointment in you. All you really did was identify a problem, as if you had no part in creating it. But, as a mentor, a guide, a teacher, you are an integral part of the learning and therefore an integral part of the outcome. In fact, using self-reflection you might ask yourself "how effective was my teaching?" We are not suggesting that students are always the most responsible learners, but to determine where the problems lies, see if your stronger learners are experiencing unanticipated difficulties, and if so, you may need to revisit your teaching process on that topic. Ultimately, learning is a shared responsibility.

Don't feel that you can never express feelings of dissatisfaction. You can reserve a disappointing comment for a more appropriate moment that matches the discussion, as long as you find a way to offer a solution or alternative. For example, at a certain learning point in a mathematics discussion, the professor says "I was surprised at how many of you chose to apply different equations to many of the similarly structure-based problems on the exam. I thought about that and I identified the issues, so I think we should spend a few minutes reviewing this to allow me to clarify certain points." While the professor is expressing unhappiness with the outcome, the tone shifts to one of surprise rather than disappointment, the action focuses on self-reflection, and the solution offered is built on sharing, not grounded in blame.

We share your frustrations and your legitimate disappointments in "less than ideal" students. We, too, frequently encounter these situations, but over the years we have observed and realized that expressions of these negative feelings with students are very counterproductive. Let off some steam privately with colleagues and not publicly with learners.

Comments, especially negative ones, should be offered in context, related to something specific, and must always carry a solution or strategy toward some positive outcome. This will enable you, as the instructor, to focus on solving the problem rather than complaining about it.

Avoiding Lecture Letdown

It is critical that before you start a presentation or just before you go into the classroom you mentally prepare yourself for the session. This preplanning or mental preparation is something that very few instructors do before they give a lecture, lesson, presentation, or seminar to *students*; but, this preparation is what they often do when they are in front of *peers* in continuing education programs, or at outside conferences. If you are like most, when speaking to peer groups (professional learners), you may experience subtle palpitations, a bit of excitement, and possibly a degree of apprehension or worry as to how you will best perform. This slight "anxiety" actually helps you to focus and prepare far in advance for the presentation. But if your everyday classroom lectures are taken for granted, your level of "happiness" will be much lower.

One way to overcome this "lecture letdown" is to review our skills assessment tool immediately before your session. Identify *no more than three items* (challenges and/or opportunities) that you plan to address in the upcoming lecture. This proactive approach to teaching will force you to mentally prepare for the topic, knowing that you have to address the skill elements that you identified. For example, in this category, *happiness*, let's say you decide to concentrate on the single opportunity "smiles." Before walking into the classroom, your mental preparation is to plan a story or scenario related to the topic, that when delivered allows you to emotionally recall the joy in the story relevant to the teaching. This advanced planning forces you to think about what you will say and how you will say it. However, if you just assume that the "perfect story" will suddenly appear at a moment's notice, then you are setting yourself up for failure.

Using Self-Reflection

One key to maintaining happiness is in adequate self-reflection. At the end of each lecture, session, or course, the effective teacher reflects by thinking "what should I have done differently?" This leads to continuous self-improvement and fosters a progressive and contemporary curriculum filled with novel approaches for optimal learning outcomes. If you decide to give an illustration, perform a demonstration, or conduct a "memory-anchoring" activity; or, if you intend to use multiple analogies, case discussions, or even plan to temporarily go off topic—at some point, analyze the learning benefits. Ask yourself, "Was that activity effective?" This will allow you to self-assess in the attempt to self-improve, even though the improvement could be minor. Just keep in mind that your efforts to try different things or incorporate new activities are subject to the time constraints of the lecture. Think of this as a "commercial break" where you allow yourself no more than two minutes of experimenting with new ideas or classroom interactions, for each hour of lecture. While there is no one recipe that fits all, you can maintain your level of happiness by using self-reflection to find the joy in each moment of teaching.

Expressing Joy

The characteristic of happiness is clearly evident by the appearance of an action common to all cultures called *smiling*. From a verbal perspective, the use of humor further fuels the happiness and tends to extend the smile to the rest of the learners. Your joyful attitude as an instructor should be evident because such happiness can stimulate the learning in your students, especially when they perceive the joy in your teaching. It is important that you offer tangible evidence of your happiness so that your students can validate the perception of your enjoyment. What better way to do this than to smile?

Beyond words, the presence or absence of a smile may indicate approval or disapproval, because a smile is part of nonverbal behavior. Studies show that teachers are judged more positively by students when nonverbal behavior is communicated in a positive manner.[12, 15, 19] A smile helps communicate the intention behind content through a nonverbal path, indicating a joy in sharing the subject.

Three Dimensions of a Smile

Not every smile needs to be overt. There are different ways to smile as a means of expressing happiness. The types of smiles are: *outside*, *in-depth*, and *inside*.

The *outside smile* is with your mouth, and it is reactionary to either your own words or to the words of others, expressing happiness, indicating joy, and appearing obvious to everyone. In most cases, the outside smile reveals the teeth and may even expand to laughter.

The *in-depth smile* is with your eyes, a window to your soul that engages people in a willing belief of your own beliefs. Some call this credibility, others call it charisma, but we prefer to call it convincing. The in-depth smile is sometimes revealed when the eyes widen for emphasis.

The *inside smile* is with your heart, revealing your personal stories and heartfelt experiences that somehow relate to the given discussion, linking emotion to content. Usually this feeling is accompanied by the outside smile or the in-depth smile.

If you can use one or more of these smiles, periodically during your teaching, you will be more effective. But, the most effective type of smile is one that is natural.

⌇⌇ Fixers of the Outside Smile ⌇⌇

In January of 2005 I was asked to coach an international group of "Global Speakers" who were preparing for a major conference later in the year. My efforts took me to seventeen different countries to work with selected speakers who were eventually gathered for last-minute rehearsals a few days before the conference.

The group shared a common interest—they were all dentists. They were clinicians, technicians, and some academicians, in disciplines from prosthodontics to periodontics and everything in between—these were professional presenters and experts in their field.

The slide designs were impeccably crafted, with magnificent, vivid photography in crisp, contrasting colors displaying depth, clarity, and just the right of amount of supporting text to explain but not overwhelm the viewer. Their expertise was, without question, evident in a plethora of well-thought-out cases, concepts, and creative expressions. Their planned interactions with the audience were to be directed flawlessly with tact and precision, carefully managing discussion and dialogue while moving the presentation toward defined learning objectives. In short, these were superb speakers, the cream of the crop, the masters of the moment! There was only one little problem— none of them ever smiled.

With everyone collectively in the arena, I said to the entire group, "I don't believe this! Not one of you has smiled in any of these presentations! You're dentists! You sell teeth for a living!"

To which one voice in the back softly replied, "Yes, but not our teeth."

To this day, whenever I coach dentists, getting them to smile, is . . . well . . . it's like pulling teeth!

—∽∾∾—

Developing a Natural Smile

The more natural smile occurs when you connect the outside smile to the in-depth or inside smile. Focus on an internal action, one that by its very nature will cause you to smile. One type of internal action is emotional recall. Recall a positive experience and then relay that memory openly, your nonverbal behavior will respond naturally to the expression. Storytelling is the most common example of emotional recall. When preparing a lecture, seminar, or presentation, consider adding two or three uplifting scenarios or perhaps some inspiring life situations and relate them to the topic. These stories or anecdotes can be woven into the teaching at appropriate times to support learning objectives. Some may consider the storytelling a digression, but the connecting of abstract concepts with real-life scenarios adds a greater dimension to the learning, and this does not have to be time-consuming. Keep in mind that your perspective (positive or negative) on the experience will be evident in your expressions and will affect a learner's level of interest.

Studies show that teachers with a more positive view of humanity (a happiness) use nonverbal *communicative acts*, which encourage student involvement in classroom interaction, while teachers with a negative view of humanity (an unhappiness) tend to use nonverbal communicative acts, which discourage student involvement.[32] This suggests that the degree of optimism or pessimism in a teacher will affect learner participation. So, whenever possible, look on the bright side to encourage involvement.

Regardless of the type of smile, there are a number of significant observations regarding the way facial expressions are interpreted. For example, smiles are reciprocated (returned) predictably; observers can tell whether someone's facial expression reflects real or feigned (faked) enjoyment; someone's smile can affect the mood of the observer; gaze can express emotions; and smiles can signal attentiveness and involvement.[23] In essence, the smile you bring to the presentation is both noticed and interpreted. But, you need to smile *naturally*. Somebody who tries too hard to smile is perceived much differently than someone who is *natural*, where the smile becomes an unconscious action while focusing on teaching and interacting with the learners. If you say to yourself, "I have to remember to smile," then your connection to the act of smiling is superficial, that is, not from the heart. If a smile lasts throughout the *entire* presentation, then it will completely lose its effect. Sustained emotions lose their effect after some time, especially when there are no contrasting emotions for balance. A smile gets noticed mainly because there are moments where the person is *not* smiling.

Incorporating Humor

"Many a truth is said in jest" is a common perception of the truth in humor. Comedy is best when delivered with timing and based on reality. Proper delivery creates a simultaneous response. Circumstances, rooted in reality, link the head and heart to the expression of sincere emotion. In essence, humor is only effective if you are confident in the delivery and you are able to make the humor relevant and appropriate. However, there may be times where your belief that something is "funny" is far from the truth. When humor is used inappropriately, there is an adverse effect on learner perception of you as a trustworthy, caring and reliable authority.[33] This is discussed in more detail later in this chapter (see "Using Inappropriate Humor," page 111).

The educational literature is filled with studies that support the use of humor as a learning enhancement for retention of information, especially in courses that students "dread" or find particularly challenging. Using humor in a presentation has both psychological advantages (reduces stress, lowers anxiety) and physiological benefits (stimulates circulation, relaxes muscles), all of which enhance the learning atmosphere.[33, 34] Humor further improves the learning environment by making a class more enjoyable.[34] Researchers have also noted that "appropriate and timely humor in the college classroom can foster mutual openness and respect and contribute to overall teaching effectiveness."[35]

There are many different kinds of humor, including spontaneous remarks, jokes, skits, and games, each of which can be included in classroom activities, discussions, problem solving, and even exams. For example, a professor might teach a complex topic using an interactive game of questions to make the learning "fun." While students appreciate the entertaining nature of learning, this is not to say that students prefer an entertainer for a teacher. Our research shows that expertise and content-related elements are significantly more preferred as characteristics of an effective teacher than the use of humor. However, it is the *combination* of characteristics, including the use of humor that adds value to the effectiveness of a teacher.

The best kind of humor is if the students can, through the humor, remember the content. Humor has been shown to aid in the retention of information based on *incongruity*; that is, a disconnection between current thought and some alternative view.[36] In a lecture, the predominance of non-humorous content *contrasted* with humor creates a momentary mismatch that focuses attention on evaluating the contrast, allowing for retention (storing) of that information. This is one of the ways that learning occurs. Humor alone, or in *silo*, will have little or no effect because there is a lack of contrast. However, if you are quick witted, and you can plan or improvise by connecting humor to the current topic, you can use the incongruity for a learning purpose.

Stretching the Rubber Band

Incongruity, or a mismatch of information, can trigger the retention of specific details. Many satirists, humorists, and other comedic personalities purposely "stretch the truth" by contrasting reality with some type of absurdity to generate humor. Imagine the humor as a stretched rubber band, which can then be snapped back by using a contrasting reality to affect long-term memory.[36] This emotional shift in tone, from reality to absurdity and back to reality, can be effective in "teaching a lesson." One way to use humor is to strategically place a humorous comment, or story, or a light-hearted discussion, *immediately before* an important learning point. The contrast between what is funny and what is serious draws attention to the difference and increases the retention of the concept.

Practice Makes Perfect

Ad-libs or spontaneous, humorous remarks create an informal learning environment.[20] But not everyone is improvisational or witty. Unless the individual has a very high level of skill and confidence and can improvise well, the humor must be *planned*.[33] Planned humor usually works because there is extra attention devoted to practicing the delivery of the material. More rehearsed content increases retention, especially when the humor is used to illustrate important concepts.[36] This practicing ensures that the humor is accurate and *well-timed*.

But this does not mean that planned and practiced humor will appear unnatural or fake. On the contrary, the more something is repeated, the more comfortable one gets in repeating it. You can use the *same* humor over and over with *different* groups, because each group is listening for the first time and reacts in a natural manner, thinking that you created the humor on the spur of the moment. Even though you may have been telling the same humorous story for years, the natural response from a new group of listeners makes the content sound fresh, as if you had improvised it on the spot. Interestingly, the damage of failed humor will equally enhance memory but in the form of a *negative response*.[36] The incongruity from a bad joke invokes a contrast in the same way that a funny comment does, only with a negative result. Thus, if you just can't tell a joke, we strongly suggest you avoid improvising, and put off the choice of incorporating humor.

The essence of happiness in teaching is evidenced through facial and vocal expressions that can make learning a pleasant experience. A genuine smile and a sense of humor are characteristics that learners prefer to see in teachers. The fun in learning is a result of your happiness in teaching, especially when you make education enjoyable for you and your learners!

ENERGY

I studied the lives of great men and famous women, and I found that the men
and women who got to the top were those who did the jobs they had in hand,
with everything they had of energy and enthusiasm.

—Harry S. Truman

In the educational sense, we describe *energy* as a characteristic of one who
demonstrates a liveliness in sharing knowledge.[1] While the previously discussed concept of "happiness" relates to the innate joy in teaching, the issue
of energy is more focused on the physical expression of that joy, in the form
of an outward enthusiasm and a visible willingness to convey information.[3]
An energetic delivery of content is appealing to students and teachers, each
having similar perceptions as to the importance of energy as a teaching skill,
and both valuing enthusiasm as being critical to the classroom experience.[37]

From a wider perspective, terms related to energy, such as enthusiasm,
liveliness, vigor, and excitement, can be collectively viewed as part of *motivation*, in the sense of a teacher's desire or incentive to engage learners in a
stimulating manner. While we will discuss learner motivation in a later section, an instructor's motivation is reflected in the level of energy used to
communicate. Thus, the skill of energy as a teacher's expressiveness is characterized by something tangible and visible that learners can judge.

What motivates a teacher can be *selective* or *collective*. If you are motivated by the subject matter, you may find that certain topics within a course
are more interesting to teach than other topics. As a result, the learners may
perceive an inconsistency in your varying levels of "selective energy" associated with changing topics. At times, you may be more vigorous in delivering
content that excites you, creating a level of engagement that learners welcome
and relish. Your being excited about the "selected" subject matter will motivate you to teach to that level of interest, perhaps creating more interaction
and discussion in order to stimulate thinking on the part of learners. This will
further fuel your own enthusiasm about the subject. Yet on other occasions
you may find a topic boring and your energy level will wane. You may mud-
dle through the content and offer little opportunities for learners to participate
in any meaningful discussions.

In a similar way, selective energy may be related to the group rather than
to the subject matter. Some professors bring a heightened sense of enthusiasm into the classroom simply because of the high caliber of the learners,
such as might be found in an advanced course or honors program. The students themselves can be intellectually challenging to the professor, inspiring
more thought-provoking issues while teaching in a more energetic manner.

While enthusiasm in any lecture is desired, the inconsistency of selective energy is difficult for students to reliably predict.

Rather than picking and choosing those topics or groups that you find most interesting, if you are motivated by the "act of teaching," then you will bring a *collective* level of energy into every learning situation, regardless of the topic or the group, helping you to maintain a consistency. Learners can reliably predict the type of behavior you will bring into the classroom each day and this facilitates the understanding of content. The evidence suggests that when the energy is tied to the act of teaching itself, both teachers and students report that such enthusiasm allows for more stimulating and effective instruction.[38]

Regardless of cause or reason, the presence of energy in an instructor is beneficial to the learning environment.[37] The challenge to educators is avoiding situations where enthusiasm is perceived to be missing.

Looking Less Lively

The appearance of enthusiasm or the lack of it can be seen in the facial expressions and the body language.[21, 23, 27, 28] Similar to happiness or joy, energy is perceptible, making it easy for learners to realize when energy is missing. Thus, if you tend to *look too serious*, or you frequently *look tired*, the learners will perceive this as a lack of energy and they may think that you are less interested in the teaching.

Many faculty that we interviewed believe learners have greater respect for an instructor who appears more reserved while delivering expertise and fostering knowledge. But by restricting expressions, emotions are suppressed and energy stays locked inside. In our experience, this commonly observed phenomenon is what we call "losing yourself by teaching," where a professor believes that he or she must maintain a stoic style when teaching in order for learners to appreciate the seriousness of the topic. But, when you *look too serious*, the more natural parts of your personality are negated or masked and you will be less likely to inject humor, fun, or lighthearted comments, which can provide contrasting emotional moments that breathe life into a lecture, seminar or discussion. The natural (unforced) act of smiling, discussed earlier, is one way to overpower a "too serious" look. Another approach is to counter your seriousness with learner liveliness. The energy in your students is at your disposal. Consider adding more interaction and discussion to your teaching and the participation level of your learners will rise, injecting a youthful energy into the environment. In many cases, this dynamism is contagious as more and more learners feed off the energy of those around them.

Invariably, it will be difficult for you to curb your enthusiasm when the entire group is energized.

There will be times when you may have the desire to deliver content with vitality, vim, and vigor, but your demeanor or physical state is just not cooperating. In other words, the mind is willing but the body is not. No matter how hard you try, you just *look tired*. Clearly we have all had days where the trials and tribulations of everyday life take their toll and keep us from looking or feeling our best. How many times have you been "under the weather," possibly sick or physically exhausted, and still went to work? Under those circumstances, you can be energy-challenged and it may be evident to others that you look drained. For the most part, learners are forgiving when instructors are clearly not feeling well, especially if those teachers are normally energetic or lively. But, if a professor is continuously exhausted or visibly worn-out all the time, then the learning atmosphere will be less desirable. For example, after several interactions with you, learners adapt to your pattern of behavior and are quick to notice if you repeatedly appear less than enthused, especially when there is a recurring lack of energy. In these situations, you may be experiencing a deeper level of fatigue that could be associated with poor health or nutrition. Or, you may be burning out.

When Energy Matures

Energy can prove distracting if it swings to different extremes, from a heightened level of enthusiasm to a somber sense of reality, each of which may be related to the *length of time* that one has been teaching. The feeling of elation or bliss is one extreme of energy, typically associated with newly appointed faculty who tend to embrace the opportunity to guide learners in a very exciting way. That feeling can eventually dissipate as familiarity with the teaching role sets in and, over the course of time, the once overtly energetic instructor may begin taking teaching "for granted" and become disinterested, lethargic, or even exhausted. Has this happened to you? If your "get-up-and-go" just "got-up-and-went" then you may find yourself not looking forward to your next class, your next semester, or even your next year.

When you ask long-standing professors if they bring the same sense of excitement to their teaching as they did early in their careers, the answer for many of them is "I don't really think about it." They later admit to having become more self-critical over the years. By then, the teaching became routine and mundane as they matured in the profession, causing them to "drift" while teaching. *Maturity drift* can be defined as being carried along by circumstances to the point of teaching aimlessly, without sufficient focus or self-reflection. When left unchecked, this drift may develop into teacher *burnout* which is essentially a deterioration of an instructor's ability to teach effectively, mainly characterized by stress, emotional exhaustion, and frustration.[39] Teachers may feel overburdened by the work itself (courses, meetings, administrative tasks, etc.); or, instructors may become cynical about the profession, becoming indifferent to the act of teaching. Studies have shown that burnout is actually a manifestation of teacher temperament, an emotional state that is affected by the emotional labor of the profession, and that some instructors are able to deal with burnout in a variety of ways in order to stay motivated.[40]

As the exceptional or "gold-standard" teachers mature, they find ways to avoid burnout by not making the teaching mundane or routine. They learn to overcome the ever-present *maturity drift* that plagues their colleagues by continually creating a new environment or a new sense of excitement, whenever possible. Sometimes, rediscovered eagerness stems from simply having a new group of students, elevating the instructor's desire to create a learning impact, ultimately creating a visible expression of energy and vigor associated with effective teaching.

If your enthusiasm is being affected by burnout or maturity drift, then find *visible* ways make changes to seminars, or discussions by tailoring each topic to that unique environment, to that particular group, and to those individuals within that group. It's as if each class is new beginning, a fresh start in some way. You can become a more effective, gold-standard teacher by using novel approaches as a way to continually sharpen your skills, while maintaining a positive outlook which sustains your energy and enthusiasm, class after class, semester after semester, and year after year.

Engaging Learners

Some may expect an energetic person to be animated and very full of life, but actions do not have to be excessive for someone to be seen as lively. The perception of a professor's enthusiasm is often seen through *nonverbal immediacy*, where instructors demonstrate emotional *intent*, such as excitement, to appear more accessible.[41] The combination of an instructor's personal investment in the content along with the positive expression of enthusiasm contributes to teaching effectiveness.[38] This underlying intent to share knowledge, when done in a lively manner, creates a greater level of interest in the learners, keeping them *engaged*, *awake*, and *attentive*. But what strategies can you employ to boost your own energy level and create the engagement you seek from learners? Table 3.7 outlines ways that you can elevate your enthusiasm, raise energy, and keep learners interested in the learning experience.

Table 3.7. Selected methods for increasing an instructor's energy level and the associated skill area

Strategy	Skill
Use positive reinforcement to promote desired recurring behavior. You will experience excitement when you see positive reactions from learners.	Caring
Express understanding for students concerns, mistakes, shortcomings, or failures, while adding personal experiences to bring the real world into the classroom. The "sharing" of feelings will be uplifting and dynamic for you.	Empathy
Incorporate humor and fun activities relevant to the learning. The planning and timing needed for effective humor will require a heightened level of energy in delivery.	Happiness
Demonstrate your belief in the topic. If you show that you enjoy the subject, your enthusiasm will be perceived by your learners, stimulating their interest in the content.	Passion
Find very simple ways to explain complex ideas. It is motivating to realize that your learners are "getting it" and this validates your teaching efforts.	Expertise
Offer the opportunity for personal guidance, tutoring, mentoring and additional help that enhance the social aspects of the learning experience. Your availability will increase your commitment and enthusiasm for teaching.	Approachable
Arrange content that flows logically and smoothly. Learners stay attentive as they follow along more easily and you will be more enthusiastic about teaching an organized topic.	Content Organization
Manage the use of time effectively and tell stories to give life to information. It takes energy and creativity to completely cover a topic in the time allotted while weaving in the art of storytelling.	Content Development
Add photographs of people to slide content to create an emotional link to information. Learners are more engaged when images of people in action or situations are visibly associated with content. The effect may be overt or subliminal.	Content Design
Incorporate audio or video to enhance concepts, especially where inspirational elements can be infused into the learning. Multimedia stimulates the senses, and the *production quality* creates an energetic display that keeps the learners more engaged, awake and attentive.	Additional Sense Stimulation

Table 3.7. (Continued)

Strategy	Skill
Create a learning environment with little or no distractions (cell phones, chattering, bad behavior, etc.). This will keep learners attentive and allow you to spend less energy on managing disruptions.	Environment
Use gestures to describe concepts or to invite interaction. The actions of the body require more energy. Consider adding movement and depth to vary proximity and animate the body, but not excessively or to the point of distraction.	Body Language Style
Vary the pace and pitch of your voice. The fluctuations in tone create a more lively sound in your words and perk up the ears of the listeners to give the perception of higher energy.	Speaking Style
Do not digress or drift from the topic. If you are mentally distracted, you will waste energy and time trying to make content flow smoothly.	Focus
Create an atmosphere for interaction, discussion, and dialogue to give learners a chance to outwardly express themselves with you and with other students. This adds to the energy in the room, compounded by lively discussion, motivating you to manage the responses.	Interaction

An energized teacher energizes students. Enthusiasm is sparked by an inner motivation or desire and fueled by the energy needed to sustain continued interest on the part of the learners as well as in the teacher. While learning is shared responsibility, enthusiasm requires individual effort. It is important that you, as an instructor, make such the effort to add life to your teaching. But you must be self-motivated. You have to *want to teach* in order to have the energy to teach the *way you want*.

PASSION

> The essence of teaching is to make learning contagious, to have one idea spark another.
>
> —Marva Collins

Educationally speaking, we describe *passion* as a personality characteristic of one who believes in what he or she is presenting.[1] From a wider perspective, an instructor's overall belief may be in the profession itself, as in "I have a *passion for teaching.*" In fact, when it comes to the act of teaching, evidence of passion is observable across multiple activities and related to other personality elements, such as in a teacher's happiness ("I *like* teaching"), energy ("I *am enthusiastic* about teaching), and inner motivation and identification ("I *am* a teacher). This further exemplifies the interrelationship of the personality characteristics in a teacher who, as a whole, can be described as a *passionate individual.* In other instances, passion can be observed in isolated situations. "I love teaching *math*" is a typical way that a teacher may describe a passion for the topic. Whenever your belief in the content is strong, apparent, determined, and committed, learners will be able to identify your passion for the subject.

Whether your passion is for the profession or for the topic makes no difference to learners, because the perception of your passion is not distinguishable according to type, only from observation. In fact, studies show that when teachers are perceived as having passion for teaching or for a teaching activity, learners experience positive outcomes.[42] However, if you lack passion, doubt yourself, apologize for being unprepared, seem unclear, and show no enjoyment of the topic, you lead learners to feel that your belief in the teaching or the subject matter is missing, and your credibility will be at risk. Students trust in your ability to be persuasive, convincing, and true to life. Falling short of such expectations may cause learners to have less faith in the reliability of your comments, opinions, ideas, and other statements. After all, if you don't believe in what you are saying, how can the learners believe it?

Maintaining Credibility

In the instructional process, a teacher's passion (belief in the content) is the foundation for credibility. In other words, the manner in which information is expressed by a teacher must be trusted and considered reliable by the learners. The good news is that learners already ascribe a level of authority and expertise to an instructor or anyone perceived to be in control of the content.[3] Therefore the teacher begins with an existing level of credibility and there is no need to establish it because it is already there. However, the effort is in *maintaining* that credibility. When a teacher is perceived as being credible, the effect on learners is *positive* in terms of teacher-student interaction, as well as in overall classroom learning.[6] The educational literature describes factors that contribute to an instructor's credibility, mainly character, competence, and caring.[4, 6, 41, 43] The combination of these elements further illustrates the interrelationship among many of the personality traits described in this chapter. A teacher's credibility is not only reflected in *passion* (character), but related to *expertise* (competence), as well as to *caring* and *empathy* (caring). As an instructor, there are a number of ways you can increase your credibility with learners. Table 3.8 outlines ways to display your enjoyment of the topic, demonstrate your passion, and maintain your credibility.

Table 3.8. Different ways to increase credibility with learners

Being More Believable		
Objective	*Approach*	*Practice*
Develop affinity	Share information	Encourage participation, treat learners equally, listen attentively to comments, reveal personal experiences, be available "outside the classroom"
Create immediacy	Be accessible	
Be argumentative	Challenge learners	Ask both easy and tough questions to stimulate thinking; use expertise to demonstrate competence; react to learner requests in a timely manner
Become assertive	Display confidence	
Be responsive	Appear approachable	
Take control	Handle disruptions	Manage compulsive communicators; establish agreed-upon rules and guidelines; deal with misbehaviors
Express optimism	Critique constructively	Use positive vocal tones; focus on what learners do correctly; reinforce good behavior; avoid sarcasm, negativity, and fault-finding
Be prepared	Appear organized	Outline topics in advance; connect concepts seamlessly; don't try to cover too much material; use technology effectively and in moderation
Stay focused	Limit learning objectives	
Add value	Simplify content	Tell stories, use illustrative examples, create real-world analogies; teach to what learners already know then expand; make the subject relevant

Avoiding Apology

Inherent in passion, and related to the competence component of credibility, is a teacher's *commitment* to the content.[6] To believe in what you are teaching, you must demonstrate "ownership" of the information, both philosophically and intellectually. It is not uncommon to feel less passion when teaching in subject areas where you do not believe that you are an expert.[44] Yet learners see you as an authority and deem you to be a credible and trustworthy source of information. If there is any perceived doubt in your level of confidence in the content, the learners will judge you as less reliable. One way in which teachers express a lack of commitment to the topic is through *apology*.

⁓ So Sorry! ⁓

Harry Wexler, a physics instructor, is asked to substitute for a colleague at the last minute by his department chair. "Harry, I have John's lecture here, will you just do me a favor and give it, since he is away next Monday?" Harry reluctantly agrees. As he walks away, he is feeling overwhelmed and frustrated, and he has never seen John deliver this topic. Harry knows the content, but has never formally given this lecture before.

Harry reviews the material and finds there is nothing unfamiliar in the content. The next Monday, Harry begins the class by saying "I'm sorry, but Mr. Tinsdale is out today and I will be covering this topic for the first time. I apologize if I don't know the content like he does, but this is not my lecture."

Upon hearing the apology, the learners will perceive Harry as a less reliable source of this information. Immediately, the class knows that Harry cannot possibly be enjoying the session. Moreover, without realizing it, Harry has likely reduced the level of interest in the learners.

⁓

Never apologize for your lack of familiarity with the content. There is no reason to ask for forgiveness from those who have never granted you permission in the first place. The learners have no control over your ability, nor do they expect to see weakness in your approach. Moreover, by announcing your anxiety you will bias the listeners who will look for any signs of your struggling with the material. The learning atmosphere needs to be clear of obstacles. Avoid adding your own apprehension into the situation, even if you are feeling less than confident with the content.

One of the better ways to appear more comfortable with material that you find challenging is to focus on the bigger picture. The overall subject matter, that is the course or program of study, may correlate with your passion for meeting specific learning objectives. For example, those who teach humanities or philosophy may be focused on developing higher-level thinking skills, whereas in math and science the objective may be to teach facts and principles, while in business courses the goal may be to prepare learners for a career. If your overall objective is clear in your own mind as to what you truly believe you want to accomplish, and you are consistent in your belief in achieving that learning objective, then you will focus on the higher-level concepts associated with the given subject or lecture.

This wider perspective will be easier for you to manage, allowing you to express more philosophical views and general concerns, rather than specific details or facts, many of which may not be in your immediate recall. Your connection to the bigger picture will ignite a passion that will be immediately perceptible to the learners, and help stem the tide of any apprehension you may be feeling for the specific topic.

Enjoying the Topic

Beyond credibility is the perception of the learners that you truly enjoy the topic. While we discussed "joy" in terms of happiness, enthusiasm, and energy, your inner or *central* joy is expressed as a core belief in the content. Learners do not have to believe in the content; rather, they only need to believe in *your belief* in the content. This core conviction is at the center or heart of your delivery, demonstrating your enjoyment of the topic. But how do you express this joy? There are several ways to tap into your belief in the content, depending on how the learning is "centered," that is, whether the focus is on your own experiences and opinions, on group interactions and discussions, or on a specific learning activity. Table 3.9 outlines three different ways that learning can be centered in order to maintain the enjoyment in teaching the topic.

Is there a link between your enjoyment of the topic and the students' enjoyment of you as a teacher? Yes. Learners perceive your joy in teaching as a positive learning experience. In reality, students "like" a teacher who enjoys the topic, and the "likability" factor has been linked to learner performance.[45] When someone likes you, it stems from a shared feeling of similarity (likeness) as in "having something in common," which is described in the literature as an *affinity*.[46] It follows that if you are well-liked and students are learning better, then you will continue to pursue affinity-seeking efforts that make the learners keep liking you. These efforts stimulate learner engagement by promoting positive reinforcement and mutual cooperation in order to share the joy in the topic, thereby demonstrating a true passion for teaching.

Table 3.9. Centered learning from different perspectives, focusing on related processes

	Paths of Knowledge	
Perspective	Process	Practice
Teacher-centered	Instructor-led action, prepared in advance and delivered didactically, where information is "pushed" to the learners	Lectures, information, outlines, experiences, opinions, stories, analogies, examples
Student-centered	Group-directed behavior based on problem solving to stimulate thinking, as information is "pulled" from the learners	Interaction, participation, discussion, role playing, debate, question-answer, audience response system, online learning
Learning-centered	Task-oriented or activity-based exercises that increase social networking and collaborative skills, where information is "shared" among learners	Individual or group assignments, tasks, projects, labs, group presentations, team-driven competitions, games, debates

MOTIVATION

> The task of the excellent teacher is to stimulate "apparently ordinary" people to unusual effort. The tough problem is not in identifying winners: it is in making winners out of ordinary people.
>
> —K. Patricia Cross

Energy, enthusiasm, and vigor are necessary elements for a *teacher* to bring life into learning. Yet, one of the most common questions asked by educators is "how do I motivate my *students*?" We describe *motivation* as a characteristic of one who instills a sense of enthusiasm in learners.[1] Our previous discussion about energy focused on your inner motivation as an instructor, but what can you do to stimulate your learners? How do you instill a sense of enthusiasm into the minds and hearts of those you teach?

The word motivation literally means "to move," implying some type of energetic action toward *doing* or *getting* something. When students have an incentive (motivation) to learn, they are more enthusiastic about accomplishing the learning task. The literature focuses on different types of motivation. Some learners are driven by an *internal* (intrinsic) desire, others are stimulated by *external* (extrinsic) matters, and some are *not motivated* (amotivational), having lost the enthusiasm for learning.[47–50]

Internal (intrinsic) motivation is expressed by intense involvement, deep interest, and high levels of concentration.[51] More specifically, internal motivation is based on the *enjoyment* of an activity. For example, a learner may be engaged in a science professor's lecture because he or she *likes* science and finds science-related topics to be interesting. At times, internal motivation may be personal, as in having a general interest in an area (sports, politics, etc.), or the motivation may be based on a situation (project, group activity, etc.). Regardless of the source, internal motivation is a function of autonomy or individual (internal) control. The incentive to perform a task rises as a person feels more in control of the process. As an instructor, you can instill a sense of enthusiasm in your learners by giving them more choices or greater control of activities, tasks, discussions, and other educational processes that allow individuals to personally connect with content in meaningful ways.

When there is less autonomy available to a learner, outside influences can become incentives. *External* (extrinsic) motivation can be fueled by perceived value, such as a reward for achievement (honors, recognition, etc.). Sometimes the external motivation is derived from financial support, such as in those who academically compete for scholarships or grants. In other cases, the external motivation may be self-induced where a person forces him- or herself to be motivated, such as a learner who asks to do on an extra-credit assignment and has to meet a deadline for its completion. Or the external motivation could be self-regulated even though it is not fun or exciting, such as an exercise or diet program to lose weight in order to participate in a team sport. The closer the motivation is to being internalized (intrinsic) the more self-discipline it takes to maintain the motivational desire. This is why it is easier to require that learners attend class (external motivation) versus hoping that they will attend because they enjoy the class (internal motivation).

As an instructor, external situations may appear to be out of your direct control, but are clearly within the scope of the learning environment. For example, a professor preparing students for national exams has no influence on the test design but can instill a sense of enthusiasm in the learners by offering a preparatory course. The external motivation for the learners is the reward of passing the national exam, and, as a result, the professor is likely to have a group that is engaged, awake, and attentive in the course. Keep in mind that this external motivational strategy may be short-lived and may not lead to a motivated lifelong learner.

When there is no internal or external motivation, a learner is considered unmotivated, or *amotivational*, and may appear disinterested or bored even to the point of behaving in distracting ways by being sarcastic, cynical, or indifferent in the approach to the subject.[47, 48, 50] Unmotivated learners cannot suddenly make a leap to being internally motivated; but, small steps toward success are the key elements to internal motivation.

⌦ Diary of a Motivational Sequence ⌫

Doreen is a sophomore enrolled in a liberal arts program at a large university. She has not declared a major and is undecided as to what she would like to do. One of the classes that she attends is Professor Kane's fine arts course in Roman architecture. The professor notices that Doreen has little interest in the subject and, at times, she makes sarcastic comments and jokes, which are considered distracting.

Doreen is an example of a student who is unmotivated. Professor Kane sees this and, rather than give up on Doreen, chooses to introduce stages of motivation to help Doreen become more interested in the topic.

First the professor asks Doreen to partner with another student to complete a joint project. This external motivation can be a mild form of *outside* pressure, especially because a fellow student (peer) is involved in the effort. Next, Doreen is given a choice of completing an assignment by either submitting a printed report or by giving an oral presentation. This type of external motivation is *self-determined* (based on her choice) and creates self-pressure.

Doreen chooses the oral presentation and soon realizes that she needs to create support visuals to help her deliver the content more effectively. The external motivation is now more *self-regulated* because Doreen has made a personal decision to add a design component to her work, which is time consuming and not exactly fun.

After her presentation in front of the class, although she has not developed a love for the subject, she clearly enjoyed the reception she received from fellow classmates. In time, this will lead to internal motivation as a result of her progressive success.

Although Professor Kane was not able to internally motivate Doreen, by using levels of external motivation as the stepping stones, he has designed a *pathway* for her to go from not being motivated at all to gradually becoming internally motivated.

⌒⌒⌒⌒

If you find a number of learners who appear unmotivated, consider changing your routine to match the varying levels of interest in the group. By providing independent, individualized learning opportunities (self-determination) where possible, students may feel empowered to take more control of the topic and thereby become more motivated, leading to positive reactions from those who may initially appear disinterested in the topic.[52]

Beware of Boredom

In a hallway conversation, you may have overheard a student say to a classmate, "This course is soooooo bor-rrr-ing!" Then, as the student followed you into the room, you realized that the comment was about *your* class! Many teachers have heard students complain about dull or uninteresting courses with the word "boring" surfacing as the all-encompassing description for something that is undesirable. Some learners see boredom as a task or activity that is devoid of energy, lacking stimulation, disconnected, relatively lifeless, and apparently empty.[53] We can argue that because education is a lengthy process, routines become commonplace, allowing boredom to set in at some point. It is not surprising, then, that learners find ways to avoid boredom by finding other interests, such as doodling, text messaging, surfing the Internet, sleeping, or overtly disrupting the class by being obnoxious, striking up side conversations, showing up late, or not attending.

Sometimes, students handle boredom by creatively "imagining" alternative circumstances that increase motivation to overcome the boring situation.[51] For example, a medical student is completely bored in an anatomy class, but he knows that attendance is mandatory. So, to cope with the boredom, he writes down a number on a piece of paper, looks at a diagram of the circulatory system in his textbook, and proceeds to count the blood vessels in each finger to see if the total is close to his written guess. By making an imaginary game out of the anatomy lesson, the student becomes more involved in this *boredom-coping activity*. The motivation to "play" and try to "win" increases, and this offsets the boredom.

While a boredom-coping activity may not enhance learning, it can help deal with the issues that are at the root. Boredom results from a lack of attention and a disconnection. Effective teachers find ways to overcome learner boredom by creating attention-getting *activities* that connect to learning. Table 3.10 lists comments learners use to describe boring situations and ways that instructors can address these issues.

In addition to activities done during class, boredom can be addressed at the start or at the end of a session. For example, you can "pre-screen" learners at the very *beginning* of a lecture by analyzing what students know about the topic before teaching it. Support materials, such as slides, that are planned and designed conceptually allow flexibility as to how detailed the discussion will be at any point. In this way, you can teach to the level of knowledge derived from the pre-screening process. At the *end* of a lecture, you can plan enough time for a *rapid recall* activity, by asking "what was the single most important thing you learned today?" Some or all of the learners can participate in this exercise, depending on class size. If you make this a recurring theme, students will adapt by listening more attentively during class, knowing they will provide feedback at the end. Another way to stimulate thinking is to use the *inquiring minds* activity, where you ask, "What questions are on your mind, that are still unanswered?" These attention-getting scenarios help students connect with the content by being more engaged in the learning. In addition, you can use the feedback from the class to bridge concepts and make better connections to the next topic.

Although boredom may be related to lack of stimulation or a disconnection, keep in mind that learners may be bored or disinterested for other reasons. For example, too much technology in the classroom, such as an instructor's high reliance on PowerPoint, results in less interaction and fewer opportunities for learners to use critical thinking skills. When there is "nothing to do" because the slides are doing everything, students can become disinterested and bored. In some cases, a teacher's boredom may translate to the learners, as in "I am bored teaching students who don't want to learn." If the teacher is bored, surely energy and enthusiasm will be missing and the learners will be less stimulated to stay interested. At other times, a student's personal issues may be causing a lack of interest and these include: substance

Table 3.10. Typical learner comments about boredom and methods for addressing the problem

Busy Battling Boredom	
Learner Observations	*Instructor Actions*
"My teacher is monotone and just reads the slides."	Practice breathing exercises, take more pauses, project to the back of the room; add physical movement and gestures to increase energy; maintain eye contact with the group, paraphrase content; remove full-sentences or wrapping bullets from slides, create interaction to allow a variety of vocal tones.
"There was nothing to do in class, so I was bored."	Build activities, tasks, discussions, and group interactions to give students "something to do" beyond listening; consider more active involvement such as games, debates, and other learning-related projects.
"I finished my project quickly so I had nothing else to do."	Consider letting those who complete tasks sooner to leave early (if not needed) or allowing them to help others (if not disruptive to the learning).
"I get bored when I have no idea what the teacher is talking about, especially when it is way over my head."	Simplify concepts using stories and examples; create interaction and dialogue by prompting learners with easy-to-answer questions to identify knowledge levels; teach to what students know, then build from there.
"The professor says the same thing over and over again, and I already know it."	Avoid repetition of the content in the same form by choosing alternatives, such as questions, slides, multimedia, debate, and other activities; challenge learners with discussion-oriented questions, allowing new ideas and comments.
"I am bored when I can't relate to the topic."	Create real-world analogies that are relevant to the learners; increase participation with interaction and discussion especially focused on concepts and learner opinions.

abuse (drugs or alcohol), lifestyle choices, stress, exhaustion, attention-deficit disorder (ADD), and other problems that are unrelated to the subject matter or the teaching style.

Sometimes learners lack motivation because they think they can't achieve positive results or they suspect that there are forces beyond their control that keep them from succeeding in class. Certain events can be de-motivating, such as failing an exam, or being forced to work on a project with someone, or being pressured into making a class presentation. These situations can cause feelings of incompetence that stem from a lack of self-confidence and, if compounded, may lead to *academic burnout* (not teacher burnout), which is a complete collapse of motivation in all educational areas.[47] In these situations, a learner can get exhausted from the stress of trying to succeed; may become indifferent (cynical) about the value of staying in school; or may feel a lack of personal accomplishment and, as result, stop participating in class, increasingly arrive late, incur excessive absences, fail to complete assignments, miss exams, and ultimately withdraw from the course.

As an instructor, it is important that you recognize the underlying issues or circumstances that cause learners to lose motivation. Effective teachers demonstrate sensitivity to learner progress by *caring* enough to take an active interest in the growth and development of the students.[54] While you may not be able to rescue every unmotivated student from the dangers of academic burnout, you could be the last hope for those who are on the edge, about to withdraw completely from a course, a program, or a complete education. You might be the external motivation that generates a positive reaction in learners who might otherwise give up.

There is also a very small group of learners who are bored because they are exceptional and your level of teaching is too slow, too simple, or unimaginative. Don't be too quick in dismissing this group, because they are often the outliers and leaders of the future. Thomas Edison, Albert Einstein, Steve Jobs, and Mark Zuckerberg are among this group, but they are not always such recognizable names. Although these brilliant minds don't learn in conventional ways, you can stimulate them and become an integral part of their education.

Generating a Positive Reaction

Motivation is the impetus or driving force behind effort. Those who believe that they can and will perform well are self-motivated to do well. One of the strongest motivators is self-confidence, that is, an inner belief in a successful outcome. In addition to self-confidence, there are a number of other factors that can motivate learners, including: self-control of the learning process, collaborative relationships with peers, interesting academic tasks, personal connection to content, expectation of positive outcomes, and clearly defined goals.[48] Table 3.11 illustrates different motivational opportunities that you can use to generate a positive reaction in your learners.

Table 3.11. Suggested techniques for stimulating learner motivation

Motivational Opportunities	
Principle Facts	*Strategy*
Motivation increases when the content is relevant to the learner.	Poll the learners to assess relevancy. For example, "How many of you have had this experience?" When concepts are immediately applicable they are immediately interesting.
Motivation is enhanced when the learner can relate the material to what they already know.	Don't teach in silo. Understand where you fit in the overall curriculum scheme. For example, be familiar with the topics covered previously by others and topics that will follow yours.
When the learner feels competent, motivation rises.	Design your learning materials from simple to progressively complex. The game show *Who Wants to Be a Millionaire?* does this by asking a few easy questions at the outset. This strategy allows the participant to feel more competent and thus boost the motivation.
Active participation shows evidence of motivation.	Encourage interaction and expand discussion opportunities (see *Approachable*, page 96 and see also chapter 5, *Interaction*, page 242).
Problem solving stimulates learners better than fact finding.	Refrain from all-fact lectures and assure assignments involve problem solving. Embed necessary facts within case discussions to enhance relevance.
Positive reinforcement is motivating.	Recognize RIGHT, Seek SMALL, Plan POSSIBLE—use any or all of these tactics (see table 3.2, page 25).
Control of an activity by the learner is motivating.	Create alternative learning activities for the same content and allow student to choose. For example, giving report options of print, video, or presentation.
Student-centered behaviors enhance motivation.	Show compassion, empathy, caring, friendliness, and a sincere willingness to listen.
Negative behaviors can suppress motivation.	Avoid pessimistic remarks, nonconstructive criticism, fault finding, intimidating humiliation, or other comments that put down learners.

While there are a number of ways you can instill a sense of enthusiasm into the minds and hearts of your learners, motivation is also a function of how connected learners feel to you and to the topic. It is important that your students like you and like what you are teaching. When there is an *affinity* or shared positive feeling for your teaching, learners are motivated to study; interact; participate; and remain engaged, awake, and attentive in the process.[46]

It is clear that learners do not seek out boring, uninteresting, unenthusiastic teachers, especially if the prospect of such can be avoided. The popularity of numerous emerging online ratings of instructors is testimony to how quickly and broadly learners actively share impressions of faculty with other learners. We are not suggesting that you alter your teaching to conform to individual opinion or group consensus, but you cannot expect your students to be motivated if they are unhappy, bored, or otherwise distracted by your teaching.

Although learning is a shared responsibility, the ability to motivate learners is a proactive effort that must begin with you.

EXPERTISE

Education is a lifelong experience.
Experience is a lifelong education.
Education plus experience equals expertise.

—Michael Bugeja

In teaching, *expertise* is a process or a journey toward a destination called learning. The expert teacher navigates learners along the path of knowledge by making complex ideas easier to understand. We broadly describe expertise as characteristic of one who logically explains and simplifies the materials.[1] However, such a generalized description merits an expanded discussion in order for you to fully understand how to develop expertise and how to use it effectively. It is important for learners to see you as an expert because you represent a reliable source of information. If the students do not think that you are competent as a teacher, then your credibility is at risk. When credibility suffers, learners lose interest, boredom sets in, energy and enthusiasm wane, and the motivation to learn disappears.

The skill of expertise is intertwined with many of the other personality traits that help keep audiences engaged, awake, and attentive. The goal is to use your abilities resourcefully in order to grow, develop, and become a more effective teacher. In that regard, the very notion of "developing" expertise suggests a continuum from novice to expert, similar to how anyone might build a skill. Therefore, the fact that expertise is a *process* allows a continual honing of this skill throughout your teaching career.

The literature defines expertise in a variety ways and it appears that the characteristics of experts, as outlined in table 3.12, revolve around the dynamic relationship among the core elements of *knowledge, experience, problem solving, talent,* and *context.*[44, 55–61]

The general characteristics of an expert are similar in teachers as they are in other professions.[44] From an assessment perspective, learners lack the experience to identify particular "expert" characteristics, preferring instead to make very general observations about a teacher's level of expertise in the classroom.[1] If students feel that they can follow along in a given topic, they are likely to perceive the instructor as having a knack for teaching. This increases learner self-confidence and motivation, helps students reach a deeper understanding of the subject, and results in higher levels of achievement.[44]

The "Know-What" and the "Know-How"

Part of your expertise is derived from having in-depth knowledge in knowing *what* to express and in knowing *how* to express it. That knowledge can be

Table 3.12. Characteristics of experts according to core elements of expertise

	Understanding Expertise
Core Element	Expert Characteristics
Knowledge	• Focuses on specific subject area for comprehension of content • Widens exposure to related subject areas • Confident and competent regarding teaching all aspects of the subject area • Understands subject matter extensively and deeply • Sets challenging objectives for learners • Simplifies complex topics • Adds stories, examples, and analogies to support concepts
Experience	• Requires time to develop (5–10 years) • Develops automatic (routine) processes for repetitive functions • Recognizes learning patterns quickly • Reads learner habits and cues easily • Shares accumulated personal experiences • Maintains composure and manages emotions • Develops self-reflective techniques to improve
Problem Solving	• Analyzes slowly but solves more quickly • Views problems qualitatively, not quantitatively • Embraces new problems as exciting challenges • Uses adaptive techniques to solve new problems • Applies in-depth analysis • Logically explains ideas • Connects ambiguous points • Makes informed decisions • Focuses on results
Talent	• Flexible planner • Adapts to diverse learners and varied situations • Deliberately practices to overcome limitations • Improvises easily • Monitors learning and offers constructive feedback • Knows the audience • Displays passion for teaching • Respects learners • Reliably predicts learner results
Context	• Adjusts to workplace conditions • Constrained by increasing tasks and responsibilities • Manages learner misbehavior • Sensitive to classroom climate • Handles institutional issues such as environmental, political, or administrative • Overcomes social barriers such as culture, language, gender, age, race, and religion

explicit in the sense of having a database of facts, figures, and other information in a specific area or domain at your fingertips and ready to be accessed when needed to support content, or the knowledge can be *implicit* in your ability to function effectively and creatively in a given field or area.[62] The *know-what* (explicit) part is knowledge *gained* from learning, whereas the *know-how* (implicit) part is knowledge *applied* through experience.

Even though your position as a teacher gives you control of the learning environment, for the most part you do need to demonstrate your explicit knowledge by simplifying the materials so as to make the subject comprehensible, which adds to the perception that the information is imparted from a reliable source. In most cases, your subject matter expertise will need to adapt to a diverse group of learners in order to keep them engaged. Novice instructors, who lack an in-depth knowledge about a subject, may be more rigid in their classroom teaching, covering a course outline exactly as prescribed. Instructors who are more expert and have the "know-how" to be flexible enough to adapt to the given learning environment are willing to use more interactive techniques that may detour from the established plan, as long as they remain within the confines of the subject matter.[44, 56, 59, 61]

Avoiding Complexity

We often see comments on student evaluations that refer to an instructor as being "too knowledgeable." Therefore, if you lack the ability to *simplify complex topics* for learners and you appear "too knowledgeable," your perceived expertise may be compromised. For example, your *speaking style* may create a learning challenge. Perhaps your exaggerated effort to elucidate evokes an educational discourse of hyperfluency in an academic register that is difficult for learners to comprehend. In other words, as in that last sentence, you may be speaking at such an elevated language level that nobody knows what you are talking about! (see "Fluency" in chapter 5, page 210). Another possible reason why you may be perceived as "too knowledgeable" is because you've overprepared the content and feel that you need to cover each and every aspect in order to make sure that the learners have a clear understanding of the topic. Or, it may be that your attention to detail is really just an effort to show the learners that you have a comprehensive command of the topic, fearing that they might see you as a non-expert if you don't offer an excessive amount of information.

It is not enough to just *know what*, you have to *know how*. An expert does not worry about covering every detail in order to demonstrate or prove the existence of knowledge. The goal of a teacher is not to simply impart knowledge; instead, the effort should be to develop analytical, creative, and critical thinking skills in learners so that they grasp the subject matter more intu-itively.[60] If you can learn to simplify more complex topics, you will end up with more time to answer questions and clarify concepts. If you are well-prepared, have organized your materials, bring energy and passion to your teaching, and set objectives that learners are able to achieve, your expertise will be both efficient and effective.

Expertise through Experience

The expression "experience is the best teacher" is mainly a testament to the time it takes to develop the *know-how*. The problem with experience is that your learning takes place after you've been tested. Studies do indicate that it takes about three to five years to gain a consistent level of proficiency in a discipline or skill area, but likely up to ten years for an expert to emerge.[44, 55] Depending on your teaching experience, from novice to expert, your ability to use expertise to facilitate learning will vary. Experience in years usually adds to your knowledge base in a subject area, but it takes more than time invested in teaching to pay dividends in terms of becoming an expert.

We should be careful as to whom we label as expert when it comes to teaching. An expert in the subject does not necessarily equate to an expert teacher of the subject.[59] While you do gain experience from repeated teaching of material, you can also learn effective teaching techniques from watching other instructors. Less experienced educators can develop expertise by observing and learning from more seasoned faculty whom they perceive as experts.[63] Beyond the existing faculty, these observations can be also done by reviewing videos of teaching in action in order to evaluate different styles, various interactions, and other classroom dynamics.[64] In fact, the sharing of "best practices" among educators is becoming more common as faculty members invite colleagues to their lectures and then ask for feedback and suggestions in order to improve skills.[65] The benefit of having more experi-ence is that you learn to teach more effectively with less reliance on support content that might detract from the topic. From a design perspective, as you grow in academia, you will realize that your slides become less crowded and hold less information, while your lectures shift to more interactive discus-sions with learners in order to stimulate critical thinking.

Making Logical Connections

Part of the expertise of an instructor is to provide learners with clear explana-tions of the concepts, theories, facts, figures, ideas, and other information associated with a given topic. The complexity of content poses a problem for students, especially if the topic is filled with collections of seemingly random facts or details. The *problem-solving* ability of an expert is demonstrated by helping learners see the relationships among what otherwise might be isolated bits of knowledge.[66] Whereas learners attend multiple courses in a given program or curriculum, they may lack the ability to make connections across related topics.

Imagine that each fragment of information learned within a specific topic is similar to a puzzle piece. It takes an instructor's expertise to recognize patterns and solve the dilemma of putting the entire puzzle together for learners to see the "bigger picture." Therefore, it is important that you develop your expertise in a subject area to the point that you see how content relates to practical experience. Your overall educational perspective is peppered with a variety of experiences that have helped you develop a more focused understanding of how the taught subject matter fits into the real world. When you explain relationships among seemingly ambiguous points, you enlighten learners and allow them to think more creatively. Consider using more real-world analogies to help students understand the deeper meaning of what you are teaching by linking content to context.

At times, you may avoid making logical connections, because you lack the in-depth knowledge to see the bigger picture. Why open up a new can of worms with new discussions, new problems, or new arguments? Rather than problem solving, some teachers choose problem *dissolving*. In other words, by continually employing the same routines, an effort is made to minimize classroom challenges as a way of improving the efficiency at teaching.

Routine expertise is associated with *experienced non-experts* who have developed a set of everyday habits to combat recurring problems by fitting each difficulty into the most comfortable solution.[59] Why not? It would appear that a problem-free environment makes for optimal teaching. But by narrowing down or eliminating problems, you inhibit the growth of your expertise as you focus on only your strongest skills. In fact, as problems arise, you may find yourself just using one approach simply because you have perfected the strategy.

However, *adaptive* experts are those who embrace new problems as new learning experiences in order to expand expertise to new levels.[59] The presence of a new obstacle requires alertness, attention, and focus on dealing with the unexpected. Such adaptive expertise is more of a continuum or process than a static or achieved skill.

⚊⚊ Acting on Instinct ⚊⚊

In order to keep theatrical performances fresh, night after night, as if happening for the first time, well-trained actors purposely place obstacles into the action of the play. They actively work to overcome new challenges, making the performance appear more realistic.

For example, an actor who is supposed to be looking for a set of keys during a scene will ask a fellow actor in the scene to hide the keys in a new spot during each performance. There is also an agreement that by a certain time if the keys are not found, a visual hint (a glance, a gesture, etc.) is given to help direct the actor to the correct location so the keys can be found.

To the audience, the search for the missing keys appears very realistic because the keys really are hidden. The placing of obstacles creates healthy challenges with just enough risk and reward to keep the role fresh and exciting, especially during those performances when the keys are found!

This is an example of *adaptive expertise* as it applies to acting.

The more flexible you are in the learning environment, the more likely you will be to try "new" things, and while some of these fresh approaches may lead to novel problems, you will find innovative ways to address those issues, thus expanding your database of solutions. For example, suppose you are considering adding some video clips into your slide presentation to support a lecture. If you are unfamiliar with how to handle any technical problems that may arise, your routine will be better served if you don't include the clips. Problem *dis–solved*! However, if you opt to include the clips, if a technical glitch occurs, your struggle with the new problem will become a learning lesson and your expertise will adapt accordingly. Problem *solved*!

Talent Plays a Role

Expertise also hinges on a certain degree of *talent*, especially in the ability to sense learner feelings or outcomes.[44] How well do you know your students? Your talent as an instructor is based on a combination of many factors, beyond knowledge, experience, and problem solving, centering squarely on your familiarity with the needs of your learners. We have reviewed numerous teacher evaluations and noted student comments such as "makes sure that I follow through with my assignments"; or, "has a knack for knowing the best ways to help me"; or, "can tell when I am having a bad day." These responses suggest teachers with the talent for knowing learners as *people*. While expressions, reactions, and nonverbal cues from your students will offer you feedback as you teach, your expertise involves flexibility in planning content that adapts to the diverse learning styles of your group. If you are unwilling to improvise based on the situation, you may appear rigid in your approach, unwilling to consider alternative expressions.

⤛ Just a Minute Man ⤜

Kevin is a tax specialist and an adjunct faculty member at a city college where he teaches an entry-level accounting course. He talked with some of the more experienced faculty about the best ways to prepare lectures and support materials. One of the more seasoned professors took Kevin aside and said, "The trick to making slides is to equate them with time. One minute equals one slide. Your lecture is an hour, so make sure you have sixty slides—no more, no less."

Kevin wasn't sure if this was the best advice, but he didn't have enough experience to suggest an alternative. So, he designed sixty slides to cover the lecture period and figured that he could "average" a minute across all the slides, knowing that some would take more or less time, depending on the content.

During the lecture, he spent more time trying to correct his timing for slides that took too long by shortening his spoken words on other slides. It wasn't long before he was completely detached from the meaning of his phrases. The class became restless, students were fidgeting, the murmuring became louder, and distractions began to increase.

To try to match the allotted time, Kevin began to speak even faster, determined to finish all sixty slides in sixty minutes, totally unaware that the learners were unable to stay engaged with the topic. By the time he was done racing through the remaining few slides, the class was confused, lost, and disconnected.

Had Kevin taken the time to monitor the behavior of his students during his talk he would have realized the futility of the slide-per-minute constraint and he might have been able to adjust the lecture to address the key learning objectives more effectively.

⤛⤜

One of the hallmarks of talent is in the ability to reliably predict learner outcomes. One instructor who prepares graduating students for national exams told us, "I can tell which students will pass, just based on the comments they make during class." His predictions have been highly accurate and he admits that his aptitude for forecasting performance is based more on "gut feelings" than anything else. Yet the ambiguity of "sensing" may be the most concrete explanation of talent. Surely experience with multiple groups allows the recognition of behavior patterns, but talent is necessary to translate observed behavior into predictable results.

Talent is difficult to measure, but we often use the term to describe a higher level of ability unrelated to what can be achieved by practice and repetition. Although talent is more qualitative than quantitative, there are efforts that you can make to add to your expertise that in time will help you look like a "natural." For example, be responsive enough to address immediate questions, comments, or opinions, not only to show learners that you respect their input, but also to monitor levels of understanding. If challenged with a new undertaking, such as working with the latest technology, keep practicing until you are more familiar and comfortable. Find multiple ways to target the teaching to appeal to diverse learning styles by encouraging interaction, discussion, debate, and other interpersonal communication so that you can reliably anticipate learner behavior and adapt accordingly.

Classroom Climate and Conditions

An often overlooked influence on expertise is the *context* in which the learning takes place (see "Dealing with Conditions" in chapter 4, page 180). In a perfect world, conditions would always be ideal and teachers would encounter no obstacles to optimizing the learning experience. But we live in an imperfect world. The impact of external factors, some of which are beyond your control, will affect your ability to develop, manage, or deliver your expertise to the extent you may prefer.

In some situations, the classroom itself is a poor learning space or incompatible with planned instructional activities, forcing alternative methods of instruction just to compensate for the limited environment. For example, a marketing professor teaches the same course to three different groups of second-year students, meeting in different locations during the week. He plans to incorporate several video clips into a slide presentation in order to show the emotional effects of music in television commercials. The classroom for one of his groups is not equipped with a sound system, so he must reconsider playing the clips for that class, especially because they will not be able to hear the music in the commercials. Although the more adaptive expert may have innovative approaches, flexibility, and other ways to deal with the limitations, the issue is that the context (surrounding conditions) will affect the impact of the teaching.[67]

As teachers mature in the profession, more constraints on time develop as a result of other responsibilities beyond the classroom, including research, community involvement, extracurricular functions, and administrative tasks. How many times have you found that there are just not enough hours in the day to get things done? While one can argue that effective time management is a skill unto itself, the conditions that influence your availability will affect your adaptive expertise potential. When you are overwhelmed you might rely on shortcuts or more restrictive and narrow approaches to teaching, simply because you don't have enough time to invest in alternative methods.

At times, the conditions that affect expertise are institutional, community driven, or even indicative of the educational system. Policies, directives, mandates, rulings, and other wide reaching issues may adversely affect your attitudes, beliefs, enthusiasm, creativity, or teaching methods.[68] As a result your ability to offer the subject matter in the most expert manner possible may be compromised. For example, a team of educational consultants are empowered by a university to initiate curriculum reform measures. Based on thorough analysis of different programs, a consensus is reached to reduce the time allotted for certain courses. In a department meeting you are told that one of your courses will be shortened by one-third of the time but that you are still expected to meet the same learning objectives. Being forced to fit content into less time will affect your teaching plans and may cause you to create shortcuts to learning in order to reach expected outcomes; or, worse yet, you may be unable to adapt to the change, become frustrated, and not achieve the established objectives.

Part of expertise is maintaining a calm disposition in light of challenging situations so that your emotions don't affect your ability to think creatively.[66] Based on the circumstances of the reduced class time, expert faculty will meet the new challenge by determining how to redistribute the learning methodology to achieve the same objectives. From a content-development perspective, an expert instructor may use the shortened time frame to teach those high-level critical issues that can only be covered in lecture format, while reserving secondary learning points for online case discussions, assigned group tasks, or other *out-of-classroom* activities to allow for the redistribution of curricular hours. It is this type of flexibility that demonstrates expertise.

Your sensitivity to the classroom climate is critical to learner perception of your expertise in managing the environment effectively. At times you may need to handle misbehavior such as lateness, chattering and other such distractions. On a larger scale, expertise can be affected by your inability to overcome social barriers such as culture, language, gender, age, race, or religion. These issues may be distracting or discriminatory, directly related to you or to your learners, causing you to avoid open communication, restrict discussions, or make uninformed decisions. In essence, your interactions *within* the learning environment can have a profound effect on your productivity as an instructor, and ultimately affect your ability to achieve learning outcomes.

Developing Your Expertise

It is important to be aware of the characteristics of experts to understand that expertise is a continual, dynamic, and ever-changing process that requires *desire*, *practice*, and *coaching*, along with constructive *feedback*. Most important is that you have to *want* to develop your expertise. If you are highly motivated you will be committed to becoming more expert in your specific area. Later, you may aspire to gaining proficiency in related subject areas to widen the scope of your expertise.

Beyond the desire is the *doing*. You need to keep actively pursuing efforts to attain a deeper understanding of your particular domain before you can even consider widening your scope. Deliberate *practice* can overcome many limitations and may lead to an acquired expertise.[58] With continual practice, the basic skills soon become very *automatic*, allowing you more time to focus on gaining higher level skills to become more and more proficient.

Practice can be improved from evaluation and review, especially in *coaching* situations. Having a coach is like having a personal trainer who watches you on multiple occasions and provides constructive feedback, while guiding you toward higher levels of expertise. One of the techniques that a coach may use to evaluate performance is *Keep-Start-Stop*. The coach monitors a session and manually records observations in three separate columns based on actions that should continue (Keep), ones that should be considered (Start), and others that should be eliminated (Stop). Immediately following or soon after the session, the coach and the instructor discuss the observations and recommendations to see where improvements or changes can be made. In the world of academia, coaches are often replaced by mentors. The most effective mentoring occurs when feedback is based on direct observation.

When you examine the elements of desire, practice, and coaching, the teaching profession is such that the desire may be ever present, but the opportunities to practice in simulated situations or the likelihood of receiving consistent feedback from an expert coach or mentor are limited.[44] You typically will use the live classroom for practice, realizing that some approaches may work and other methods may fail as you develop your expertise. In addition, a coaching expert may not be available in your academic setting, based on budget restraints or access to a qualified individual. Perhaps the lack of rigorous practice and the limited availability of coaching are the reasons why it takes ten years to reach a high level of expertise! So how do you become an expert if these opportunities are few and far between? As an alternative, institutions use internal resources such as evaluative processes to provide feedback for instructors.

Evaluating Expertise

It is not uncommon for an expert to be judged by results, especially because results are *measureable*.[44, 62, 66] In education, outcomes are usually measured through performance on standardized tests, exams, or other instruments that are scored. There is considerable debate as to whether learner performance is a clear indicator of a teacher's expertise.[44, 69-73] However, because the goal of teaching is learning and the measurement of learning is though performance, it is not surprising that expertise is associated with achievement. An instructor should be efficient in the teaching process and effective in achieving outcomes.[62] As a way of monitoring your own development of expertise, feedback is necessary and essential.

While you can gain experience from observing others, you can develop a greater expertise when receiving feedback from being observed, as is done though evaluation and ratings from learners, peer review, and self-assessment. The combination of all three of these observation perspectives is a *triangulation* that provides for an optimal assessment of effectiveness.[74]

Self-Reflection

While academic evaluations generally provide feedback on a number of teaching attributes, it is sometimes difficult to distinguish specific ratings for a single aspect, such as expertise. In addition, observations from learners and peers may be done on a limited basis, sometimes only once in the course of a semester or year. Therefore, in addition to the observation and feedback from others, experts use *self-reflection* as a more immediate and continual means of improving expertise.

Self-reflection helps you analyze your perspectives in relation to other views; lets you consider the ethical, emotional, and logical consequences of your actions; allows you to clarify your reasons for using specific approaches or strategies; and helps you understand the particular choices you made that led to either positive or negative outcomes. After each teaching activity, ask yourself, "What can I do differently?" Look for ways to improve upon your current approach. One of the more common methods for self-reflection is to watch a video recording of one of your classes. This is similar to observing other experts using videos of teaching.[64] The ability to see yourself in action can give you insights into the elements of your style.

If you have the desire to grow and the opportunity to practice with coaching and constructive feedback, you can develop expertise by advancing your understanding (knowledge) over an extended period of time (experience), making logical connections (problem solving) that adapt to the diverse needs of your learners (talent) within the confines of your environment (context), in order to be efficient, effective, and continually self-reflective.

INSPIRATION

Teaching is more than imparting knowledge, it is inspiring change. Learning is more than absorbing facts, it is acquiring understanding.

—William Arthur Ward

There appears to be a paucity of literature on the study of *inspiration* as a skill in teaching, although many articles and books refer to teachers who "inspire" learners through determined effort. From an assessment perspective, we describe inspiration as a characteristic of one who makes the learners feel encouraged to incorporate learned concepts.[1] The *encouragement* may appear to be self-driven, stemming from a learner's inner confidence to act without a push from someone else. However, it is from the actions of the teacher that the learner is inspired. This is why studies allude to inspiration using related action-driven terms such as *motivate, stimulate, persuade, influence, energize, ignite, infuse,* and other similar words that describe the desired *effort* of teachers to have a lasting *effect* on learners. Because all of these expressions point to a long-term result or *learning outcome*, we see inspiration as being more than motivation; it is something "beyond teaching." If learners decide to investigate a topic after class, that is motivation. But if learners want to be just like the teacher, that is inspiration. As an instructor, your ability to bring an *added value* to your teaching efforts can be quite inspiring.

The starting point to develop this skill is to work toward encouraging learners to *do something* with the knowledge you've shared. There is more to education than memorization, assignments, and taking exams. While it may appear obvious that the application of learning is typically seen in the workplace, students can be inspired to develop lifelong learning habits early on in their education that allow them to become critical thinkers, social collaborators, and exemplary leaders. To blaze a trail toward a deeper understanding of applied knowledge, learners need someone to show them the way. They need a leader. Using *leadership* techniques, an inspirational teacher guides learners along an educationally rewarding path toward accomplishing goals and objectives. To that end, good teachers can become good leaders in a number of leadership-driven ways, most notably through *behavior modeling, transformational teaching,* and *mentoring*.

Leading by Example

"Do as I say, not as I do" is certainly *not* the motto of the inspirational teacher. Instead, the ability to be a shining example to which learners will aspire is what ignites the fire that fuels achievement. If you want learners to place the same value on what you are teaching as you do, then you will have to lead by example and model the very behavior that you seek.[75] *Behavior modeling* starts by setting an example for others to follow. Each day, each session, each class is an opportunity for you to demonstrate your commitment to the topic, your attention to detail, your high level of preparation, and your willingness to interact.

Inspirational teachers can influence learners by modeling a behavior beyond the classroom. For example, an accounting professor who spends two Saturday mornings each month during tax season to prepare returns for senior citizens at no charge demonstrates a sense of community and charity that goes far beyond the classroom. Learners may be inspired by the professor's behavior and might decide to get involved with local programs that yield a similar sense of community and charity, even if unrelated to their specific field of study. A student may model the professor's behavior by donating time preparing meals at a homeless shelter or tutoring young children in reading at a local library. The same sense of community and charity are evident even though the activities are very different and unrelated to the taught material.

As an instructor, you may model many different behaviors that inspire learners. You could get involved in extracurricular activities, coordinate meetings or events, involve others in joint research projects, supervise study clubs, raise money for a foundation, support a social cause, and even help in the professional development of new teachers. These displays are seen by learners as going beyond the normal expectation of a teacher and, as a result, may stimulate a greater sense of the educational experience, beyond facts, figures, and exams.

Your attempt to model behavior does not have to be on a big scale; it can occur in everyday activity. For example, if you want to teach learners to respect *your* time, then you will need to demonstrate *your* responsibility for being on time, finishing on time, allowing time for interaction, and making time for challenged learners. Students have to observe your behavior before you can expect them to mimic it or embrace it. Therefore, you should try to exemplify a visible consistency between what you say and what you do so that others can follow the behavior you model. As an inspirational teacher, you will need to set high standards and live by the same values that you advocate. Last, but not least, you cannot inspire if you cannot interact and communicate.

Teachers as Leaders

The inspirational teacher transforms a learning environment into a life-changing experience. When we interviewed faculty and students, and asked if they had an inspirational teacher, almost everyone said "yes." Upon elaboration on "what makes a teacher inspirational," there was no one common response. However, it was very quickly apparent that there was no mention of the subject taught! The comments were about personality characteristics, and the teacher's ability to expose students to life's lessons. Inspiration represents the expression of *life-related* principles, beyond a single topic or educational program. These ideals are not necessarily part of a curriculum; but, they certainly serve a purpose in the development of values such as responsibility, ethics, sharing, teamwork, commitment, trust, assistance, and other elements that affect the learner's perspective on life. When learners embrace these demonstrated principles, teachers are seen as leaders because larger connections are made.

The majority of teaching involves a transactional process where an instructor expects something in return for their teaching. Usually this return or transaction is in the form of academic performance. These teachers feel highly rewarded when students demonstrate a high learning outcome, evidenced through exams, assignments, or other assessments. Yet, the inspirational educator expands on the process, using *transformational teaching* to stimulate critical thinking, establish meaningful relationships, and captivate learners with a compelling vision of their future.[76]

The transformative teacher is seen as one who creates a convincing reason for learning by expanding the world for the students beyond assessments and exams. You can provide your learners with a glimpse of the bigger picture through various activities, such as conducting industry site visits, arranging field trips, inviting guest lecturers, or letting the worldwide web offer a worldwide view by embarking on virtual tours of other countries and cultures.

As you expand learner horizons you are perceived as a leader, namely, someone who can *influence, motivate,* and *stimulate* an entire group while offering *individual* attention to those seeking greater guidance. These leadership characteristics are demonstrated when transformational teaching follows the four major principles of *transformational leadership*, described in the literature as: idealized influence, inspirational motivation, intellectual stimulation, and individualized consideration.[77, 78]

Leadership-driven teachers use *idealized influence* to act as strong role models for what learners can expect to experience in their future. In many cases what is truly inspiring is the charisma of the teacher in creating such a vision and fostering the true value of education. *Inspirational motivation* is used by teachers to set high standards and raise expectations of learners with the intention of teaching students how to work together toward a common goal. The elements of teamwork and sharing become part of the learning process, motivating each individual to support one another and raise the collective knowledge of the group. This type of leadership trait is also true of coaches who inspire teams by getting players to motivate one other and raise the level of their "game." Leader-oriented teachers also use *intellectual stimulation* to apply the skills of expertise by encouraging learners to find innovative solutions to complex problems, connecting major concepts across topics and courses. The most powerful use of transformational teaching is seen through *individualized consideration*, where a teacher focuses on the specific needs of each learner to help him or her reach a higher potential.

Teachers as Mentors

Learning is a shared responsibility and you will get a sense of which learners are inspired by you because they will seek you out and ask for more guidance. In some cases, a *mentoring* relationship evolves where a teacher counsels, guides, and advises a student for the purpose of educational and career development.[79] There is considerable evidence of the positive effects of mentoring on learners, such as better retention, greater comfort with the learning environment, higher grade point averages, and other reinforcements that help keep students motivated and focused.[80] Regardless of the process, the important element is the genuine and trusting relationship between the mentor and the learner, or mentee. As an instructor, you can become a very inspirational force in a learner's life when you choose to take someone *under your wing* and serve as an exemplary role model while being interactive, challenging, insightful, encouraging, nurturing, supportive, understanding, and protective.

As a result, mentoring advances the concept of a rewarding and long-term, mutually beneficial relationship where, ideally, the teacher fulfills a desire to counsel, guide, and shape the future of a willing, eager, appreciative learner. A mentor shares detailed subject matter expertise to give a student more advanced knowledge in a given field, helps set realistic academic and career goals, displays highly professional behavior as a role model, and provides a level of emotional support, especially during times when the learning environment becomes challenging.[79, 80] Table 3.13 outlines strategies that you can use when mentoring learners.

Being a mentor takes time and commitment, but the rewards can be invaluable when you consider the feeling that you get from shaping the career of an individual who truly appreciates advice from an experienced expert willing to provide personal guidance and emotional support.

Emotional Intelligence

When you lead by example, transform the learning experience, and mentor individuals, you inspire others by making emotional connections on an interpersonal level. But to develop the skill of inspiration requires an *intrapersonal* perspective, that is, an introspective view of how you express *yourself.*

Table 3.13. Strategies for becoming a better mentor

Becoming a Better Mentor	
Mentoring Effort	*Strategy*
Set academic and career goals	• Assess learner abilities (strengths, challenges, etc.) • Require specific details about what a learner wants • Monitor progress toward educational/career goals • Stimulate critical thinking • Help envision a compelling future (share "the dream") • Develop personal and professional potential • Encourage continual self-reflection
Share expertise	• Assure the acquisition of skills and knowledge • Challenge, evaluate, reflect, then repeat the cycle • Use tutoring skills to foster advanced subject learning • Sponsor a learner in activities outside the classroom; seek visibility, group involvement, internships, etc.
Be a role model	• Share life experiences to show personal choice • Reveal personal feelings to build a strong relationship • Demonstrate ethical and moral behavior • Be consistent in a variety of settings • Facilitate learner observation of interaction with leaders, peers, or other professionals • Demonstrate willingness to create a network of support • Illustrate conflict management skills • Show how to deal with a challenging work/life balance • Be willing to continue mentoring for many years • Support and sponsor "the dream" into a "reality"
Offer emotional support	• Address learner fears • Identify and share problems • Respect and encourage learner solutions • Create the opportunity for positive reinforcement • Give moral encouragement to build learner self-confidence • Establish a supportive relationship • Share responsibility for learner mistakes • Seek to protect, shield, and defend from negativity

The literature describes this as *emotional intelligence*, which allows you to manage and control your feelings, through self-awareness and self-expression.[31] When learners see your passion for positively expressing your feelings, emotions, opinions, and beliefs, they become infused with the same level of self-confidence in similar self-expression.[77] In a sense, your emotional intelligence lets you become more aware of what makes you "tick," checking to see how in touch with your feelings you are and whether you feel good about your choices, decisions, and everyday lifestyle. The higher your emotional intelligence, the more likely you will be to express your feelings as freely as you express your knowledge, all the while appearing self-confident, self-motivated, self-reliant, and self-reflective. Too often, the academician sees the transfer of knowledge as the primary skill of an educator. But what makes a teacher truly inspiring is the ability to bring passion, empathy, happiness, energy, and other emotional aspects into the act of teaching, beyond the factual exchange of information.

From a development perspective, there are ways that you can measure your emotional intelligence. Similar to how IQ (intelligence quotient) scores are derived from standardized tests, there are EQ (emotional quotient) models that help measure your ability to manage and control your emotions. For example, one of the more popular templates is the Bar-on Model that measures your EQ across five main areas or *domains*: Interpersonal, Intrapersonal, Stress Management, Adaptability and General Mood.[81] Figure 3.2 outlines the EQ domains and the related sub-skills.

The intensity or focus placed on the fifteen "sub-skills" or components of the Bar-on model are reflective of the type of work that a person does, with

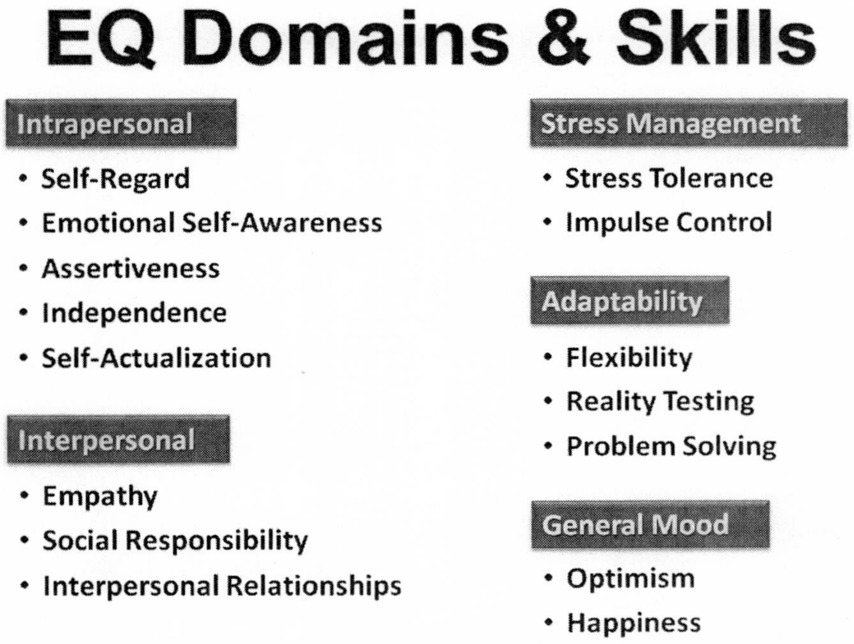

EQ Domains & Skills

Intrapersonal

- Self-Regard
- Emotional Self-Awareness
- Assertiveness
- Independence
- Self-Actualization

Interpersonal

- Empathy
- Social Responsibility
- Interpersonal Relationships

Stress Management

- Stress Tolerance
- Impulse Control

Adaptability

- Flexibility
- Reality Testing
- Problem Solving

General Mood

- Optimism
- Happiness

Figure 3.2.   Bar-on Model of Emotional Quotient (EQ) domains and sub-skills

particular areas being more challenging than others, depending on the profession. Therefore, these skills require greater attention in order to manage and control related emotions. The EQ components of *flexibility, assertiveness, independence, problem solving,* and *self-actualization* are found to be highly desirable skills for college and university professors.

As you achieve a higher level of emotional intelligence you will also make deeper connections to your content, allowing you to combine the power of your expertise with your passion for teaching, while providing learners with both knowledge *and* understanding. As a result, students feel more energized and engaged in the learning process because they see the knowledge from a more complete perspective.

Your ability to transform teaching into a greater experience will require you to model the behavior and mentor learners, thereby converting you from a teacher to a leader. In the process, without a doubt, you will be inspirational.

SELF-CONFIDENCE

The way to develop self-confidence is to do the thing you fear and get a record of successful experiences behind you.

—William Jennings Bryan

The confidence that you have in yourself is based on how you value your own ability to reach your goals, using your skills and knowledge. The more you trust in yourself, the more you value your expertise, the higher your confidence will be in achieving positive outcomes. However, from a learner's perspective, a teacher's self-confidence is recognized or perceived through visible or tangible actions. We describe self-confidence as a characteristic of one who appears prepared and in control of a presentation or discussion, regardless of the audience size, level of expertise, or rank.[1]

The audience preference for attributes of "level of expertise" and "rank" is more closely associated with those of *professional* learners (versus *student* learners), such as seen in groups of peers or superiors. One professor put it this way, "I have no problem talking to my students in any class that I teach. But if I have to speak at a conference, I can get nervous." Another experienced instructor commented, "Presenting to my department chair or, worse yet, the dean, is intimidating. These people are very judgmental and pick apart everything I say. But, teaching the students is easy!" You are more likely to experience some discomfort or anxiety when presenting to a group of colleagues, especially if you feel that the group knows as much as you (or more) or if some members of the audience have a higher rank or power, such as a dean, department chair, or other administrator. These feelings are not unusual and not limited to teachers. It is not uncommon for certain students to refrain from participation because they are afraid to speak in class. Many people have anxiety about being the center of attention or under the scrutiny of others.[82]

When observing educators, a visible lack of self-confidence is more common with novice instructors or with those teachers who are "new" to the topic itself. For example, a seasoned professor who is asked to conduct a class for a colleague may feel unprepared and therefore be less confident in the ability to cover the topic effectively. Compounding this issue is the fact that student learners initially accept a teacher as an authority on the topic.[3] As a result, the instructor is granted or assigned a level of self-confidence at the outset. For instance, a second-year medical student assumes that the instructor is confident by virtue of the status of the teacher as a practicing clinician.

This assumption is less true for professional learners who approach the learning from a peer perspective. These learners usually have similar experience with the content, perhaps working in the same field as the teacher, although not having the same level of expertise in the knowledge of details. Therefore when the same teacher wears the hat of a clinician and lectures on a specific medical topic to a group of practitioners, the learners are not students, but professionals. This group shares a degree of familiarity or experience in the field and is less likely to automatically ascribe a level of self-confidence to the speaker; instead, they will wait for that characteristic to be demonstrated. In the absence of such a revelation, there is the likelihood that the clinician, having to demonstrate confidence, may appear apprehensive and may end up visibly expressing nervousness. Before we discuss ways to express self-confidence, we must first understand the issues related to the feelings of uneasiness associated with delivering content.

Conquering Fear

Studies show that the highest degrees of social *phobia* or fear are associated with *performance*, such as in public speaking or when speaking up during a meeting or even in a class.[82–84] When it comes to teaching, perhaps the term "phobia" is a bit extreme. In reality, the uncomfortable feeling of uneasiness when speaking in front of others is generally described as being *nervous*. Table 3.14 lists responses given by teachers, with varying levels of experience, when asked to describe exactly what was causing the nervousness during different speaking situations.

The uncomfortable feeling of nervousness when speaking in front of others is sometimes relative to personal perspective. If the words "I" or "me" go through your mind (as in "what will they think of *me*?" or what if *I* can't answer a question?"), you will experience nervousness because the focus of the activity is internal, centering on the *self*. Instead of being learner-centered, you are self-centered. This invariably leads to feeling self-conscious, which results in a higher anxiety or nervousness while delivering the content, worrying about your ability to engage the learners. However, if the focus is external, centered on the students, then your efforts will be directed toward *doing something* for the learners, as in "How will this help *them*?" "What can be done to make this better for *them*?" As an instructor, you should be *proactive* (focused on doing something for the learners) instead of *reactive* (focused on worrying about learner reactions to you). Tangible *actions* (nonverbal signals, inflection, interaction, etc.) can help you to concentrate on issues outside of yourself. These actions are illustrated through the *performance* skills, discussed in greater detail, later in this book (see "Body Language Style" in chapter 5, page 186).

Time and visibility also affect the feeling of anxiety that can occur when speaking. The process of connecting thoughts to words is nearly simultaneous, giving you no time to edit, other than a momentary pause. Beyond the

Table 3.14. Causes of nervousness as described by interviewed teachers

What Makes You Nervous?
I am afraid I won't look like I know what I am talking about.
I am worried about what they think of me . . . as if I am not what they expect.
I don't want anyone thinking that I am wasting their time.
Sometimes I feel that the audience is judging me on everything I say or do.
I feel like I need to prove that I am an expert.
The biggest fear for me is if they don't like me.
It worries me if I can't answer a question.
I don't want them to think I am lightweight or inexperienced.
Because I am young I am afraid they won't respect me as a teacher.
I have been teaching many years and I get nervous when I have to use the new technology.
The worst feeling for me is if I think I am boring them.
I am intimidated when my department chair or the dean is in the room.
I worry that my accent will make them think I don't know my content.
Because I am short, they may think I can't be an effective speaker.
I need a few minutes to get comfortable, so I am worried about the opening moments.
I say "um" a lot, so people may laugh or think I don't' know the topic.
The fear for me is that I may "go blank" and forget what I am going to say.
Being in a wheelchair makes me wonder if people are just feeling sorry for me.
I get nervous if I have to speak immediately after someone very recognized or well known.
I am very self-conscious because I have a speech impediment that is very obvious.
I worry that my voice makes me sound too young.
The more people in the room, the more nervous I get from being watched by so many.

voice, the high visibility of your complete presence, offers no shield for facial expressions and body language, making the communication effort even more conspicuous.

⟳ Full Exposure ⟳

There are many forms of communication. For example, letters, faxes, e-mails, and even text messages offer the *written* word. When you write, you have time to edit and restate your words until you are ready to send them out for response. Phones and voice mail are used for remote *speaking*. When you talk on the phone, you have less time to edit, but you are free to sit comfortably, and it doesn't matter how you may be dressed or how you appear. Voice mail even gives you a chance to plan your response in advance.

These two methods of communicating are less stressful simply because you can't be seen and you get more time to collect your thoughts. When you are less visible, you will have less fear. For example, online courses, such as webinars or podcasts offer less visibility and therefore produce less anxiety.

But classroom lectures, small-group discussions, and one-to-one conversations are usually face-to-face, requiring your complete presence. When you have greater visibility, especially in face-to-face situations, you can experience more anxiety in communication.

⌇⌇⌇

Intimidating Issues

Beyond the uneasy sense of nervousness, you may feel *intimidated* by the learners' poor response to the content. What is intimidating is more related to the act of teaching and the intended results, rather than the nervousness associated with being observed in a teaching activity. While there are many reasons why the delivery of information can be a daunting task, the most often cited are: *looking foolish*, *being judged*, *appearing boring*, and *wasting time*.[85, 86] Table 3.15 offers suggestions for overcoming these more commonly identified intimidating issues.

Table 3.15. Suggested actions to overcome particular fears or worries when speaking

Fighting Intimidation	
Feeling	*Actions*
Looking Foolish—feeling unprepared, possibly unable to address questions or comments related to the topic	Manage information in a consistent manner by explaining concepts using visual aids and descriptions. High-priority learning points can be connected to stories, examples, or analogies. A presentation can be supported with photos or graphic elements. Processes can be illustrated with animations or videos.
Being Judged—belief that the learners are judging every word or every action	You should become the judge by evaluating and observing learners to continually assess attentiveness to the topic. Make an effort to have greater eye contact with the students. Create interaction, using thought-provoking questions and judge the level to which learners have command of the content.
Appearing Boring—concern that the talk will be boring, either because the topic is boring, or it contains too much material	Find significance in the high-priority concepts within the topic to convey relevance and importance. Limit the amount of extraneous details in the content. Create connections to real-world applications of the materials. Add more interaction to keep learners actively discussing the topic.
Wasting Time—worry about learner expectations being met, either from the delivery or from the quality of the content	Make better use of time by adding relevant (quality) content. Plan more interactivity. Ask questions, stir discussion, and create controversy. Involve learners to allow time to be productive and not wasteful.

Regardless of the type of learner, an effective teacher must be prepared and ready to take control of the learning situation in a convincing manner in order to be able to meet the established learning outcomes. In short, *prepared* teachers are rarely nervous or intimidated.

Demonstrating Confidence

A confident teacher is primed and organized—one who walks and talks with authority while making logical connections to content in a way that keeps learners engaged. As an instructor, you have to feel *comfortable* with the act of presenting material to learners. Naturally, *experience* with a variety of learners and learning situations will help you gain a greater level of comfort. This is why self-confidence is more of an issue for those with less educational experience (novices) or for those new to a particular experience (unfamiliarity). In addition to practical experience or just plain practice, there are ways that you can develop a more confident approach to teaching. Table 3.16 identifies various active communication efforts that can help you express your self-confidence in learning situations, while enhancing other related skills.

Closely related to a teacher's self-confidence is the level of *emotional intelligence*, which is the ability to manage the learning environment by handling distractions, interactions, and other daily pressures that may otherwise affect mood, performance and self-motivation.[31] The act of teaching is not purely intellectual because so much of the work is emotional, especially considering your daily interactions with multiple learners and, hence, the managing of multiple personalities. If you have high self-confidence and a strong sense of emotional maturity you can effectively control the classroom climate to keep learners engaged, awake, and attentive. The very fact that you feel "in command" of the learning experience allows you to continually be self-reflective, which is a key component when developing expertise (see "Self-Reflection" in the "Expertise" section of this chapter, page 77).

In essence, the relationship between expertise and self-confidence is cyclical in nature when you consider that each feeds the other. Expertise is the knowledge and experience that supports self-confidence, which is your personal belief that you can affect a positive outcome which will result in learner success.[87] It follows that the more self-confident you are in the teaching, the more competent you become as an instructor, further fueling your self-confidence in trying new ways to engage learners. As you exhibit this kind of "competent confidence," quite certain of your abilities, your learners gain a greater level of understanding of the topic. From greater understanding comes deeper learning and, invariably, educational success.

Table 3.16. Communication activities that promote self-confidence, linked to related skills

Communicating Self-Confidence		
Activity	*Description*	*Related Skills*
Accepting	The capacity to immediately empathize with the existing situation, regardless of preconceived notions. This enables you to recognize diversity and tolerate adverse opinions.	Caring, Empathy
Accuracy	The ability to quickly get to the point. This is useful during question and answer moments.	Content Development, Interaction
Action	The external expression of a strong choice, represented in a physical manner using the body and voice. This helps develop control of nonverbal and verbal cues.	Body Language Style, Speaking Style
Adapting	The capacity to acclimate to a particular situation, although not necessarily accepting the circumstances. This aids a teacher during those times where a sense of logic and common sense appear to be lacking.	Expertise, Approachable
Advancing	The ability to move a story forward, from "point A" to "point B," based on the natural progression of logic or emotion, without digressing. This is a critical skill in order to direct learners toward an objective or outcome.	Expertise, Content Organization, Content Development, Speaking Style, Focus, Interaction
Anticipating	The quickness of expecting the unexpected based on a history of predictable outcomes. This skill also develops with experience, since learning situations tend to repeat.	Expertise, Interaction
Attention to Detail	The talent for fine-tuning a perspective without cluttering the concept or overexplaining the idea.	Expertise, Content Organization, Content Development, Content Design

Table 3.16. (Continued)

| | *Communicating Self-Confidence* | |
Activity	Description	Related Skills
Certainty	The tenacity to take responsibility for an expressed choice. A professor who cannot be decisive is seen as weak.	Passion, Expertise, Inspiration
Clarity	The flair for simplifying an issue without overstating or underestimating relative importance.	Expertise, Content Organization, Content Development, Content Design, Focus
Conflict Management	The capacity to see both sides of a situation while facilitating a positive outcome.	Caring, Empathy, Approachable, Interaction
Cooperation	The quality of effort that always adds value toward a common goal.	Caring, Empathy, Interaction
Creating a Sense of Urgency	Exacting a pressure that identifies and targets the specific importance of a concept or idea. The art of persuasion is based on this principle, and useful in debate, discussion, or argument.	Expertise, Focus, Interaction
Creating Analogies	The ability to find similar, real-world applications of defined parameters for a given issue. Comparisons to transportation, health, family, food, or life experiences are useful analogies.	Empathy, Content Organization, Content Development
Deduction	The natural transition used to show the reasoning behind a given line of logic. In teaching, this skill is used to connect a group of concepts into a flowing story or theme.	Expertise, Content Organization, Content Development
Flow	The functional layout of scripted logic placed on a defined timeline and paced in a pleasing manner.	Expertise, Content Organization, Content Development, Speaking Style

Table 3.16. (Continued)

	Communicating Self-Confidence	
Activity	*Description*	*Related Skills*
Focusing	The aptitude for finding the center of attention at any given moment of a situation. The lack of this skill causes instructors to confuse learner understanding of the content.	Content Organization, Content Development, Content Design, Focus
Intention	The emotional connection to content, represented in a mental manner using the mind and heart.	Caring, Happiness, Energy, Passion, Motivation
Justification	The internal measurement of belief in a personal choice. Expressed outwardly, this validates information in the form of credibility.	Passion, Expertise
Listening	The level of attentiveness to audible content and patterns of speech. A good listener hears the sound of silence between spoken phrases in order to grasp the pace of a learner's voice. This avoids interrupting, overlapping, or cutting off the dialogue.	Approachable, Speaking Style, Interaction
Logic	The sequential and predictable display of related information, whether legitimate or flawed, that leads to a decision.	Expertise, Inspiration
Maintaining Integrity	The facility to sustain a strict adherence to a value proposition or perspective without losing sight of the objective.	Passion, Expertise, Personal Appearance, Focus
Observing Visual Cues	The ability to detect and decipher actions and reactions, such as movement, gestures, facial expressions and other noticeable forms of feedback.	Body Language Style, Interaction
Providing Resolution	The capacity to reduce complexity into simplicity, while seeking the best outcome possible.	Expertise, Content Organization

Table 3.16.   (Continued)

	Communicating Self-Confidence	
Activity	*Description*	*Related Skills*
References and Alternatives	The components of support for a given line of logic. Professors with more experience are likely to have a wealth of backup information at their fingertips available to overcome argumentative objections.	Expertise, Content Organization, Content Development, Content Design, Focus, Interaction
Relationship Building	The knack for finding similar interests, desires, or needs, while creating a common bond in the process.	Empathy, Approachable, Interaction
Selectivity	Choosing the unique and relevant details of an issue specific to the immediacy of the situation.	Content Organization, Content Development, Focus, Interaction
Setting	The ability to preset the context, conditions, parameters, or guidelines relevant to a particular line of logic. Educators always provide a necessary bias (selective data) to support a point of view.	Expertise, Environment, Content Development, Content Design
Sharing	The willing effort to offer others a chance to enjoy a particular experience. This skill reduces nervousness (butterflies, jitters, stage fright, etc.) because it forces an instructor to focus externally (on others), rather than internally (on self).	Caring, Empathy, Happiness, Energy, Passion, Approachable, Interaction
Shifting Focus	The process of directing or giving attention to a particular view (person, group, support item, etc.). Teachers use this to draw attention to support materials (a display visual) or to others in the room (during interaction).	Body Language Style, Content Design, Additional Sense Stimulation, Focus, Interaction

Table 3.16. (Continued)

Communicating Self-Confidence		
Activity	*Description*	*Related Skills*
Support	The effort given to promote or defend a particular choice. An instructor uses this as a collaborative skill when advancing a particular line of logic shared by at least one other person.	Empathy, Interaction
Timing	The ability for positioning the important component of an issue at the key moment of interest or discussion.	Expertise, Content Organization
Using Virtual Space	The talent for representing thought processes through visible action. Instructors can use physical movements (gestures, expressions, etc.) to identify the unique and specific components of a concept or idea.	Additional Sense Stimulation, Body Language Style

APPROACHABLE

Ability is what you are capable of doing.
Motivation determines what you do.
Attitude determines how well you do it.

—Lou Holtz

We describe approachable as one who appears friendly and receptive to comments and interaction.[1] The literature uses the term *immediacy* to identify behavior that reduces the perceived "distance" between people, whether physical or psychological.[41] At times, a teacher may be distant from a learner more in the psychological sense, as in being too knowledgeable (an *expertise* issue), less open (a *body language style* concern), insincere (a *caring* matter), or unable to relate (an *empathy* problem). To appear more immediate, an instructor should develop a collaborative and supportive relationship with learners to achieve desired educational outcomes. If students feel comfortable "getting to know" a teacher, a level of trust builds and the likelihood is greater that interaction will be open, honest, and forthcoming.

As an instructor, it is in the best interests of the learner if you can find ways to "connect" by being available and accessible beyond the classroom, especially when students seek help or advice. For example, having an "open-door policy" to the extent that your schedule permits provides an assurance to learners that support is within reach through appointment or posted office hours. Inside the classroom, the perception of availability is seen through a variety of immediacy *cues*, such as eye contact, smiling, movement, gestures, and vocal expressions that you can use to establish a sense of warmth and friendliness. Learners have shown a more positive reaction to more approachable teachers and there is evidence of increased learning as a result.[3, 41, 45]

With respect to the act of teaching, you can create an impression of being more approachable by encouraging learner participation. This is the *proactive* version of interaction because the responsibility is on you to stimulate behavior, rather than *reacting* to learner questions, comments, or other participation (see chapter 5, "Interaction," page 252). As with many of the interrelated personality elements described in this chapter, approachability is interwoven among skills such as caring, empathy, happiness, energy, motivation, and inspiration.

Think of being approachable as being "responsive" to the needs of your learners. But don't confuse responsiveness with anticipation. You might end up waiting a long time before getting something to respond to from the learners. Instead, you should find ways to promote participation in learning activities, allowing your students to become more involved and, as a result, more engaged, awake, and attentive.

Stimulating the Interaction

It should be no surprise to you that not every learner is a willing participant. Studies show that class participation varies by age, gender, years in college, class size, and course level.[14, 15] While it may be interesting to observe demographic differences, the purpose of this skill is to foster interaction among all learners, to avoid having only a few students dominate the interaction. As an instructor, you will likely need to instill a willingness on the part of all of your students to interact; or, you may find that only a small percentage of your learners actively participate, as the evidence seems to suggest.[88]

In our faculty interviews, many of the professors indicated that "class participation" accounted for a percentage of the grade, although many of these instructors defined "participation" very differently. Some only expected that students answer questions when asked; others required in-class presentations as a measure of participation. Some expected students to have already-prepared questions for the teacher, while others suggested learners have research-supported data for all discussions as evidence of participation. Some instructors merely expected attendance or presence as meeting the requirements for class involvement. The spectrum is wide when it comes to understanding what teachers mean about the level of participation or interaction.

In many situations, professors tend to over-prepare and leave little time for any interaction (see "Too Little Time" in chapter 4, page 128). If the lecture, seminar, or presentation is prepared with the intent of having interaction as part of the learning, then instructors will need to stimulate the activity. The stimulation for class participation is not simply based on offering a reward for such effort. Part of the responsibility for interaction is related to the perception of the learners, based on the course level. Evidence suggests that students tend to be more interactive in higher-level courses than in introductory ones, citing maturity (years in college) and familiarity with the content over the course of time.[15]

The incentive for students to interact is also affected by the degree to which a teacher instills a sense of enthusiasm in the learners (*motivation*), is viewed as genuine and sincere (*caring*), offers a level of respect for student contributions by seeing and understanding from the student's perspective (*empathy*), and appears visibly receptive to student comments (*interaction*).

Naturally, the stimulation of interaction may backfire if only a small percentage of the group continually offers to interact, answer questions, lead discussions, and so on. The remaining students may eventually expect the more talkative ones to always offer comments and provide answers throughout the class, thereby limiting the instructor's original intent behind group interaction.[88] To encourage participation across the entire class, a professor should offer interactive opportunities to as many students as possible, at least across a series of lectures if not during each one.

Selective Discretion

There is a thin line that separates those who choose to participate and those who are chosen. It is up to the instructor to decide who interacts, when, how often, and so forth. Such power in the classroom must be used wisely, and too often, professors wield a damaging sword by arbitrarily selecting students for interaction who simply are not prepared. The result is usually embarrassment or disappointment on the part of those selected unexpectedly who could not rise to the occasion. Soon after, *receiver apprehension* sets in among the group, with many learners fearing failure if asked to contribute.[13] The teacher's approachable nature suddenly seems less so, and the classroom climate feels a bit colder.

Some professors use the argument that because learning is a shared responsibility students should always be prepared for interaction when they get to class, as a teacher can and will call on any student at any time during any class. However, regardless of the logic behind this argument, the student who feels "put on the spot" will likely be less confident in future interactions and will learn *not to participate* unless forced to do so. In our research, many students commented on their reticence in asking or answering questions after having the experience of failing to respond correctly when called upon by the instructor. A lack of confidence on the part of the student hinders participation.[14]

As an instructor, you will need to be aware of the impact of choosing arbitrarily, especially if the result of your action causes a decrease in participation. Of course, any level of participation is better than none, so every teaching opportunity should involve some degree of interaction. It doesn't matter how many learners are in the room or how much time you have to speak, students who are *actively involved* are motivated to learn.[89] The effective professor understands how to motivate learners to become actively involved so that they feel they can ask any question or make any comment without fear of failure.

No Time to Talk

Regardless of a learner's willingness to interact, the *opportunity* must exist. The most difficult environment is one in which the instructor does not create the opportunity for participation, thinking that by inviting interaction, time may be taken from the planned lecture. This results in a teacher who appears unapproachable, exhibiting a behavior that is non-immediate, which may be considered a teacher *misbehavior*, but to learners simply represents poor teaching.[41] There are many ways that teachers limit the chances for participation, particularly when interaction is *interrupted, delayed, postponed,* or *intimidated.* In all of these situations, the perception of being approachable is compromised because learner interest is disrespected, discouraged, dismissed or distanced.

Interactive Interruption

At times, your own expertise or experience may get in your way because you can reliably predict learner questions or comments. As a result, you will find yourself interrupting the interaction prior to its completion in order to address the comment or question. By preventing learners from completing the verbal expression of a thought or idea, you will reduce additional participatory efforts from others. In essence, you will teach people how *not* to interact.

⚊⚊ Comic Relief ⚊⚊

Have you ever been to a comedy club? One rule of "stand-up" affecting audience behavior is that after the first joke is told, the audience must be allowed to laugh until they are completely silent. If the comedian interrupts the laughter, the audience learns *not* to laugh by suppressing the verbal expression of the emotion.

Legend has it that the comedian Robin Williams experienced this early in his career. His stand-up routines were filled with extremely witty phrases delivered in rapid-fire fashion. The moment he said something funny, he would follow it with something even funnier, followed by something even funnier. Audiences realized that if they laughed too loudly, or even at all, they would not hear the second or third comments. Not wanting to miss anything, the crowd learned to suppress the laughter so that by the end of the comic routine, no one was laughing at all, yet everyone agreed that "he was so funny!"

The irony of this taught Williams to restructure his comedy to include longer bits and planned pauses to allow listeners to react completely to the experience.

⚊⚊⚊

Allow your learners to completely express themselves before you offer a reply. Patience is a virtue. By not interrupting, you will appear more receptive to interaction. Moreover, you will develop better listening skills and prevent misunderstanding if you wait for a comment to reach its completion.

Delayed Gratification

In our observations we have heard many professors say "Please hold your questions until the end." Some say this not because they don't want to be interrupted in the middle of the lecture but rather because they don't think they're going to have enough time to cover the topic. Of course, if the lecture is well planned, time will be available for both content and interaction (see "Length x Time = Difficulty" in chapter 4, page 127). Others say they prefer not to be interrupted because it distracts from their flow of content. One instructor said to us, "Singers are not interrupted during a performance!" The difference, of course, is there is no comprehension required when listening to a musical performance.

Yet, by delaying the interruptions, the teachers get to manage the *available* time for lecture and can then limit the number of questions in the *remaining* time. One instructor we interviewed summarized the problem by saying, "I have a lot to cover, so I tell the students to hold any questions to the very end. Then, I take one or two or however many questions as I have time for because I would rather skip some of the questions than lose time teaching the material."

Delayed gratification takes the learning out of context. A student seeking clarification of an important point within the topic desires immediate explanation to comprehend and understand more fully in order to build a foundation for subsequent content. But if the question is delayed until the very end of the lecture, even though a teaching opportunity still exists, the learning opportunity is not in context. Upon hearing a student's question near the end of class, the entire group will have to "think back" to the reference point in the lecture (assuming they can recall the moment) that links the question to the related content. Conversely, the professor is an expert who can easily put any question into context, thereby connecting to the reference point very quickly. The benefit of the answer may only help the student who asked the question, but may not be of similar value to the rest of the learners because of the time lapse between the originally explained content and the delayed response to the inquiry.

If a student question is taken immediately, the instructor can respond in a number of ways: clarifying content to answer the question, connecting the question to other points made in the lecture or to points made in previous discussions, comparing the question to another student's related inquiry, offering the student a chance to express more of an opinion, or posing new ideas to the group based on the student's original question.[90] The rest of the students hear the response in the current context of the topic and, as a result, may gain greater clarity about the issue. It is apparent that many more teaching opportunities exist when interaction is welcomed as it arises, rather than when it is delayed.

Postponed Curiosity

At times, participation is deflected and postponed to a later time, beyond the lecture and outside of the classroom. For example, if an instructor says, "If anyone has a problem or a question, come and see me after class." This appears to be a welcoming invitation, but students we interviewed offered a different perspective, seeing the option of "asking later" as a sign of weakness. One student said, "When I hear that, I think maybe I'm the only one who has this problem, so I don't want the professor to think I do not understand something that the rest of the class does." Students do not always judge the "see-me-after-class" invitation as an opportunity.

The postponement reduces your own effectiveness as to the clarity of your teaching. By addressing a learner's concern after your session, rather than during class, you may not realize the gravity of a problem. In most cases, this is not an isolated incident, and it may be symptomatic of a larger issue. For example, if during your lecture one student says, "I don't understand what you mean," you may notice that a number of other students also appear confused. You can immediately clarify your statements so that everyone understands. But, if you postpone the explanation and offer only individual private feedback, the whole concept of encouraging interaction is lost and your ability to address the needs of a larger group will suffer.

Keep in mind that there are times where a postponed response is appropriate, especially if questions or comments deviate from the current theme or are specific to a particular learner. When classroom discussions go "off-topic" they can disrupt the learning. You can very politely say, "Your concerns apply to a variety of topics beyond the current one. Therefore, these issues can be better addressed at a later time." In other instances, a particular point may stimulate a number of other questions, comments, or opinions that extend beyond the objectives of the current session. After responding to a few of these interactive moments, you can move ahead in the lecture by saying, "This is a very thought-provoking issue and I am more than happy to answer any further questions after our session today." This postponement is helpful for topics that normally require much more time to filter through various perspectives, theoretical arguments, or philosophical concerns. In fact, the ability to discuss these views after class extends the learning beyond the classroom, adding to the educational experience for both the teacher and the learners.

Intimidation Factor

At times, interaction may be restricted due to a learner feeling intimidated by an instructor's knowledge, power, or rank. Research indicates that the greater the perceived knowledge of the professor, the less likely the participation from the learners.[14] Because the instructor is seen as an authority on the topic, students might fear they will not meet the expectations of the professor if they offer any questions or comments. In other words, learners might feel unworthy of contributing anything of value or uncomfortable challenging the teacher's views, so they resist participation.

It is possible that it is not the instructor's *knowledge* so much as the complex academic speech or *hyperfluency* that may be intimidating the learner, thereby affecting the understanding of content (see "Fluency" in chapter 5, page 210). Such a challenge can also happen during interaction if the manner in which the professor speaks is "above" the comprehension level of the learners (see "Avoiding Complexity" in this chapter, page 69). Be careful of using your intellectual prowess to criticize the interaction of your students. Your invitation to have them participate will be very unwelcomed if students fear your disapproval or criticism.[14] In fact, students also demonstrate anxiety if their fellow students disapprove of their comments or questions. One student remarked, "It's one thing if the professor thinks I don't know something, but I would hate to have the rest of the class thinking the same thing."

If you can use your knowledge and authority as a beacon not as a weapon, and if you can treat each response as a help not a hindrance, then students will be more inclined to interact. If you do offer criticism, do it constructively and with a purpose toward fostering a better understanding of the issue. While the fear of the professor's criticism or peer disapproval can limit participation, instructors should make every effort to structure the learning so that students feel less intimidated and more willing to participate. The opportunities for interaction are both verbal and nonverbal and support the notion of a learner-centric approach to teaching.

Rank and power of a teacher can intimidate a learner who fears that questioning a professor's views may be interpreted as questioning the authority or undermining the teacher's power. One department chair, who is also an active teacher, explained a recurring dilemma in this way: "At the beginning of each academic year I find that the students are reluctant to be interactive during class. I have to go out of my way to encourage participation by assuring them that first and foremost I am a teacher. It is important that they understand that my academic powers are to enhance the teaching and not to be punitive or judgmental to students that are inquisitive or who challenge my views. Year after year, the students keep telling me how they were initially so afraid of me and the mere fact that I was a department chair in active teaching scared them." These same sentiments are voiced by deans, university presidents, and provosts, all of whom maintain roles as active teachers but do not want to be seen as wielding a coercive power over learners that intimidates openness and discussion. To overcome this perception of power and rank, you need to go out of your way to dispel the issue by being more understanding and mindful of these student fears, while promoting active involvement.

In essence, the approachable teacher invokes a perceived closeness or immediacy that motivates learners to become an integral part of the learning, without hesitation or fear. Enhanced interaction and participation invariably leads to students' encouragement and a more effective learning process.

PERSONAL APPEARANCE

Clothes and manners do not make the man; but, when he is made, they
greatly improve his appearance.

—Henry Ward Beecher

If a condescending joke is truly funny, make yourself the subject—you will
increase the number of people laughing by at least one.

—Joe Harsel

The way you appear to learners is an image that is collectively expressed
through related skills of *self-confidence, interaction, body language style,
speaking style,* and the ability to seem *approachable.* We describe personal
appearance as one who looks and behaves professionally.[1] The operative
word, *professionally,* is seriously subjective. Who is to decide? After all,
what may be considered fashionable, stylish, or tastefully acceptable varies
across colleges, workplaces, cultures, and generations. There are many books
and articles that offer a variety of perspectives on how to dress, act, speak, or
carry oneself in different situations, in many cases based on social norms.

While personal appearance factors do not appear to be instruction-related
issues, they do have an effect on teacher likeability. Evidence strongly suggests that the clearest indicator or predictor of self-reported learning is the
likeability or warmth of a teacher.[3, 19, 41, 45, 91–94] This is not surprising, given
the fact that teachers need to influence learners by keeping them engaged,
and learners are more engaged and have a higher regard or *affinity* with a
teacher who is warm and likeable.[3, 4, 46, 95] The "likeability" factor is influenced by attractiveness, approachability and formality of dress, leading to the
logical conclusion that how you look and behave will affect learning outcomes.[45, 92, 93, 96] This is apparent in evaluations of teachers, both inside the
classroom and online, such as the very popular site *RateMyProfessors.com,*
where students rate more attractive professors higher and give them more
positive feedback than their less attractive counterparts.[45, 92, 93, 96] Apparently,
there is no discounting of the effect of personal appearance on a learner's
overall impression of a teacher.

Don't despair! While it may seem disheartening to think that students can
be swayed by a pretty face, there are a number of other factors beyond personal appearance that affect learning outcomes, including expertise, empathy,
passion, and all of the other personality skills discussed in this chapter, not
to mention the content and delivery skills covered in the next two chapters.
So don't give up on your academic career just because you aren't exactly a

Hollywood heartthrob! Some things are clearly out of your control. Even though you can't just become a better-looking person, you can find ways to look better. Your individual expression is clearly observable in the context of the learning environment and therefore merits attention. To that end, developing personal appearance as a *skill* requires your truthful attention to the image you have of yourself and the image you choose to display.

Self-Appraisal

How you *look* and *behave* begins with a self-reflection and ends with a reflection of yourself that others get to experience. From a psychological perspective, research has continually shown a strong correlation between low self-image and low self-esteem, citing those who feel less attractive or less good about themselves as having a lower self-worth; and, this reflects on lower performance and negative social behavior.[97] Perhaps our image-conscious society has created a problem that affects our jobs. The concepts of splendor and fashion are highlighted constantly in the media, and social status is often assigned based on appearances, while those who may not live up to the cultural standards of beauty are disadvantaged. Although it seems completely illogical to compare our standards with that of celebrity, it still happens. In light of such social comparisons it is easy to understand how one can succumb to a lower opinion of oneself. On the other hand, it is not uncommon for instructors to use affinity-seeking strategies, such as maintaining a pleasant appearance, to build stronger interpersonal relationships with learners.[95]

Personal appearance is one such affinity attribute that is affected by the way you dress, your grooming habits, and other physical displays of your persona which are part of the overall "look" that learners observe. However, personal appearance is really more about having a *personable* appearance. It's more about attitude than attire. It's more about attentiveness than attractiveness. It's more about teaching than trending. Moreover, the language choices you make based on appropriateness and social correctness are verbal expressions of your "behavior" with learners. If you dress poorly, and your appearance is distracting, or you make inappropriate comments or jokes, your level of effectiveness as teacher will easily be compromised.

If you feel challenged or disappointed in some aspect of your personal appearance, you can control your ability to positively impact students by placing greater efforts into other teaching skills. Remember that your *image* is a balanced composite of many skills. Understanding these will allow you to easily compensate for what you perceive to be shortcomings or negative feelings.

Dressing Appropriately

The evidence exists that in addition to attractiveness and approachability, the formality of dress contributes to the overall "likeability" factor of an instructor.[45] Therefore, what you wear will create a visual impression for your learners. When the environment or setting is not an issue, both men and women should feel comfortable maintaining gender as an expression. A woman should not avoid wearing a dress just to try to blend into a room full of men, thinking that she must dress like a man to be accepted. At the same time, a wild haircut may be acceptable at an art school but the same style might be frowned upon at a medical school. We should celebrate our individuality but not overstep accepted boundaries.

One easy rule to follow whenever you are unsure as to how to dress for any speaking occasion is to be dressed at least *one level above* that of your audience to the extent of the highest expected formality for the occasion. So, in a typical university classroom, if your learners are dressed in casual clothes, you should be dressed at least in *business-casual* attire (one level above them), although it would not be problematic for you to appear in business attire (a business suit, for example). However, if the "culture" of the environment dictates a different formality, you should try to observe the norms and not attempt to alter expectations.

⟿ Just Wear It ⟿

One of my clients is Nike, a leading sports apparel company, known mostly for footwear but dominant in overall sportswear and related accessories. When I first visited the company to schedule a complete presentation skills workshop program, I wore my normal business attire (suit and tie) for the meeting.

The vice president of human resources responsible for setting up the seminars asked me how I planned to dress for the workshop sessions and I responded that I would wear something similar to my current business attire. She said that she appreciated my formality but asked if I would be willing to dress more business-casual instead of business, losing the jacket and tie elements. She told me that the dress code within the company is to foster a sporty, relaxed, casual look, similar to their apparel lines, and employees had continually requested that invited speakers and consultants follow the same casual code if possible.

I could have argued the point, citing the rule of dressing one level above the audience, while maintaining my sense of style and comfort. But organizational "culture" always supersedes general guidelines, especially when specifically requested by the host. I had no problem dressing less formally than I am used to, because that was considered "appropriate" for the occasion.

⌒⌒⌒⌒

Some people may choose to follow a more traditional approach to attire using the BASIC principle: a **B**elievable **A**ppearance is **S**imple and the **I**mage is **C**onservative.[85, 86] In other words, you can elect to maintain a sense of personal style, but lean toward a more conservative look, especially if the planned outfit garners too much attention. However, what you wear can reflect individuality, power, or status. Fashion carries a sense of individual expression and should not be compromised, unless the expression is distracting in some way. In fact, the U.S. Senate is a perfect example of how women choose to showcase individuality. Many of the female representatives wear colorful outfits, such as bright red business suits, to stand out from the men, who are typically dressed in dark blue or dark gray suits. You will easily notice this the next time you view a state-of-the-union address.

Fashion is a difficult choice to manage, and as you gain experience in your environment you will easily learn what works and what doesn't. To that end, there are some specific areas that you can manage in order to look more professional in terms of dressing appropriately, by *focusing on the face*, *considering proximity*, and *thinking of technology*.

Focusing on the Face

Your face carries your message through your voice and your expressions, and it can communicate any of the six universal emotions of happiness, sadness, fear, surprise, anger, and disgust.[21] Therefore, you should avoid anything that distracts learners from seeing your face. Your clothing, accessories, hair style, or other cosmetic choices can lessen the impact of your expressions. For example, from a clothing perspective, avoid outfits that draw attention to your form, rather than your face. This is not to say that you need to sacrifice your gender or personal style to try to look androgynous. Rather, you have to understand that if the attention is to the fashion of your form, then you will be taking the focus away from your face. While this may feel socially flattering, in a learning environment it can be counterproductive. If your wardrobe choice is too noticeable, too trendy, too colorful, too avant garde, too funky, too sexy, too loud, or too distracting in some way, then you may wish to reconsider the choice if you find it interfering with the communication of content.

If you plan to use body language and movement to enhance your delivery (see chapter 5, "Body Language Style," page 186) and you are wearing a business suit, the choice of buttoning or unbuttoning the jacket makes a difference for men but not for women. For the men, while the jacket may look better when buttoned, it is better to have freedom of movement in the upper body to allow for natural gestures. With the jacket buttoned, if the wrist is raised higher than the elbow to gesture toward the screen, the jacket will buckle, gape, and pucker unnaturally, billowing out near the chest, as the button presses against the torso. This is because men's jackets are cut boxier. If the jacket is unbuttoned, you will not be restricted when gesturing and you will appear natural.

Considering Proximity

In smaller settings, such as a seminar room or classroom, your facial expressions are more visible and therefore more challenged by items surrounding your eyes and mouth, since these areas carry emotions, language, and intention. For example, more facial hair, such as a full beard or full mustache, will mask the fullness of certain expressions, such as smiles or frowns. We are not telling you to be clean-shaven but consider trimming facial hair, if possible, enough to allow expressions to be more readable. The eyes and the eyebrows carry emotions as well, and the length of your hair can inadvertently cover one of your eyes when you move or turn your head. If your hair reaches your shoulder or is longer, consider keeping it away from your face, pulled back perhaps or at least restricted from blocking your expressions. You don't have to give up fashion; rather, you just have to keep style from taking the focus away from your face while you are teaching.

Thinking of Technology

At times, your clothing choices may facilitate the presence of related technology, such as sound and video. For instance, a *microphone* is often used in larger group settings. If you are using a wireless microphone that clips on (a lavaliere mic), be sure to wear clothing that makes it convenient to hold the clip-on mic and the attached battery pack. For example, wearing a straight dress with a high neckline and no belt will make it quite challenging to attach a clip-on mic and battery pack. The mic will have to be clipped by gathering or pinching the dress material together, and this will look unnatural. The mic may even dislodge if there is sudden movement that causes the fabric to stretch. To compensate, we have seen teachers who end up holding the battery pack in one hand and the microphone in the other, close to the mouth, unable to gesture or move naturally for fear of moving the mic away. Instead, consider clothing that carries the advantage of centering the microphone, such as a tie, a V-neck collar, or a button-down shirt or blouse. In addition, try to wear clothing with a waistband or belt that can hold the battery pack. In fact, wearing a suit jacket allows the battery pack to be placed in a side pocket or inside pocket, hidden from view. In addition, avoid wearing fabrics with rough textures as these may cause a rustling or hissing sound over the microphone as you move.

There may be times where your appearance is viewed through the eyes of a camera, such as in broadcasts, video conferences, or even in large group settings where *image magnification* places you on a screen for people to see you from a distance. Whether you have a professional directing the media or you are personally in control of a webcam, the camera environment relies heavily on lighting and backgrounds to create the impression that you are at a very short distance away. Similar to our discussion of keeping the focus on your face, certain dress code issues can become distracting.

Highly reflective items are the most distracting objects on camera. Avoid shiny lapel pins, earrings, mirrored jewelry, and other items that will cause glare, especially if the reflection is happening inconsistently when you move. Earrings are only a problem if they are too obvious, or noisy, or dangling in a way where the light keeps reflecting back into the audience. One of the most common mistakes is getting up on stage to speak at a large conference wearing the identity badge one is given at such events. Usually these clip-on or hanging name tags are plastic and create a very obvious reflection. Just remove the name badge before you get in front of the camera. No one is able to read your name from a distance anyway.

In some camera situations, clothing can cause unwanted visual effects. Depending on the camera equipment, shirts, blouses, or even ties and scarves with thin vertical stripes can appear to "vibrate" through the camera. This is especially true with the high contrast of thin dark lines on bright white, or even with plaids and houndstooth patterns.[85] Below your face, at the neckline or collar area, accessories such as ties, scarves, or necklaces should be conservative so as to harmonize with your attire and not become the dominate element. Consider solid colors or subtle patterns, where possible. The important thing to remember is that when technology enters the learning environment its limitations cannot be ignored. Work with the camera, the microphones, the lighting, and all the other production elements to ensure that your teaching presence is clearly optimized.

Appearing Distracting

While dressing appropriately can contribute to your personal appearance, other issues may be compromising. Beyond the more obvious concerns of poor hygiene, sloppiness, or a disheveled appearance, factors that contribute to an unprofessional look may also be related to the manner in which a teacher manages the learning environment. For example, in addition to traditional classrooms, instruction may take place in laboratories, production areas, simulated workplaces, public venues, or other physical spaces, all of which should be kept clean and orderly as different groups of learners use the spaces. As an instructor, if you have a disorderly arrangement of materials or a lack of attention to neatness, especially where cleanliness and order are expected, your perceived ability to manage your environment will appear distracting.

Although a professional "look" is desired, the more complete picture of personal appearance also includes the way you "behave," which can become distracting through poor attitude or demeanor, most evident in verbal discourse. Therefore, when comments or humor are *inappropriate*, learners are distracted and dismayed.

Making Inappropriate Comments

In the "Caring" section at the beginning of this chapter we discussed the making of negative comments, being sarcastic, and finding fault as having an adverse effect on learners. From a personal appearance perspective, comments may also be considered "inappropriate" when they cross the borderline of decency, morality, or ethical conduct, and are perceived as teacher *misbehaviors*.

The literature identifies teacher misbehaviors as generally falling into three categories: incompetence, indolence, and offensiveness.[12, 98, 99] Whereas incompetence (lack of ability) and indolence (laziness) indicate severely deficient or nonexistent teaching skills, *offensiveness* is typically in the form of rudeness or mistreatment that is more reactionary or immediate to the situation. For instance, an open comment that humiliates a learner for poor performance is considered inappropriate and may even be seen as a personal attack. Any displeasure you have with a student should be discussed privately. Even if you are disappointed with the entire class and want to verbally admonish them as a group, your condescending remarks will be seen as intimidating and unpleasant. If your goal is to "teach them a lesson" then do just that—*teach them*—that's the lesson!

At times, even when teachers have the best of intentions, seemingly positive behavior may be inappropriate. Instructors who make comments that suggest special treatment for certain students may be seen as "playing favorites." Excessive praise or misplaced friendliness can easily seem improper, especially to learners who feel less favored or at a disadvantage, if the remarks are perceived to show favoritism.

Other inappropriate remarks that have no place in the classroom include politically incorrect comments relating to lifestyle choices, religious beliefs, or ethnic backgrounds. Temper your language to avoid sexist statements, cultural commentary, and self-centered power displays that often segregate learners. Offensiveness, especially verbal abuse, is not only considered unprofessional behavior, but the apparent lack of caring negatively impacts the learner's perception of a teacher's trustworthiness.[12]

Using Inappropriate Humor

We discussed the more positive aspects of using humor in the "Happiness" section of this chapter. But when humor is used inappropriately it reflects on a person's style or character, beyond the intended effect of being funny (or not funny). Humor is directionally challenged. It is acceptable to poke fun at yourself, but not at others. Research shows that the use of self-disparaging remarks or self-deprecating humor adds to an instructor's appeal by increasing rapport with the students.[20] However, more aggressive humor, such as sexual innuendo, insults, or sarcasm, especially when directed at others, is unwelcomed. Off-color comments, sexual jokes, or statements that might be considered offensive to anyone listening are inappropriate.[33] In fact, humor aimed at a select portion of the group may make those targeted feel embarrassed.[100] Thus, a quick comment directed at under-achieving students, such as "Those of you who scored under 50 know exactly what I mean," may sound funny or lightly sarcastic to you, but it won't to those who failed. Moreover, the comment will not enhance learning. If your joking is "at the expense" of others and someone other than you is "paying the price," then consider the humor inappropriate. Some jokes will seem fine because everyone laughs, but some people laugh only to feel included. Those same people could later misinterpret the humor or find it offensive or demeaning. When in doubt, if the humor may be misconstrued, then don't use it.

One way to decide the appropriateness of a comment is to imagine your statement offered to a superior or subordinate, discussed on the TV news, or written up in the newspaper. If the comment would then be an embarrassment to you, it shouldn't be said. Even if the humor is deemed acceptable at the moment, if it has any potential of being *misinterpreted*, then it should be thought of as inappropriate and better left unsaid.

Learners have expectations of teachers to be both professional and professorial, regardless of the topic, course, or study discipline.[17]As a credible source of knowledge, you have the responsibility to look and behave appropriately in all of your teaching activities in order to model for your learners the professional behavior expected of you.

PERSONALITY — SUMMARY AND STRATEGY

As we look ahead . . . leaders will be those who empower others.

—Bill Gates

Table 3.17. Highlights of the personality skills

Personality Skill	*Key Points*
Caring appears genuine and sincere	• A caring teacher is a more credible source of knowledge and contributes to a more positive learning environment • The presence or lack of caring is seen through visible or vocal actions • Caring is evident when learners are supervised, guided, and attentively watched over • Caring is actively supported through encouragement, positive reinforcement, and constructive criticism • Sarcasm and negativity are counterproductive in a caring environment
Empathy sees and understands from the perspective of the audience	• Empathy implies a shared understanding of mutual experiences • To exercise empathy an instructor recalls experiences that match the current feelings of the learners • Words that evoke shared emotions enhance empathy
Happiness evidently enjoys teaching	• Colorful personalities have an advantage • Happiness can be seen through concrete visible actions, such as body language and vocal tones • Displaying anger or showing disappointment adversely affects happiness in the learning environment
Energy demonstrates a liveliness in sharing knowledge	• Students notice the lack of energy more than its presence • Burnout is a deterioration of an instructor's ability to teach effectively, characterized by stress, emotional exhaustion, and frustration • The combination of an instructor's personal investment in the content along with the positive expression of enthusiasm contributes to a high-energy teacher
Passion believes in what he or she is presenting	• Belief in content is the foundation for credibility • Happiness, energy, and motivation are interlinked to passion

Table 3.17. (Continued)

Personality Skill	Key Points
Motivation instills a sense of enthusiasm in learners	• Some learners are driven by an internal desire, others are stimulated by external matters, and some are not motivated at all • Rapid recall is an activity that focuses on key learning points • Motivation includes: self-control of the learning process, collaborative relationships with peers, interesting academic tasks, personal connection to content, expectation of positive outcomes, and clearly defined goals.
Expertise logically explains and simplifies the materials	• Expertise is a continual, dynamic, and ever-changing process that requires desire, practice, and coaching, along with constructive feedback • Experts use multiple teaching strategies, are highly flexible, and use continual self-reflection • Experts have the ability or talent to be in tune with learner feelings or outcomes
Inspiration makes learners feel encouraged to incorporate learned concepts	• Inspirational teachers are influential to the lives of the learners far "beyond teaching" • Leadership-driven techniques that inspire learners include behavior modeling, transformational teaching, and mentoring • Inspirational teachers have a high level of emotional intelligence
Self-Confidence appears prepared and in control of a presentation or discussion, regardless of the audience size, level of expertise, or rank	• Self-confidence starts by knowing one's fears and limitations • The main reasons for feeling intimidated include: looking foolish, being judged, appearing boring, and wasting time • Prepared teachers are rarely nervous or intimidated • High self-confidence and a strong sense of emotional maturity help effectively control the classroom climate
Approachable appears friendly and receptive to comments and interaction	• Approachable instructors develop collaborative and supportive relationships with learners to achieve desired educational outcomes • Stimulating interaction increases opportunities for approachability • A prerequisite to being approachable is to be available
Personal Appearance looks and behaves professionally	• Image is a balanced composite of self-confidence, interaction, body language style, and speaking style, as well as being approachable • Personal appearance is affected by style as well by behavior • Inappropriate language or humor compromises professional and professorial behavior

4

Process

Professors known as outstanding lecturers do two things; they use a simple plan and many examples.

—Wilbert J. McKeachie

By definition, a *process* is a planned course of action, a pathway, or a procedure that can be developed and put into place to achieve an outcome. An instructional methodology can be comprised of lectures, discussions, interactions, independent work, and technology-based activities. The related teaching behavior can be isolated into skills of *organization* and *expressiveness*.[1] The *process* elements, discussed in this chapter, are organizational in nature. The *performance* elements, discussed in the next chapter, are more expressive behaviors. There is debate in the literature as to which behaviors, organizational or expressive, contribute more toward student achievement. Some findings have shown that behaviors of organization are directly linked to actual *achievement* outcomes, while expressive behaviors are directly related to learner perceptions of the *amount* learned. However, there is general agreement that the presence of both behaviors produces an optimal learning environment.[1–3] Our research of learner preferences also supports the presence of both behaviors as contributing significantly to teaching effectiveness.[4]

From a *process* perspective, it is apparent that students learn better when content is structured, clear, concise, well designed, and offered in a setting conducive to learning. The challenges for teachers involve lack of organization, overabundance of material, clutter of details, poor use of technology, and inability to manage the learning environment. When one or more of these obstacles are evident, the negative effect on teaching effectiveness can be significant.[1, 3, 5]

Conversely, the opportunities to enhance the learning process are seen when teachers provide concrete examples, add stories and analogies to connect ideas, design support visuals that are easy to read, include a variety of

115

activities beyond lectures, and respect the limited time available for learners to grasp the amount of material presented. As you minimize challenges and maximize opportunities, you can continually focus on addressing the needs of your learners, based on their preferences.

The common thread in developing the process skills is *content*. To better understand these skills, a perspective on student feedback is necessary. Table 4.1 outlines the positive and negative keywords expressed by learners related to the process skills.[4] Some of these comments come as no surprise to seasoned educators who have seen similar words and phrases on student evaluations and other forms of feedback.

From an organizational perspective, the process elements described in this chapter focus on the skills needed to plan the teaching material and manage

Table 4.1. Feedback on process skills from both student and professional learners

Process Skill	Feedback from Learners	
	Negative	Positive
Content Organization	confusing ideas, disorganized, abstract references, slides unrelated to content	good construction, well-thought-out, easy to follow, gives good examples
Content Development	rushes through material, too many points, too much information	clarity, tells stories, elaborates, uses cases
Content Design	cluttered slides, too much animation, text too small, long sentences, paragraphs of text, words not visible on background	good contrast on slides, good PowerPoint design, background not distracting, uses pictures to explain topic
Additional Sense Stimulation	poor sound quality, video unclear, too many "special effects"	multimedia, helpful animation, hands-on activities, uses clickers for questions
Environment	too dark, room too cold, people walking in and out	starts on time, comfortable seating, good view of presenter and screen

the way the information is offered to the learners. Figure 4.1 illustrates the significance that *student* learners attach to each of the process skills.

These learners express the highest preference for content organization; content development; content design; and, to a lesser extent, additional sense stimulation and an optimal learning environment.[4] As you develop your effectiveness using the skills assessment tools, any of your "process" challenges should be addressed according to the significance noted in figure 4.1 so that you can prioritize your efforts based on learner preferences. For example, if you find that you are challenged in the areas of *content design* and *additional sense stimulation*, you should work on content design first, because this is a more highly preferred skill as perceived by student learners.

This chapter focuses mainly on developing content from a planning and design perspective. The following sections: *content organization*, *content development*, *content design*, *additional sense stimulation*, and *environment* offer perspectives, insights, references, and recommendations to help you better address the needs of your learners and enhance your overall teaching effectiveness.

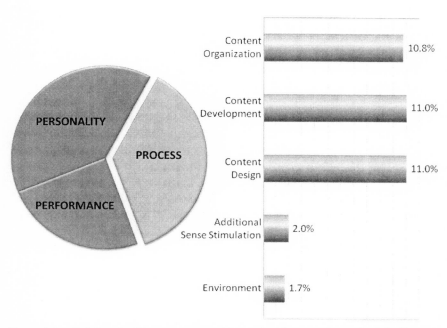

Figure 4.1. **Relative significance expressed by student learners for each of the Process skills**

CONTENT ORGANIZATION

It usually takes more than three weeks to prepare a good impromptu speech.

—Mark Twain

We describe content organization as a characteristic of one who applies real-world situations to simplify content.[4] If the content is not organized, the students do not follow along and soon become disinterested. The effective professor guides the learners along a path of understanding that is orderly, structured, and well-thought-out, providing a measure of *clarity*.

Teacher clarity is part verbal and part structural.[6] The *development* of content, discussed later in this chapter, focuses on *verbal* clarity; namely, the skills of offering information in various formats to help sustain the learning process. But, *structural* clarity is found in the *organization* of ideas, activities, interactions, and discussions in order to help learners understand lecture material and easily follow the logic of the content.

Connecting the Dots

You may recall a childhood moment of artistry when you had to connect a series of numbered dots to reveal a picture. The key to the artwork was in the creative choices made by the designer in identifying which portions of the underlying image (the dots) would serve as the connectors. Organizing content can follow a similar pattern if you identify the key points of a topic (the dots) and then build the connectors (references, examples, etc.) to ultimately reveal your picture (learning outcomes). By breaking the topic into units or learning segments, you help learners understand the relationship between sections and thus they more easily grasp the information.

Clarity in content organization is related to how the learning material is *sequenced* in order to establish relationships between the dots, including the manner in which the professor verbalizes the connections. Studies show that student retention and achievement are positively influenced by the orderly arrangement of key points in a topic combined with transitional phrases that show the relationships among these points.[7] Well-organized content is important for learning.[5] From a clear structure, learners can delineate subsections that are more difficult to comprehend allowing them to revisit a section and understand the relationships among ideas. However, if your lectures are chaotic collections of random facts and figures, then your students will have less control in their understanding of the disorganized material, resulting in poor learning outcomes.[8]

Traditional Structure

Organization of content, in a traditional sense, usually follows a pattern starting with an *outline* of the topic, where the learners understand exactly what will be covered as the professor explains briefly the relationship among the parts of the outline. This scope or breadth of detail helps learners focus on the important elements in the topic and the sequential order in which these items are likely to appear and be discussed, all of which relates to the preset learning outcomes established by the teacher. The use of predetermined or standardized learning objectives typifies many instructional curriculum designs.[9] To make these objectives cohesive, individual topics throughout a given course or program must tie together seamlessly. Each topic can be subdivided into major content areas or related sections.

By breaking a specific topic into sections, the information is more manageable by both the teacher and the learners. During a lecture, the instructor makes *transitional* statements that signify the end of one section and the beginning of the next, clearly connecting the two areas (see "Phrasing" in chapter 5, page 208). Without this connection, students cannot see the relationship between the parts. As each portion of a topic is revealed, *comparisons* emerge, such as contrasting one section with another or showing similarities across sections. The final phase of the session is a *summary*, which basically reviews the original outline to verify the points that have been covered while clarifying the relationships among the main ideas presented.

This process of *outlining-transitioning-comparing-summarizing* is just one approach to providing a clearly organized delivery of content. In fact, the *order* in which content is presented can alter learner perception as to the level of importance of information based on its priority in a given outline.[1] For faculty who are less familiar with different teaching strategies, consider organizing content from higher to lower priority to help students retain important concepts.

Randomization is also possible. Research shows that the sequencing of information within an organized structure can *deviate* from the order of the proposed outline, allowing instructors to cover material in different ways and not be bound to a single step-by-step approach to teaching.[7] Using the same analogy of a connect-the-dots diagram, imagine a more complex scheme where the dots are connected in such odd patterns that you need to wait until the very end to see the complete picture. Thus, a more seasoned professor may choose to jump around among outlined topics while establishing relationships between sections using a chunking strategy, where distinct pieces of information are grouped together linking pre-existing knowledge with new concepts.[8] However, because the connecting dots (sections) seem scattered, the professor must tie the concepts together and ultimately reveal the big picture of the learning at the very end. Without this final picture, learners will be lost. For example, an accounting professor perhaps outlines a lesson that discusses three different depreciation methods but chooses to cover each method randomly, not in the sequence noted on the outline. If comparisons are made and the depreciation methods are linked together logically (as to when to use each one), the learners are better able to grasp the concepts and gain a greater understanding of the *bigger picture* of depreciation.

Whether you choose to adhere to a sequential outline or bring together separate sections of content, your growing experience as an instructor will allow you to experiment with various approaches in order to continually foster the most effective learning environment.

Abstract or Concrete

Clarity is important in content organization, but one of the most challenging obstacles to clarity is the instructor's use of abstract references. The learning effect of using abstract references is described in the literature as *receiver apprehension*, where learners perceive they are unable to process information immediately because connecting elements are missing or too abstract to identify.[6] Such apprehension has been shown to lead to negative learning outcomes and reduced student achievement or involvement. During class, as learning is taking place, direct references or assigned tasks should be clear and concrete, to avoid receiver apprehension. Outside of class, such as for general research assignments, references can be more abstract to encourage self-directed learning.

During class, throughout a presentation, lecture, or discussion, you are very likely to link facts and figures to references or sources of the data. If your references are vague or abstract, your learners will be forced to make sense of the nonfigurative comments by creating more tangible representations on their own. This effort separates a cohesive group of listeners into a collection of individual perceivers of the content. Each learner will attempt to visualize, quantify, interpret, or investigate his or her own version of your perspective. For example, suppose that during the course of instruction, you say, "Just look around and you can see examples of fast-paced activities." The generality of the statement opens a door in the mind of each individual to fill in the blanks: where to look, when to look, and what types of fast-paced activities to look for. The intent of your message is subject to many interpretations, making it more abstract. Each listener is momentarily distracted and this reduces your ability to keep the group focused on the content. However, your statement can offer more details such as, "Go to the cafeteria during a peak lunch hour. Stand near one of the checkout counters and observe the fast-paced actions of people wanting to pay and go as quickly as possible." The specific directions focus the learners on the same page or picture of what you intended. They know where to look (cafeteria near a checkout counter), when to look (peak lunch hour), and what to look for (people in a hurry). The intent of your message is more concrete when the group can visualize the same image or description. Table 4.2 shows some comparisons between abstract statements and more concrete versions, offering specific details for greater focus.

To elaborate on a point, explain a situation, or make an association, you may introduce the illustration with phrases such as "for example," "for instance," "let's say," "suppose," "what if," or "case in point." To keep learners focused, avoid generalizing and incorporate *concrete examples* wherever possible. To illustrate, a business law professor, discussing the different forms of contracts, offers the following statement: "One type of contract is a promise for an act. For example, person A promises to do something for person B in exchange for something of value." The professor's example contains several abstract elements, most notably with the word "something."

Table 4.2. Comparing the difference between abstract references and more concrete links to content

Abstract	Concrete
You can research this and you will find a lot of good information.	If you research the phrase "translucent glass properties," look for results that link to the website "Scientifica.uk.com."
Read the textbook for next week and we will have a discussion.	Read chapter 14 for next week and pay particular attention to the section on the role of the Federal Reserve System. I plan to center our discussion around the advantages and disadvantages of the system.
I recall a study that identified behavioral problems in children with diabetes.	Cohen's 2004 study on behavioral problems in diabetic children.
Does anyone see a problem with this story?	Based on what we just learned about punctuation, what three mistakes did the writer make in this story?
Are there any questions?	Are there any questions about the causes of pH imbalance?

The learners will have to envision specific details to complete this picture. The professor could have illustrated the example more concretely, saying "One type of contract is a promise for an act. For example, Ellen promises to wash her mother's car for twenty dollars." The added details paint a more concrete picture of the example. The people have identities (daughter/ mother), the act is described (washing a car), and the value is specified ($20).

Keep in mind that you don't have to give infinitesimal, specific details just to avoid being abstract. In the above example, the learners do not have to know the last names of the people, the brand of car, the time of day, the weather conditions, or even how long the car washing activity might take. Providing too many details is unnecessary, but clarifying a few abstract elements will help your learners stay more focused on the intended message in the example. This should not be confused with "spoon feeding," where you are removing any analytical thinking for the students.

Interestingly, it is possible to use abstract references as a *teaching tool* if your objective is to develop the organizational skills of your learners. For instance, to exercise the research and analysis traits of your students you may say, "Take a look at the problem I posed and try to figure out how to solve it. Use whatever resources necessary." Without explicit directions, it would appear that this assignment is too vague. Yet, because the *intention* is to force learners to think independently, the vagueness helps them make personal decisions regarding the manner in which they will each handle the assigned task. In this case, the use of an abstract reference serves a learning purpose.

Practical Application

Part of an instructor's expertise is the ability to place content into the context of the "real world" in order to demonstrate the practical application of information (see The "Know-What" and the "Know-How" in chapter 3, page 67).

In higher education, the majority of faculty do not possess a *teaching degree*; rather, their expertise is within a given discipline from which they combine practical experience with content knowledge. It is not uncommon for a full-time finance instructor to have worked several years as a stock-broker before joining the academic environment. An adjunct faculty teaching music history three times a week may conduct an orchestra on other days. A tenured medical professor still attends to a one-day-a-week practice. As an instructor, you integrate knowledge, experience, wisdom, and even your own beliefs to organize content in such a way that you deliver information effectively while developing the learning skills of your learners.[10] Thus, if you enhance a curriculum by introducing cases based on real situations while including your views or opinions, your learners build skills related to inquiry (who, what, when, where, why and how), and controversy (agree/disagree), and not just those of memory.

Beyond practical experience, a number of faculty have exposure to various forms of professional development activities, such as attending established courses or programs, networking among faculty in other institutions, encouraging peer reviews, and seeking additional feedback opportunities to learn new techniques for organizing content. The benefit to learners is that a teacher can bring both practical experience and continual professional development into the classroom in order to shape content to the needs of newer and more diverse groups.

CONTENT DEVELOPMENT

Spoon feeding in the long run teaches us nothing but the shape of the spoon.

—E. M. Forster

We describe content development as the ability to develop a concise and clear message.[4] In terms of teaching, this "message" relates to the meaning, significance, and intention of the communication toward some learning objective.

In a world of deadlines, data, and overlapping multiple tasks, time is of the essence. The learners want it quick, they want it easy, and they want it now! While they can get overwhelmed with the details, they seem to desire the highlights, preferring the instructor who streamlines content, favoring quality over quantity. It is not surprising then, that the current generation, time starved and task challenged, prefers that content be clear, concise, and to the point. The preference of learners for quality content is based on clarity and crispness.[11] Whereas content organization is based on *structural* clarity, content development is a function of *verbal* clarity. When complex topics are presented succinctly, students feel empowered to learn. In fact, student ratings have been shown to be more positive when instructors provide clear explanations of content.[12]

Yet, the mere reduction of content for the purpose of being concise is not sufficient. The one-way street of an instructor lecturing and students listening leads to passive learning, an environment in which learners participate less. Learning is a *shared responsibility*, and the educational literature promotes the idea of a "learner-centric" university where collaboration exists between students and teachers.[13] The objective of content development should be focused around sharing the expectations of the learners while managing the material required for competency and comprehension.

While acquiring the basic knowledge of content is important for learners, it has been a long-standing belief that the *synthesis* or compiling of diverse elements from multiple sources (courses, for example) is what leads to creating new meaning.[14] When ideas are integrated or connected to the real-world, students discover for themselves how the learning applies in life, and they are motivated to learn more.[15, 16] This shared process of teaching and learning helps instructors create content that encourages student development. To that end, teachers are faced with the age-old question: How much should be taught in the given time? The answer has to do with *expectations*, *exposures*, and *expressions*.

Realistic Expectations

Part of content planning revolves around the commitment of the learners to the material. When students know what is expected of them, they have a better chance of learning. The educational literature discusses the importance of an instructor's clarity in outlining the *time commitment* that learners should dedicate to a course in order to perform satisfactorily.[17] Too often, however, students underestimate the amount of time and effort needed to complete assignments, conduct research, read articles, and so forth. The effective instructor develops content in a manner that makes the material manageable in the learning environment, beyond just the classroom. It is not enough to build an organized syllabus, course outline, agenda, or some type of material management system and simply *expect* the learners to follow your plan in the hope of understanding. Part of the vested interest in learning is in the use of the knowledge.

Therefore, your expectations of your learners should also include the *practical application* of the content you develop. What would you like the learners to be able to do when they come out of your session? Should they recognize the complexity? Should they realize that there is more reading material to explore? Should they have a complete understanding of that learning module? Do they need to apply learned concepts immediately? Should they use the learning as part of another related course? Is there a case attached to the learning that they must investigate or discuss in order to fully comprehend everything? Whatever the outcome, make sure your expectations are realistic, achievable, and applicable to continual learning or real-world practice. In general, faculty tend to pack too much information into the learning lesson. As a result, the students tend to not understand the material in depth.

Multiple Exposures

In developing content, where the goal is clarity and conciseness, seasoned professors find ways to present the same information on more than one occasion. Research shows that planned *repetition* invokes specific neurological functions in the brain to facilitate learning.[18] We are not talking about repetition in the sense of reciting, or replaying information over and over until committed to memory, as in rote learning; instead, we see repetition of key concepts or principles as a means to increase *understanding*, perhaps leading to a discovery of new meaning or greater comprehension. The synthesis of information is enhanced through multiple exposures to the content. Repetition plays a role in the *selective retention* of important information. Studies show that learners distinguish information of higher importance based on the initial exposure to content presented, and can glean additional information if the content is repeated or restated multiple times.[19] In other words, if students are given the chance to experience the content more than once, they will learn additional details to gain a wider perspective of the topic.

In a well-designed curriculum, content is not limited to a single lecture or presentation. Usually, the learning objectives allow for repetition of important concepts in several lectures within a program of study. For example, a philosophy professor says, "If you recall the writings of Sartre that we discussed a few weeks ago, his existentialist view involved freedom. Today we see how his contemporary, Albert Camus, focuses on the futility of existentialism in this story of Sisyphus." The professor reinforces (repeats) the philosophical issue of existentialism by contrasting the two writers, weeks apart. The students are offered another view of the same concept. From a content development perspective, clarity increases with multiple exposures to the same idea, repeating key learning points in several related topics within a course or across a group of learning modules that are interwoven, much like a web, across the entire curriculum.

Multiple Expressions

When learners have multiple exposures to similar content, clarity increases; but, if the manner in which the content is presented is *similar*, redundancy may result, and the students may not see the information in a "different" light. In other words, content development is not a one-stop shop, mainly because there are limitations to any *single expression* of a teaching methodology. Whether it be a classroom lecture, a small group seminar, a case-based discussion, or an online course—whatever the single expression or form might be—there will always be limitations.

For example, an online course containing archived content lacks a live instructor to give immediate responses to student questions. A case-based discussion can easily be dominated by those most familiar with the case, while alienating those least familiar, forcing a professor to manage the input of the learners. As an instructor developing content, you begin by understanding what the limitations are so that you can align your expectations of the learners with the limitations of the given format. Therefore, while individual teaching methodologies may each have limitations, it is the sum total of the multiple expressions of the content that leads to a more complete learning experience.

To maximize the efficiency of these different formats, you will need to plan the content in advance. Many instructors that we interviewed indicated that they preferred to give three repetitions of the content, across a variety of formats, to instill the learning. For example, an instructor might have the lecture recorded as a *podcast* for learners to listen to at a later time and support the given lecture with a downloadable version in PowerPoint, which can include notes and annotations. When using multiple expressions to deliver material, you should add additional content items to supplement the learning, thus limiting the amount of information covered during lecture time (see "Creating Handouts" in this chapter, page 163).

Multiple formats of teaching are at your disposal and you will need to prepare content in a manner that supports the network or lattice of curriculum design, only some of which is delivered through lectures and seminars, thus maximizing the use of classroom time.

Length x Time = Difficulty

Regardless of the teaching venue (lecture, seminar, discussion, etc.) your biggest limitations to covering the topic will be *length* and *time*. Simply put, in a one-hour session, you cannot teach the theory, the background, the practice, the advantages, the disadvantages, the future applications, and everything else related to the topic. It is not possible. Our research found that learners expressed the futility of excessive information as a proverbial *data dump*, where an instructor *tries to cover too much material in the given time*. This scenario is not uncommon, but the challenge here can be viewed as a two-part dilemma: "too much material" and "too little time."

Too Much Material

Your goal is to simplify the content whenever possible and limit the learning objectives of the lecture, seminar, or presentation to a few key issues. However, many faculty believe that taking a more simplistic approach to content is akin to *dumbing down* the material. Simplifying and dumbing down are not the same thing. *Simplifying* is the act of making learners understand a more complex topic, allowing them to exercise analytical thinking while building a foundational knowledge of the basic principles. *Dumbing down* is the eliminating of *all* complexity and requiring students to just memorize certain facts for the sake of exam performance. To simplify the content, you can incorporate strategies in the learning process so that the students can understand the fundamental principles as a starting point toward developing an ability to grasp more complex issues. But, be careful! Bestowing an abundance of the basics can backfire.

Learners have difficulty immediately absorbing a number of concepts, one after another, and, as a result, they usually employ "note-taking" strategies to save information for later review. If you are covering too much material in a given lecture, you may be placing the burden of learning onto the note-taking efforts of the students, expecting that after they leave your session, they will read the notes over and over. The difficulty with note taking is that not every learner focuses attention on the highest-level information in the same way.[19] Each person places a priority on content, yet there is no standard way of taking notes. Therefore, you cannot meet the "too much material" challenge by simply shifting excessive content to the notebooks of your learners and expect that each of them is equally taking away the most important points in the topic.

Covering too much material impacts a number of other skill categories. By having a wealth of content to deliver, you end up with cluttered slides and complex diagrams (*Content Design*) and, to be accurate, you narrate the slides (*Speaking Style*), reading every word, every line, every bullet. You don't simplify the topic (*Expertise*) as you make more and more abstract references (*Content Organization*). You speak quickly (*Speaking Style*) and pick up the pace in your actions (*Body Language Style*). You drift from the topic (*Focus*), ask fewer questions (*Interaction*), and rarely encourage participation (*Approachable*). Many of your skills suffer in the vain attempt to deliver too much material.

Where possible, spread your content across multiple expressions, including online teaching, case reviews, and self-directed student learning. Consider facilitating active learning through discussions and small-group learning exercises, while encouraging learners to team-up and collaborate on problem solving. These cooperative learning techniques promote responsibility and interaction.[20]

Too Little Time

In many cases, you may find that you are teaching to the *given time* rather than to the learning objectives. For a one-hour lecture, you may be preparing a full hour of material, leaving no time for interaction, questions, comments, discussions, repetition, or other interpersonal communication with the learners. But interruptions inevitably occur, and by the end of your session, it seems as if you had too little time available to teach the topic effectively.

⤳ The 6-Minute Mile ⤳

Cameron, now a very distinguished professor of pharmacology is currently in his seventies. He recalls an experience he had as a young teacher in his late twenties. As a relatively new instructor at the university, Cameron was invited to give a 20-minute presentation in front of a high-profile clinical audience to describe his cutting-edge research, which had taken him years to develop.

The audience was important, he was very enthusiastic, and just like any novice instructor he wanted to jam-pack as much information as possible into his presentation. He was thinking more about his reputation than what the audience's take-away message should be.

In earnest and with great attention to detail, this junior faculty developed his full 20-minute presentation, covering all aspects of his untiring research efforts. He couldn't have been more prepared and ready for his big moment to arrive.

However, on the day before his presentation, the conference coordinator told Cameron that they had to squeeze somebody else into the agenda, one who also had something very significant to say. The young instructor's jaw dropped as he was told his 20-minute presentation would be shortened to just 12 minutes. He was clearly disappointed.

Refusing to go down without a fight, he decided to plead his case directly to the head of the program, Dr. Eldrige, a prominent, soft-spoken, very distinguished, seasoned professor. Cameron patiently waited outside Dr. Eldrige's office for what seemed like an eternity, hoping for a chance to see the elder educator.

Suddenly, the office door opened and Cameron jumped up, immediately pleading, "Sir, I cannot believe what has happened to me! I am so upset! They cut my 20-minute presentation by 8 minutes! Eight *full* minutes! I desperately need to talk with you about this!" The older professor calmly said, "Listen, I'm really busy. If you want to talk, then talk to me as we are walking."

As they walked from one building to the next, Cameron explained how the conference coordinator cut his presentation nearly in half and he didn't know how he could possibly cover all of the content without those 8 precious minutes. To become familiar with the finer details of the project, Dr. Eldrige said, "Tell me what it is that you are trying to present."

So, as they walked, Cameron started describing the presentation, the research, the findings, the methods, and conclusions. They continued to walk as Cameron talked in a very concise manner, summarizing the information with short key phrases, clearly explaining everything to help the professor understand. The young instructor concluded his argument as he said, "So, Dr. Eldrige, you can plainly see the importance of those extra 8 minutes!"

The older professor stopped and said, "Well, since we started walking, I've been timing you, and it's taken you only 6 minutes to cover the details of your presentation in a way in which I completely understood. Considering that you have 12 minutes, which is double what you need, you can certainly cover your material in the given time!"

⚊∿∽⚊

We are not suggesting that whatever the content, just cut it in half and you can deliver the same message. Don't get caught up in trying to squeeze information into every minute. Instead, build your session with a 20 percent leeway for other learning activities. By focusing on the most important elements of the topic, you will be able to manage the material, the interruptions, the discussions, the interactions, and everything else that occurs in the dynamic environment of the classroom, in the given time.

Teacher Time vs. Learner Time

At times, the content must stay "as is" and remain unchanged regarding the amount of material to be covered. You may be wondering how to develop content so that two hours of material will magically fit into one hour of time. Rather than trying to fit content *within* the given time, consider distributing the content *around* the given time, using external assignments.

From a content development perspective, *teacher time* is the time you spend inside the classroom. Everything else is *learner time*. The ability to distribute content between teacher time and learner time gives you greater flexibility in planning your topic, letting you expand the given time for the learning session by assigning activity that supports the learning yet takes place outside the classroom. Some of the teaching can be transferred to the learners in the form of self-directed learning through "outside" assignments, making the students accountable for their education. Research suggests that when learners take responsibility for learning, the outcomes of higher education are more positive.[20]

Using a *before-during-after* approach, the teacher time (during class) is surrounded by learner time (before and after class) to expand the given time available for a topic. From a *before* standpoint, some professors develop content that includes a *pre-assignment* for the learners, either a worksheet, some research material, a pertinent article, relevant literature, or other type of work that enables students to enter the learning session empowered with a higher level of understanding of the *yet-to-be-learned* topic.

If basic (foundational) knowledge can be gained through pre-assignment, then instructors focus on fewer, yet higher-priority concepts, *during* class, allowing time for class participation, interaction, and discussion, as students learn the topic. Many instructors continue the content development plan, extending the given time to *after* class with a *post-assignment*, better known as homework, which encourages students to do additional work to see how learned concepts are applied. Keep in mind that many teachers push too much material into the "before" and the "after" time, which can quickly lead to *academic burnout*, a condition that adversely affects students.[21]

The *before-during-afte*r process is a collaborative effort. A professor's responsibility is to maximize the efficiency of teacher time and make courses exciting inside the classroom, while motivating students to continue the learning outside of the classroom.

Once Upon a Time . . .

While the challenges of length and time involve *managing* the material, there are many opportunities for *enhancing* that material. One of the more common teacher characteristics preferred by learners is an instructor's ability to *use stories or analogies to enhance content.*

For example, if a history professor discusses the fact that the Egyptians mummified corpses, the learners will be exposed to pertinent information. However, if the instructor tells an interesting *story* about visiting a museum where the step-by-step mummifying process was revealed, the students will gain an enhanced perspective. The same professor might add an *analogy* by explaining how part of the mummifying process is similar to wrapping food to be stored in the freezer. The comparison to a real-world, everyday experience (preserving food) creates a modern link to an ancient process (mummifying). Analogies draw comparisons in order to show similarities, placing concepts into current context. Your ability to create compelling and interesting moments using stories and analogies throughout the teaching allows learners to experience the *practicality* of the topic, while anchoring concepts.

If you can tie a relevant, real-life scenario to the topic and present the anecdote in an interesting manner, the impact of the lesson is greater. Depending on the nature of the story, and the manner in which it is told, it is possible to have a profound effect on the audience, where the learners become captivated by the details in the story while at the same time absorbing the information.

You can also use stories and analogies as part of a *reflective learning* process in which students are asked to immediately apply learned concepts. For example, an economics professor is discussing ethical principles regarding a professional's need to avoid conflicts of interest. After outlining the generally accepted ethical principles of conduct, the instructor tells a story to illustrate a dilemma, giving the group time to think about all the possible issues surrounding the challenging scenario. The students reflect on already-learned concepts and reference the basic principles to figure out how to resolve the issue, perhaps with a productive debate on the topic.

While stories can be *spontaneous*, arising out of the experience of the instructor to address an immediate issue, *pre-determined storytelling* is more likely to foster reflective learning, where students may make comments or expand on the given story to delve deeper into the topic.[22] To be most effective, plan your stories in advance. Ask yourself, "Is there a scenario I can describe or a story that I can tell that will have an impact?" It is not a waste of time out of the lecture to converse in this manner. It's not chatter or casual banter. Storytelling is a planned instructional technique that can be used at any point in the teaching. The best ways to use this technique is to write down the goals and key learning objectives of the lecture and then make sure that any stories or analogies you use support one or more of the objectives. This will ensure the relevancy of the added material.

Storytelling Strategies

The educational literature supports storytelling as a means of reflective learning, especially where a teller reveals specific elements so that the listeners relate to the teller's experience more fully.[22] The goal is to develop a story in such a way to cover three major components: time, place, and circumstance (conditions) in order to make the story believable and real enough to give a clear picture of the setting. By saying "when" it happened, "where" it happened, and "what" happened, listeners will be able to focus as a group. When done well, this strategy is effective in anchoring the story in memory and connecting it to your associated learning objectives. This is also the basis of problem-based learning.

⟅⟅ All in the Details ⟆⟆

"Many years ago I was at a trade show and everything was hectic." It would appear that the components of *time*, *place*, and *circumstance* are present in this one sentence. But the components are vague. The lack of detail will cause each listener to substitute a more exact reference for these unspecified ones.

The phrase "many years ago" will be interpreted differently by different people. The phrase "trade show" will make listeners drift into whatever personal reference to a trade show they may know. The phrase "everything was hectic" is completely open-ended and subject to interpretation. When elements of the story are not specific, an audience member is left to his or her own experience to help the story makes sense.

Let's change the story. "I remember in August of 1998, I was in Las Vegas, Nevada, at a computer trade show called COMDEX. There were 100,000 attendees crammed into the Flamingo Hilton hotel and there was no air conditioning. Everything was hectic." Suddenly, the elements of time, place, and circumstance have been met, and the story has a defined measure of *clarity*.

It is this attention to detail that focuses the minds of the entire audience on the same story, the same conditions, and the same specifics.

Stories not only help relate experiences, but they can rely on the element of surprise, contain extraneous details, and act as digressions, all for the purposes of enhancing learning.

The Aha! Statement

Somewhere in your story, consider the element of surprise. The *Aha* statement is a piece of information that brings a moment of amazement that causes the learners to experience a surprising discovery, a new revelation, or a brief epiphany, as if they say to themselves, "Aha!" The Aha statement has a "mesmerizing effect" on the learner. This moment of enlightenment, described in the literature as a *hook*, seizes the attention of the listener causing an immediate reaction.[23, 24] The hook can be a slice of selected research, a trivial fact, a controversial opinion, a unique statistic, or a current event.

The purpose of the Aha statement is to encourage learners to think about what was said and decide if they agree or disagree with it. This hook encourages students to exercise their personal opinions, silently, thereby investing something of themselves into the learning. Regardless of whether they agree or disagree with the Aha statement, the point is that they are actively involved in thinking about it. The Aha statement is normally given at the beginning of a story, but the effect of such a hook can come at any point along the way, or even at the end, depending on where the impact is desired.

Expecting the Unexpected

As authors and copresenters, one of the presentations that we give to professional learners makes the *Aha statement* near the end of the lecture. Using the underlying theme of "concept to creation," we show photos of the stages of gestation: from a splitting-cell through the development of the embryo, to a picture of the yet-to-be-born infant sucking its thumb in the womb. We relate this theme to our learning objective, which is to show educators how to develop content from an initial concept to a complete presentation.

We want to let the audience experience a familiar yet preconceived pattern of growth, leading to a very predictable outcome, while matching the process to the typical manner in which content is developed for lectures. We point out that if students can predict the outcome of the teaching they may be less interested in the learning process along the way.

As the imagery shows the stages of development of the baby, the surprise factor (the hook) is in the revelation of the person carrying the child—it is a man! Our photo depicts the very debatable *Time* magazine cover of the Man of the Year showing the very pregnant Mr. Lee Mingwei. This *unexpected hook* supports the learning lesson to the educators in our group that they may have to rethink traditional approaches to teaching in favor of something completely different in order to stimulate interest in the topic.

In this case, we not only describe how to create an Aha moment, we allow the audience to experience it at the same time.

In fact, when comparing two audiences, one seeing only the stages of gestation and the other seeing the stages plus the Aha moment, we found that the second group had greater recall for all key points in the presentation simply because of the impact of the Aha moment. It forced the group to recite the pattern in their head and recognize the surprise element, which, in turn, allowed them to recall related concepts more easily.

〰〰〰

If you can get the learners to perceive a preconceived pattern, something that appears quite predictable, and then you suddenly introduce a change to that pattern, the impact of the learning can be heightened.

Aspects and Suspects

Your stories can be very detailed, provided that every detail serves a purpose. Details take the form of aspects or suspects. An *aspect* is an important element in the story designed to capture the audience's attention. A *suspect* is an extraneous detail, added to stimulate thought. A suspect forces learners to sort through what they have gleaned from basic principles to decide if a detail is relevant or not relevant. Stories with aspects and suspects allow students to solve the mystery and actively participate in the learning. This balance becomes a critical element in writing cases.

Students in humanities, the arts, history, law, and literature have to go through a narrowing-down process when they research a subject, finding that not everything that is discovered is relevant. In the real world, the problem with information is not availability but usability. From a storytelling perspective, learning to sift through or weed out unnecessary elements can help students learn to focus on the most important information in the story.

For example, a medical professor addresses a group of residents, giving a case scenario of a patient, but throws in some extraneous facts to create a differential diagnosis. Could it be this? Could it be that? The *process of elimination* is critical for medical students, and instructors deliberately incorporate unnecessary or extra information that may not be pertinent to the case in order to help the students learn how to weed out what is unrelated and arrive at a proper diagnosis. These extra facts and descriptions within cases are included for a very particular purpose.

⤳ Food for Thought ⤳

As dental residents in clinical training, we used to go on medical and surgical rounds every morning with patients who had medical problems and not dental problems. This was part of our expanded training to understand differential diagnosis.

One day, we were presented with a patient, a man in his mid-forties, who had tiny, raised bumps around his eyes, which looked like hard nodules under the skin. We had to ask medical history questions of the patient, then read about the case and figure out the patient's ailment. The professor kept saying that we had to look at *everything*.

So I looked around, and all I could see was an egg sandwich in front of the patient. I thought that the professor could not possibly have expected me to look at an egg sandwich, which I was sure was the just the patient's breakfast, considering we did our rounds at 6:45 AM. But the professor kept insisting we look at the whole scenario.

Eventually, I realized that the environment, with the patient and all, was set up in advance. Apparently, this patient had a condition named Xanthelasma. This is the condition of excessive cholesterol, which builds up as plaques under the skin and can also clog the arteries. Suddenly, it occurred to me that the patient ate too many egg sandwiches! So the visual cue of seeing the plaque in the patient and seeing the egg sandwich was all designed to have the impact that it had.

While I've never in real life, since then, seen a patient that had Xanthelasma, to this day I remember the disease and what causes it. I still recall the details of the environment because it was designed to help me *think for myself* as to how to figure out the problem.

The professor did not randomly pick somebody with the hope that we might experience all the learning objectives. The patient was pre-selected; the case was pre-designed, and the egg sandwich was pre-planned, all with a learning purpose in mind.

〜〜〜〜

An Expression of Digression

In keeping with the theme of adding extraneous details to a learning exercise, some professors choose to instead use *digression tactics*. A digression is a deliberate and completely unrelated departure from the topic that initially merits attention, but then appears to add no value to the learning. However, by the very end of the lecture, seminar, or presentation, the instructor connects the digression to the topic in a very specific manner, which links directly to the learning.

〜〜 Form Follows Function 〜〜

We recently observed a teacher and were told that this seasoned professor had a unique lecturing style. He was talking about a very intense topic in architecture. His title for the presentation was "Focus on the Form."

The teacher kept reiterating how an architect has to identify the significant components of a structure even though other extraneous information, which some call "fluff," needs to be considered. As the presentation became more complex, the students were beginning to drift, shifting in their seats, becoming clearly inattentive. Suddenly, the instructor announced "We need to refocus and reset so that we can delve deeper into this area!"

He immediately displayed a horizontal bar chart with four data elements (bars) representing three different flavors of ice cream. Each flavor had a code number associated with it and all the bars were at zero. He asked the students to take out their cell phones and text-message the code matching their favorite flavor to a special phone number. Within seconds, the bars started to grow based on the text voting, until all votes were cast.

The students were impressed. Few of them even knew about these online polling programs that enable text message input to dynamically update slide content.* After the voting ended, the professor continued the lesson, forging deeper into the architectural discussion. The ice-cream voting was never mentioned as being related to the topic at all. Fifteen minutes later, he repeated the "refocusing" activity, this time asking students to vote on which of four movies they considered to be their favorite.

Once again, text message results were tallied as each of the bars elongated to reflect the votes, but the professor never related the activity to the topic, continuing instead to deliver a more complex discussion. The digression to something so completely unrelated did have an effect on the students. They were much more attentive.

He used this "digression tactic" a third time, asking students which of five animals they would be willing to adopt as a pet. Again, the activity of the voting and the growing bars was repeated. During his forty-five-minute lecture, the three "refocusing" sessions took no more than one minute each to complete.

Finally, at the end of the lecture, he ultimately connected the three digressions back to the topic by saying, "When we look to create architectural masterpieces, the essence is that you create the right flavor, one that becomes memorable and that others are willing to adopt. So remember to focus on the form and don't forget the fluff."

* There are several online polling programs (such as *polleverywhere.com*) that let you create polling questions that dynamically link results to a PowerPoint presentation for real-time anonymous interaction, limited to a "single vote per person" per poll.

⚉⚉⚉

You can connect seemingly unrelated digressions using the format of the lecture itself to achieve or enhance the learning objectives. As a teacher, you should have a variety of tools and techniques at your disposal that can be implemented in different lectures at different times during the course or the program. Keep in mind that digression tactics will lose the intended impact if overused.

Real-World Analogies

While stories contain details and can be lengthier, *analogies* serve as shorter comparisons that can be sprinkled or peppered throughout a lecture, seminar, or presentation. Effective analogies are those that are *real-world* and yet *distant* from the topic. From a real-world perspective, there is an advantage in drawing a likeness between something in your content and an everyday activity. When this happens, learners transfer the benefits of the real experience to the comparative element in your topic. For example, an English professor is discussing the poetic rhythm of iambics using a verse from a Shakespearean sonnet, specifying the recurring patterns of accented and unaccented syllables. The instructor makes an analogy to a current piece of music, specifying how musical notation is written to create similar stress and emphasis. The learners relate the real-world musical reference to the classical poetry of the sonnet and a connection is made to the idea of "rhythm."

To make analogies carry a stronger connection, make the real-world comparison to a distant reference, outside the scope of the topic. In the previous example, the professor might have chosen to compare the stressed/unstressed syllables to waves on the ocean, where the peaks represent accented syllables and the dips represent the unaccented ones. Just as one wave follows another, the pattern in iambic meter is the same. This version of the real-world analogy compares the poetic rhythm to nature (waves on the ocean) and the learner understands that if the rhythm is "true" in the world of nature, then it must be true in the world of poetry. Hence, the more distant the real-world comparisons, the stronger the impact of the assumed truth.

Typical real-world analogies include references to transportation, nature, household appliances, food, family, and entertainment. The more the reference applies to an everyday experience, the faster the connection is made by the learners.

Think in Thirds while Recapping

One way to help learners gain a more in-depth perspective on the topic is to consider developing your content in a manner that bears repeating. Many instructors create content using *repetition* by following this familiar colloquial theme of "thinking in thirds":

Tell 'em what you're gonna tell 'em.
Tell 'em.
Tell 'em what you told 'em.

This type of structure, called a *Main Points* presentation, previews the highlights of the topic, perhaps showing an agenda or outline, then covers the important points in greater detail, and ends with a summary of the learned concepts.[23] Repetition occurs within the lecture, seminar or presentation in the form of recapping, and this structure can be quite effective when planning content where a few important pieces of information need to be learned.

From a content development perspective the objective is to break the topic into thirds. The first third of the presentation should offer a snapshot or overview of the entire lecture, mentioning the higher-priority concepts. The next third elaborates on the details of the key concepts mentioned in the first third. The last third, as well as during various intermittent intervals, allows opportunities for recapping. If the content is very complex, you will need a greater amount of recapping. Keep in mind that you are not repeating the same concepts over and over again in the same way. Recapping can be done in various ways. For example, a law professor who teaches core concepts might recap by using cases to illustrate the learned concepts.

Whether you provide cases, give real-life examples, or create imaginary scenarios, the extended learning is in the repetition (recapping) of information as seen in relation to different circumstances. In fact, as you recap, student responses to your questions or comments may trigger further exploration of concepts, if not grasped.

Simplify and Diversify

You *simplify* content by focusing on high-level information, covering only what is necessary to create impact. You *diversify* by assigning additional content for "after class." The assignment of a task makes content take on a different form. For example, you might say, "As a supplement to this lecture please read the two case presentations at the end of chapter 41 and review the research paper I mentioned, as we will expand on those findings when we meet next week. In addition, the presentation I just showed you is posted on our Blackboard site, supported by references, and you may want to listen to the podcast of this lecture to review anything you might have missed." The diverse educational opportunities in the assignment allow the students to learn at their own pace without trying to cram detailed notes into a fifty-minute lecture.

But don't display all the readings and references during your presentation. Having too much additional material listed can be overwhelming. The students will think that there is no hope of remembering all the details, and perhaps no chance of writing it all down in the notes. In fact, if the learners become apprehensive and believe that they are not going to learn the details right there and then, at least to some degree, then they will switch off, stop listening and give up.[6] You will have lost your impact trying to cover too much content.

Even in your assignments, be careful that you don't overwhelm learners with too many *supplemental* materials, unless these are typical of your teaching process. If you *routinely* post presentations, offer podcasts, and assign readings, then students will feel less overwhelmed because the pattern is expected. However, always keep in mind that yours is only a portion of the learner's coursework and the combined assignments of all instructors may innundate even the most promising students. Collaborate and coordinate with other faculty, when possible, to manage assignments effectively.

Unfamiliar Territory

A challenge that we often hear is "I've been asked to give a lecture where I barely know the topic." So how do you cover the material that you know little about? You start by focusing on only the *highest-priority* information within the topic and then you relate these concepts to your own experiences, if possible, or to the experiences of others, such as leaders in the field or other notables.

The teaching is based on making connections with more general concepts, rather than burying yourself in the details of the unfamiliar. You may find opportunities to create interactive discussions to allow learners to offer opinions on core issues central to the topic. By the time you teach it, you will not be an expert, but you certainly will know the goals of that lecture, and this may be enough for the students to leave with an understanding of core concepts.

CONTENT DESIGN

Everything should be made as simple as possible and no simpler.

—Albert Einstein

Content design is a tangible representation of content from both an organizational and developmental perspective. An electronic presentation that is clearly designed and easy to deliver is effective. Learners have a high capability of recognizing quality or the lack of it in the design of the supporting teaching materials. Therefore, it is not surprising that while learners do not know the content itself, they can identify a preference for good content *design*. We describe content design as a process through which one creates support visuals that enhance the message without detracting from the delivery.[4]

The educational literature uses a variety of terms to identify the elements related to content design. The term "media" is used to encompass all types of presentation support materials used by instructors, including whiteboards, flip charts, overhead transparencies, 35mm slides, computer-generated slides, electronic presentations, multimedia, visuals, images, animation, video, audio, Internet access, audience response systems, podcasts, webcasts, broadcasts, simulations, and other forms of expression that are used in the learning environment.[23-32]

Although a number of software design programs are available, Microsoft PowerPoint is currently the most widely used application.[33, 34] In fact, regardless of the software used to design content, the term "PowerPoint" has become an accepted description for an electronic presentation of visuals and images (more commonly called "slides") used to support lectures in a variety of settings, including the classroom.[23, 24, 26-31] It is important to note that while many of these terms are used interchangeably in the literature, our intent is to describe the elements of effective content design in relation to the support materials used to enhance learning.

Technology Is Tangible

Nearly all instructors have control over the design of their support materials. Unfortunately, not every presentation is designed effectively for the purposes of learning. There is debate in the literature as to the extent to which the media used to support content affects learning. Some argue that the effective use of technology to display relevant support information has been shown to positively affect student performance, participation, and satisfaction in the learning environment.[30] In light of this, faculty are constantly challenged to gain proficiency with current technology in order to meet learner expectations, and research indicates that PowerPoint presentations are only effective to the extent that they stimulate interest.[26] Regardless of how you may wish to view the effect of technology-based teaching materials, the underlying issue is that once introduced into the learning environment, any media used to enhance learning needs to be successful or it will become a hindrance in the teaching process.

Instructors who lecture and simply use chalkboards can be very effective teachers, and the chalkboard itself functions as a visual cue, supporting the notion that the use of any visuals in the learning environment promotes a deeper understanding of the topic.[31] Technology, however, allows teachers to extend the reach of the chalkboard to create dynamic, interactive, and more visual representations of content. If you use a projector to display content to support your lecture, the learners are aware of the display and will judge the stimulus as part of the learning experience.[26, 29] Design issues arise because, unlike writing or speaking in a given language, there is no one agreed-upon way to create and display visual content.

The most important effect of visual support is as an aid in stimulating learner interest in the topic. Research shows that over 70 percent of learners surveyed agreed that PowerPoint-type presentations helped maintain interest in the topic.[31] However, it is not the *design* of the presentation that stimulates interest; rather, it is the manner in which the instructor uses the designed support material to connect concepts in a meaningful way. As much as a PowerPoint presentation may create student interest, a poorly designed presentation can cause passivity if students feel the slides are doing all the work and no real involvement in the topic is required.[26] This leads to the challenge of creating support material that truly *supports* the lecture but does not try to *replace* it.

In our research of learner preferences, many comments about visual design centered on the problems in *viewing* the information, regarding both content and contrast.[4] With regard to readability or legibility, students identify poorly designed slides more readily than well-designed ones and this is compounded by the fact that many instructors are not well versed in the nuances of using software programs like PowerPoint to create effective visual content.[27, 34–37] For multimedia presentations (video, sound, animation) the level of software sophistication is quite high, and very few teachers have the time, resources, and equipment at their disposal to incorporate more advanced elements into lectures (see "Familiarity and Comfort" in chapter 5, page 238). Regardless of the technology used, it appears that learner preferences start from an *expectation of quality* and more easily discern visual inconsistencies using a very critical eye. It is more common to hear students complain about a presentation than to rave about it, especially because each media format has some type of limitation and no single support mechanism satisfies every need of every learner. Table 4.3 summarizes the benefits and limitations of different support media used in presenting material, arranged from electronic to manual.

Technicalities of Reducing Clutter

Learners feel challenged by design regarding issues of *content* and *contrast*. The preference is for displayed media to be *visible* and *readable* based on the amount of information and on the degree of contrast between foreground and background elements.

From a content perspective, effective design is based on quality not quantity. The usual procedure when creating visual support material is to sit at your desk and use a software program, typically PowerPoint, to design slides to use during your talk. The nature of graphics software is to not restrict you in any way as to how much information you can put on any given slide. You must use your own discretion. However, if during the design process, all of your text won't fit on one slide, you will likely reduce the *text size* enough so that all the information fits.

Unfortunately, when text is too small, the learners will be unable to see the displayed content from a distance. Recommendations for text sizes are generally stated as "less than 30 words on a slide; no less than 24-point type size; 6 lines of text with no more than 6 words on a line, etc."[25] The challenge with these guidelines is that readability of content is based on *distance* more than any other factor. One way to ensure that content will be readable from any distance, regardless of the learning environment, is to use the **8-to-1 Rule**: Eight times the *height* of the image is the maximum viewing distance to read 24-point type.[23] If the image is 6 feet high, people seated as far as 48 feet away will still be able to read text sized as 24-point type.

You can test this calculation easily on your own computer, by displaying the slide on your PC screen and standing back at eight times the height of the screen. For example, if you have a notebook computer and the screen is 12 inches high, walk back 8 feet and see if you can read all the text on the displayed image. If you find yourself leaning in toward the screen to read, your text sizes are likely smaller than 24 points. To be on the safe side, try to make your text 28 points or higher and this will ensure that all of your learners will

Table 4.3.   Comparing the benefits and limitations associated with commonly used presentation support formats

Presentation Support Comparisons		
Format	*Benefits*	*Limitations*
Electronic presentations (e.g., PowerPoint), computer-generated slides	• Highly portable, can be stored on notebook PC, flash drive, CD, or accessed online; no limitation to number of images regarding portability • Full-color visual content at no additional cost • LCD or equivalent projectors usually available • Visuals can be advanced using remote control • Presentations can be designed differently for delivery and for handout purposes • Design can include builds, overlays, and interactive elements such as action buttons and hyperlinks • Navigation through content can be linear or nonlinear (using hyperlinks) • Multimedia clips (sound, video, animation) can be embedded or linked • Ability to add custom animation to enhance or highlight information • Can link to other software applications, websites, etc. • Visuals can be easily "hidden" to streamline presentations for specific groups • Allows for immediate edits, updates, and changes to content to maintain timeliness of information • Presentation can be easily disseminated electronically for review or archive.	• Tendency to force content into available visual space, causing visual clutter and small text • Possible overuse of animation such as moving text and exaggerated transitions • Poor design choices, such as too many typefaces, contrasting colors, intermittent sounds, distorted graphics, low-quality photos or video, and broken hyperlinks • Duality of purpose in trying to use visual presentation as the handout or leave-behind • Dual display may lead to reading content directly from PC without making eye contact with audience • Use of audio requires external speakers with larger groups • Depending on projector brightness, ambient light may reduce visual contrast • Screen savers, e-mail programs, and other alerts, if not disabled, may interrupt presentation • Mouse pointers, if built into remote, may inadvertently appear on screen • Embedded audio or video if not set to play automatically will require manual "click" rather than remote operation

Table 4.3. (Continued)

	Presentation Support Comparisons	
Format	*Benefits*	*Limitations*
Electronic presentations (e.g., PowerPoint), computer-generated slides (continued)	• Smooth transitions between images allow for better continuity of delivery • Dual display (PC and projector) allows for quick glances to content on PC while maintaining eye contact with audience • PC allows for other software programs such as using a word processing program to capture ideas and comments, similar to using a flip chart or whiteboard but with an ease of disseminating the notes	• Possible hesitation or resistance from more seasoned faculty to develop proficiency with design software beyond the basics • Moderate learning curve to develop proficiency with more advanced graphic effects
Multimedia (sound, video, animation); rich media; 3D animation; display simulators; interactive whiteboards;	• Appeals simultaneously to multiple senses creating a rich experience • Can be used to demonstrate complex actions such as software applications, medical procedures, construction models, and other processes • Useful for case presentations where human interactions and life situations are portrayed and discussed • Ability to pause and replay portions of content for review and analysis • Special effects and multimedia can have lasting impact and heighten or stimulate interest in topic	• Production-oriented (multiple formats) versus presentation-centered (still images) demanding greater expertise in creativity and design • Possible overuse of numerous, exaggerated, or unnecessary animations • Hardware and software components can be costly • May require specialized equipment for presentation of sound, video, or animation • Requires familiarity with technical details, terminology, constraints, and operations • Steep learning curve to gain proficiency and comfort with various software or hardware components

Table 4.3.   (Continued)

| | Presentation Support Comparisons | |
Format	Benefits	Limitations
Multimedia (sound, video, animation); rich media; 3D animation; display simulators; interactive whiteboards; (continued)		• Updates, changes, and edits can be difficult and are done with more sophisticated software, which is very time consuming and labor intensive • Possible difficulty in integrating production elements within topic to support learning objectives • Tendency to use technology and special effects to entertain rather than educate • Possible resistance from nontechnical faculty to learn or incorporate advanced media • Possible technology or equipment incompatibilities or limitations with hardware and software
Internet or web-based technology; podcasts; webcasts; broadcasts; videoconferencing	• Ideal for broadcasting, distance learning, and online collaboration where multiple presentation formats are used • Can be used for online learning either live or archived for later retrieval	• Familiarity, expertise, and experience needed to reformat, supplement, or redesign existing curriculum to fit new delivery formats • Possible resistance from faculty to learning, using, or adopting more sophisticated presentation formats

Table 4.3. **(Continued)**

	Presentation Support Comparisons	
Format	Benefits	Limitations
Audience response systems (ARS); classroom response systems (CRS); student response systems (SRS); web-based polling programs	• Allows for anonymous interaction • Possible integration with mobile devices to increase use (no need to give out "clickers" to everyone) • Polling limits responses to one "vote" per participant • Responses can be mapped demographically • System can identify participants and nonparticipants • Results can be immediately charted and displayed in current electronic presentation	• Participants can forget, lose, or misplace "clickers" or keypad devices • Technology must be incorporated into learning process requiring modification of lecture or discussion • Ability to use mobile devices for responses may also lead to distraction
35mm slides	• Portable, can be carried in carousel • Slide projection equipment usually available • Slides can be advanced using a remote control • Full-color visual content at no additional cost • Slide emulsion has maximum resolution of 5,200 lines allowing for accurate colors and visual details • Projected image distance can be greater without sacrificing visual clarity • Multiple projectors can be used to create side-by-side comparisons, or wide displays	• Setup: eight different ways to load slides into carousel, only one is correct. • Multiple carousels can be bulky to carry • Constraints per carousel: 140 cardboard/plastic-mounted slides, or 80 glass-mounted slides • Slide projector bulb burnout is common • Slides can "jam" in projector; slight delay as slides change • Costly to produce; few slide production facilities available • In-house production equipment can be expensive • Slides must be recreated to reflect updates, changes, etc. • Information not as current or timely due to cost and convenience of making new slides

Table 4.3.   (Continued)

Format	Benefits	Limitations
Presentation Support Comparisons		
35mm slides (continued)		• Slides can become dirty or aged and discolored • Manual "cropping" of slide content difficult as compared to digital cropping • Projector distance requires a more darkened room for better contrast
Overhead transparencies, acetates, foils	• Portable, can be carried in binder • Overhead projectors readily available • Annotations and markings can be made for spontaneous ideas or comments • Nonlinear option to choose a transparency out of sequence (from the stack) • Sheet of paper can be used to mask portions of transparency to reveal information in stages (builds)	• Overhead projectors phasing out in favor of more modern technology • More costly if printed in color • Color printing restricted to location and availability of printer • Transparencies can be heavy or bulky, if many are carried • Transparency material sensitive to heat/humidity • Requires physical change from one transparency to another resulting in the "blast of white light" moments of distraction • When changing overheads, incorrect placement may cause the projected image to appear tilted or slightly askew • To facilitate changes, presenter may stand closer to overhead projector and obscure view of the screen for some audience members • Tendency to clutter transparencies with too much text to avoid multiple sheets • Requires reprinting to keep information current or timely

Table 4.3. (Continued)

	Presentation Support Comparisons	
Format	*Benefits*	*Limitations*
Chalkboards, whiteboards, flip charts	• Can capture spontaneous ideas, comments, interactions • Content can be changed or erased quickly and easily • May provide a fresh medium for the "Net" generation who more commonly sees electronic presentations (such as PowerPoint). • Inexpensive supplies	• Good handwriting is needed for legibility • Seating distance is restricted by size of writing • Instructor turns away from the audience, breaking eye contact while writing and will have to speak louder to be heard • Content is usually erased or discarded after session and not reused or archived

be able to read the content on your slides from any distance. Some charts, diagrams, and other images may not always meet this test, but if you can make an effort to keep text sizes larger, your content will be more visible from a distance.

Designing content for readability from a distance will invariably limit the amount of information that you can place on one visual. When text is too small to read or when there is too much text, the visual is described as "cluttered" or "busy." When content is cluttered or busy, the audience must take the time to read and comprehend the information and the listening process is delayed or ignored.[25, 26] With less text, the learners can scan the visual content more quickly and have more time to stay attentive to your discussion of the topic. In addition, the displayed image remains visible throughout that part of your discussion; and, with less clutter, learners can revisit the visual multiple times as a means of support for the words you are saying. This repetitive type of process aids in learning.

These are suggested ways to reduce clutter on any visual:

- No bullet points wrapping to a second line
- No sub-bullets or sub-sub bullets
- No punctuation marks, except commas
- No complete sentences

Many instructors fail to design content using these parameters. There are several reasons why instructors choose to make slides that are "too busy."

Some teachers crowd the visuals with detailed content as a recall mechanism for complex information, similar to having speaker notes, except that the notes are on the slides.[34]

In our experience with junior faculty, residents, and those who present research, it is common to see an abundance of information appear on the visuals, such as detailed statistical data, background history, and scientific methodology in order to help a presenter cover the topic in depth. This content design issue also affects several other skills, such as *content development* (too much material), *expertise* (too complex), and *speaking style* (narrates content). Through some of our interviews with more seasoned faculty, one pattern that was reported is that as the years of teaching experience grow, the amount of content on visuals is reduced as a way to resist overwhelming the learners. These teachers compensate for the smaller amount of displayed content with performance-based skills, such as *speaking style, body language*, and *interaction*, to engage learners, keeping them focused and attentive.

Other instructors create cluttered content in order to make the topic appear more difficult, as if the subject carries greater weight or value because of the complexity of the details. While this busy design choice affects the skill of *expertise* (not simplifying the topic), the deliberate inclusion of excessive content is a pattern that we have observed in faculty when they are presenting to peers, especially in outside venues, where a greater number of professional learners exist (seminars, conferences, symposiums, etc.). These faculty attempt to show peers and other colleagues the vast amount of detailed work that went into the content, as though they need to justify their presentation by implying greater importance. This effort also affects the skills of *self-confidence* (intimidated by the audience) and *expertise* (too complex).

Still other teachers place a great deal of content on a visual because they intend to give a duplicate copy of the presentation to the learners to use as notes. There are a number of issues related to designing handout materials and these are addressed in depth at the very end of this section on content design.

Regardless of a teacher's reasoning for creating clutter, when content is burdensome for the viewer, especially when there is much to read, the instructor may compound the problem by reading the content aloud at the same time. While this is a challenge in *speaking style*, it is also a matter of design. Full sentences, multiple lines of text, and many levels of nested indented phrases are all very difficult to paraphrase, summarize, or memorize. Thus, in order to be accurate, the speaker has a tendency to read back the complex content. While repetition in different formats (slides, textbook, live discussion, etc.) is helpful in learning, duplication of existing visual content through vocal delivery is redundant and provides no added benefit to the listener. Students can already read, so by reading for them you offer no added dimension to a better understanding of the topic. By reducing text to short phrases, you will discuss a given point more naturally and thereby add more depth to the topic.

However, too much brevity on visual content may be problematic as well. If your slides do not have enough meaningful content, it is possible that only those learners who are most attentive and better at note taking will gain the level of understanding you expect. Unless your topic is focused on imagery, a presentation of only still pictures (photos) may be easier to deliver but learners will be left to decide which points in your speech are most important in relation to the displayed image. There should be enough content on the visual support for the learners to gain some important information but still feel the need to stay attentive to your explanation for a more complete understanding.

In other words, the slide content should *stimulate the interest* in listening to the instructor. It serves your purpose as a teacher to allow some attention to the visual content, but only insofar as it connects to your underlying explanations and interpretations.

Avoiding Content Distraction

The well-established use of computer-generated content has opened the door to the possibility of visual distractions. In the use of graphic design software, such as PowerPoint, the ability to add custom animation to make text or objects move has added another dimension to the concept of the "still image."[29] In many cases, it is the overuse of these effects that draws attention not to the content but to the action given to the content. When a paragraph of text flies onto the screen it is the animation of the text box that is noticed, not the content within the box.

Text should not move. Text is the anchor upon which the eyes move to read. If you move this book side to side, you will not be able to read the text. In a presentation, if text moves, the reader will not be able to focus on the content until it stops moving. Therefore, the movement itself has no residual value. If it did, then one could argue that text floating from the top of the slide downward carries a different meaning than text flying in from the upper left corner, rotating three times, and stopping in the bottom right. The permutations would be endless and no one would be able to agree on any meaning assigned to text movement to create a standard for learning.

Transitions are animated changes from one visual to the next. These actions should not be used randomly or excessively, as attention will be drawn to the transition and not to the content. If you decide to use slide transitions, choose an effect that matches the geometric pattern of the new slide, not the shapes from the current slide. For example, if the current slide is a text chart and the next visual in the presentation is a pie chart, choosing a transition that starts from the center and opens into the full image will match the circular shape of the pie chart. When in doubt, use no transition and simply let the next image appear.

A Matter of Contrast

Although the visual design of content may not be intuitive to teaching, visibility and consistency are important concerns in the comprehension of displayed information. Our research gathered a number of comments from learners regarding visual design issues including: "I can't read the text against the background"; "The slides used many different background colors"; "It was hard to see the colors on the slides"; and so on.[4] The evidence suggests that learners prefer proper visual *contrast* when viewing support media.[26] As an instructor and as a designer of your support materials, an understanding of contrast will help you create visual content that is easy to read from a distance, allowing your learners to be more attentive and less distracted.

Contrast is related to the absorption of light. The more light that a viewed object absorbs the farther away it appears. Looking at the extremes, black is the absence of light and therefore *absorbs* all light to appear farthest away. White is the presence of light and therefore *reflects* all light to appear closer. The range of color between these two extremes varies in contrast from darker to lighter, with darker colors absorbing more light than brighter colors and darker-color items appearing more distant than lighter-color items.

When light is projected, the visual information (specifically text) displayed from a distance is easier to decipher if set against a darker background. For example, the credits at the end of a movie are set in white type on a black background. The "crawl" of text at the bottom of a TV news station is set with bright text on a dark strip. For presentations, where ambient light can be controlled, the objects in the background should be darker than the ones in the foreground in order to gain the highest contrast in color tones.[23, 25, 26, 38]

Based on light absorption, white backgrounds in slide design are less effective because the priority information is dark (black text, typically) and recedes from the viewer, while the white background reflects light into the audience. This contrast is visually distracting when viewed from a distance for extended periods. From a teaching-effectiveness perspective, you want the higher-priority content (the text) to appear closer to the learners; therefore, you should use darker-color backgrounds and lighter-color foregrounds.

Using Color

Studies have shown that the background color of the visual produces an emotional response from the audience.[39] Although there may be a number of different cultural interpretations of colors, the physical effect of the color is always the same.[40] There is some debate in the literature as to the accurate measurements of the psychological emotional effects of color, but there is general agreement that, physiologically, color affects the central nervous system and the longer you see a particular color, the more it affects your emotions, either positively or negatively.[39]

Some colors, such as blue, are frequently described as "secure, comfortable and soothing."[39] These colors have a calming effect and are easy on the eyes over a longer period of time. It is not surprising that blue backgrounds are commonly used in presentations. Conversely, vibrant colors, such as red, may be more difficult to look at for extended periods, making these less favorable background color choices. Despite the inability to arrive at a standard measure or recommendation for the effect of color, the evidence suggests that the various reactions to particular colors indicate preferences that can be useful in design choices.[40]

In a slide presentation, the background color determines the emotional response because it recurs more often than each different foreground color, many of which tend to change frequently. Our research found that learners prefer consistency in recurring design elements because too many changes are perceived as distracting.[4] Therefore, during a presentation, it's best to stay consistent with the background color.[29] In addition, based on our earlier discussion of *contrast*, it is suggested that the background color be darker than the foreground colors. Darker tones will provide better contrast.[39] From a teaching-effectiveness perspective, you can select colors that produce an emotional response, while maintaining proper contrast among all visual elements. To that end, table 4.4 summarizes the generalizations made about the effects of different colors on emotions and may be used in selecting a background color for a particular purpose.[23, 24, 41]

The Finer Details of Design

Well-designed images clearly guide the viewer through the intended pattern in the layout to gain a better understanding of the content. When a visual

Table 4.4. Emotional effects of selected background colors

Effects of Color	
Background Color	*Emotional Context*
Black—the absence of all light; anything on a black background appears closer to the eye; offers best contrast for any photos that do not fill the screen; good for financial or historical data that cannot be changed	• Power and strength • Extinction and nothingness • Surrender and relinquishment • Emotionless and distant
Blue—easiest to read from a distance when combined with yellow or white shadowed text; useful for conservative (worst-case scenario) topics or discussions; darker blue (navy or indigo) provides better contrast; *cooler* color (temperature)	• Calm and vulnerable • Sensitive and secure • Loyal and comfortable • Traditional and conservative
Red—*warmer* color (temperature) that increases the heart rate; useful for motivational topics that stimulate groups to action; consider a maroon or dark red to reduce intensity; for contrast, avoid black, blue, or any dark text against a red background	• Impulse and encouragement • Passion and desire • Vitality and intensity of experience • Stimulation and energy
Green—stimulates opinions; useful for audience involvement, discussions, or teaching theoretical concepts; consider teal (blue-green) for teaching processes (more conservative); contrast is better with darker greens such as forest or olive	• Analytical and precise • Accurate and attentive • Opinionated and self-assertive • Organized and in control
Purple—(violet or magenta); difficult to use as a background for critical or serious information; better for entertainment-based content (visual and performing arts–type events); useful with lighter, more informal, presentations (such as an introduction to a general course)	• Magical and enchanting • Unimportant and unrealistic • Irresponsible and immature • Entertaining and delightful

appears, the "eye movement" of the viewer is affected by the design elements. The "eye" seeks a *focal point*, or *anchor*, from which to begin examining the image to process the information.

The anchor, or "starting point," varies, depending on the nature of the visual (text, graphic, data-driven chart, photo, diagram, map, etc.). For languages that read left-to-right, such as English, the starting point on a typical text chart is in the upper-left portion of the visual, where the first line of text is likely to appear. But not all slides are designed the same. Text sizes change, data-driven charts are used, artwork appears, lines are drawn, and shapes are placed in varying spots. As you design visual content for your learners, use anchoring to help guide the eye of the viewers to those elements on the image you feel are most important. The most common anchoring techniques involve *graphic elements* (shapes and artwork); *revelations* (builds and overlays); and *text arrangements* (parallel structures, typefaces and fonts, and capitalization methods.)

Using Geometric Shapes

General geometric *shapes* are the initial graphic elements that guide the eye because shapes have no boundary of language, custom, or culture. A geometric pattern (angle, line, or curve) is a visual cue not a verbal one. A square is the same shape in Toronto as it is in Tokyo. The bullet symbol that precedes a text line is purely visual, yet the ensuing text is read as language and interpreted in some context. The border or frame of a text box catches the eye before the text itself is comprehended. Text and data elements on a visual are interpreted by each individual viewer, but the geometric shapes are seen similarly by the entire group. Your effective use of geometric shapes can help anchor attention to specific areas of the image so that the group finds the same focal point from which to process information.

Table 4.5 is a brief list of the more common geometric shapes and where they can be used most effectively in the design of the visual.

Incorporating Artwork

Although nonspecific geometric shapes are more universal, often you'll find the need to use actual objects or artwork to describe something. The most commonly available artwork, called *clip art*, is a collection of symbols, graphics, and images found in software design applications, such as Power-Point, or available from other sources. These artistic renderings can be strategically placed in foreground or background areas, to add visual context to information, helping learners grasp concepts more quickly.[27] The association of imagery with spoken language is a way of "visually speaking" in order to clarify content. For example, if the content is related to "efficiency," then a picture of a clock or a stopwatch might be used to support the concept of "saving time." Or if a discussion is geared toward "global ramifications," a world map might serve as the backdrop.

Table 4.5. Commonly used geometric shapes and suggested uses

Geometric Guide	
Shape Type	*Common Uses*
Bullet (●,■,♦,❖,○,□,✓,✚,⊼)	Anchor for text lines; always left-justified, never centered, solid shapes (●) better that open ones (□) or thin lines (✓); avoid symbols that are iconic, ornate, or too obvious (✈,✂,☺)
Arrow (⇨,⇧,⇕,⇔,→,➜)	Shows direction or relationship (⇔); when used for guidance, pinpoints an exact location or element on the visual; stem of arrow should be thicker (⇨) when pointing to graphical areas and thinner (→) when connecting words or small items
Universal (□,○, ▭ , ◯)	When filled with text and color, these shapes contain important information; when unfilled, are best used as *overlays* (appearing after the visual is displayed) to focus attention on a part of the image; designed for more general areas rather than specific points (where an arrow might be better); sometimes used over text to identify a key word; border color should contrast well with underlying background
Relational (△,⬠,◇,⊕)	Typically annotated with related text indicating a pattern, process or relationship (such as a cycle with arrows or a flowchart); best when limited to one distinct shape or one defined sequence

Some clip art can be displayed as a *silhouette* (solid shape only) to reduce artistic details yet still maintain the symbolic meaning. For example, a silhouette of a coffee cup is easy to interpret, but a silhouette of a stack of coins will only look like a cylinder and lose its original meaning.

Clip art images, if filled with too many artistic details, can actually become a negative distraction, especially when the visual is displayed for a longer period. The learners can get caught up in the artwork and begin to forget about the message. This can happen from the use of graphics that have a cartoonish or silly appearance or from very sophisticated renderings that resemble a Rembrandt painting. The graphic design elements themselves should not become the focus of your visual support content.

A more obvious distraction is a *distortion*. If you alter the natural appearance of a design element, the learners will concentrate on trying to figure out what the graphic looked like before the distortion. For example, an economics professor shows a visual that includes a picture of a globe in support of a discussion of world markets. However, to fit inside an open area of the visual, the globe has been stretched vertically. The elongated, oval-shaped globe appears unnatural, focusing the attention of the learners on the distortion, rather than on the intended association of the globe signifying "world" markets.

Orientation of artwork can be another form of distortion. If you have to *rotate* a piece of clip art, you probably picked the wrong clip art, because the audience is going to have to re-orient the object in their minds just to place it in context. A more difficult orientation issue occurs with text when placed vertically, such as along the Y-axis of a data-driven chart. When the normal orientation of text is horizontal, then any change to that visual anchor will be a distraction. You may even notice learners tilting their heads to the side to read the information. While these distortions may seem minor in relation to the context of an entire presentation, they are similar to typos in print and only serve to distract your learners rather than enhance the clarity of the content.

One of the best uses of the artwork is to incorporate *photographs*. A photo is the real-life symbol of an idea. While photos may be scenic, such as a landscape or environment, photographs of *people* in real-world situations are much more effective for conveying an emotional connection to content.[26] Where possible, consider enlarging the photo to fill the entire background. Foreground elements, such as text, can be placed over photographic backgrounds, creating *depth* of field (similar to a three-dimensional effect) for the viewer. For photos that include people, avoid having any text or graphic element covering the eyes of a person, as facial expressions are a critical to emotional connection. Do not alter the natural appearance by stretching or elongating the photo to the point of distraction, unless you intend to draw attention to the distorted image.

Keep in mind that photos usually contain hundreds of thousands of colors in various degrees of brightness. If you add text or other elements on top of a photo, be aware of light and dark spots. You may have to adjust the *brightness* of the photo to reduce its intensity in order for lighter text to be readable over the photo. Effective contrast among graphic elements contributes to a better understanding of visual content.[4, 23, 27, 29]

If your photo will not fill the background, consider using a black background to reduce the contrast from another color. For example, if your visuals have blue backgrounds and you use a photo on a slide that does not fill the screen, put a small black frame or border around the photo to separate the background from the photo, allowing for greater contrast. Avoid brightly colored frames or borders around photos because brighter colors appear closer and will reduce the deeper tones in the photo, drawing more attention to the frame than to the photo.

If you use multiple photos on a visual and they are not overlapping (as in a collage), align the photos horizontally along the top; or, if placed vertically, align along the left for a more natural scan and comparison. If the photos do not align, a slight distraction will occur.

Revealing Elements in Stages

Eye movement on a visual is affected by the amount of information visible at any one time. While it is helpful to reduce clutter, not every image can be simplified to just a few short phrases. When faced with busy content, consider revealing information in stages or sections.

For text, this technique is called the *build sequence*. For example, if you have a text chart with five bullet points and you prefer to discuss one point at a time, you could display the heading and the first bullet point only, followed by discussion, followed by the second bullet point, and so forth. This build technique is used to reveal elements of a visual in stages in order to maintain a steady focus for the learners. A variation of this technique is to use the *dim-down*—or *gray-down*—approach by darkening (dimming) the color of the already-discussed item—usually to a shade of gray—then revealing the next item. This focuses attention on the brighter and most current element while maintaining visibility for what has already been covered.

The build can be done in reverse, as well. For example, you might display a data table containing five columns and six rows. While the visual is displayed, you could reverse-build the data items that you are *not* focusing on for the moment by making those items gray (dimming the color) and leaving bright the items you prefer to discuss. This will focus attention on the brighter or *highlighted* elements in the visual. Another reverse-build method is the concept of a "knockout," where a block of contrasting color appears beneath the data to draw attention. Consider the same tabular example of five columns and six rows, set against a royal blue background. To highlight all the items along row four, a black rectangle appears beneath the data, creating a knockout of the blue background on that section of the visual. Using shapes to create knockouts is usually easier and faster from a design perspective than selecting individual data elements and changing colors.

Another sequencing method that helps with data clutter is when you reveal a *section* of information at a time. Text blocks, data groups, and graphic elements—each of which contain complete thoughts—can be revealed in segments called *overlays*. This technique is useful for visuals that contain many graphic elements that may seem chaotic when viewed all at once.

Usually, if it takes you a great deal of time to design the visual, you may have to allow the learners a bit of time to digest it, by revealing the image in sections. Regardless of visual complexity, if the learners can see the components appear in segments, the complete image is easier to understand. Imagine a busy puzzle. If you watch the pieces of the puzzle fall into place, you can appreciate the whole picture when all is revealed.

For example, a history professor displays a map of Europe from 1941, showing some regions shaded gray representing countries under the control of the Axis powers. In addition, three large arrows are shown to illustrate the planned direction of attack from allied forces stemming from various points. Also shown are the names of key cities across the region. The complete visual is complicated and will take time to discuss, and knowing this, the professor decides to use overlays. First, the image is revealed showing only the map of Europe without any color shading or graphic elements. Next, the professor reveals only the shaded areas to indicate the countries under control. Next the names of key cities are introduced and discussed. Next, each arrow appears, individually, as the professor outlines the strategy of the allied troop deployment from different directions. In the end, the entire image is displayed with all of the elements, but the learners are able to see the story unfold, in sections, to gain a better understanding of the concept.

Use builds and overlays only for those visuals that require a step-by-step revelation of content to help with the understanding of the bigger picture.

Nuances of Parallel Structures

While geometric shapes capture the eye first, text on a visual requires language comprehension. A shape directs you quickly to an area, but text explains or supports the delivery of content. Because slide content is meant to be read quickly, for ease of comprehension consider keeping the text *parallel*, especially in bulleted lists. To test this, examine only the *first word* in a list of bulleted items; and, see if they follow the same pattern. For example, if the first word of a bullet point ends with "ing" and the first word of the next bullet point is a plural noun ending in "s," and the first word of the next bullet is a verb, then clearly the three statements are not parallel. This random pattern distracts the reader.

Consider making the statements parallel in structure. If the first word is "Teaches," then each subsequent statement should answer a "What else does this do?" question. Other phrases might begin with "Helps," "Gives," "Makes," "Offers," and the like. However, if the first word is "Teach*ing*," then each statement should answer a "What else is this do*ing*?" question. Other phrases might begin with "Help*ing*," "Giv*ing*," "Mak*ing*," "Offer-*ing*," and so forth. The learners will notice the parallel pattern and scan the visual more quickly and better comprehend the relationship among the statements.

Choosing Typefaces and Fonts

The letters of the alphabet are geometric shapes that carry added complexity. They must not only be scanned visually but must be read and interpreted as language. Because contours precede context, the design or shapes of the letters (the typefaces and fonts) affect the eye movement of the learners prior to the comprehension of content. If the lettering is distracting, the clarity of the content is reduced.

Technically a *typeface* is a character's design and a *font* is an attribute applied to that design (italic, bold, underline, etc.). When selecting typefaces in computer software applications, the term "font" is more commonly used. From a design perspective, there are only two kinds of typefaces or fonts, serif (fancy) and sans serif (plain). You can be sure that all the fonts you have on your computer fall into one of those two categories. Fancy typefaces have little curls (or serifs) at the ends of the letters, plain (sans serif) typefaces don't. Serifs appear to connect the letters within a word and sans serifs seem to separate each letter from one another.

When visuals are more cluttered with content, text sizes tend to be smaller. As a result, the eye movement is slower when scanning the fancy (serif) fonts but faster with the plain (sans serif) fonts.[42] Think of the font as a road. The more hooks and turns, the longer it takes to travel that road. Fancy fonts have more contours (hooks and turns), so they are read more slowly. *Reading speed* affects comprehension, especially with longer phrases or multiple lines, where slower scanning of text eases the processing of content.

To help your learners, you can develop a design strategy with font choices. For example, if you decide to use two different fonts (the suggested maximum on a single visual), then you might choose a serif typeface for the heading (title) and a sans serif typeface for the body of the chart. This layout will slow the eye down in the heading (which has the key words), and will speed the eye up in the body of the chart (where there tends to be more text). This is an effective blend of the typefaces because your learners will spend less time reading the majority of the sans serif text (scanning the fonts more quickly), make fewer assumptions about context, and have more time available for listening. Comprehension is then derived from your expertise and explanation. You probably underestimated how much control over your content that you could have.

When you are not presenting content but providing it, as with hardcopy print handout materials, the focus is entirely on content, and therefore print guidelines are used (white backgrounds, serif typefaces, etc.). For example, a newspaper may display headlines in sans serif type, such as Helvetica for a quicker scan at the copy stand; yet, the body of the paper (each story) is in a serif typeface, such as a Times Roman, slowing the reading speed to aid in comprehension.

When content is projected on a large screen, and fonts are several times the normal size, there is less of a differential in reading speed between serif and sans serif type. However, sans serif fonts read significantly faster when content is viewed on a computer monitor under lower luminance conditions, or when type sizes are smaller, or for those with visual impairments.[42] Moreover, the computer screen *resolution* tends to break up the edges of serif fonts making the reading more difficult with smaller text sizes. This is why application software is designed with sans serif fonts for ease of readability. For the same reason, a website or blog is easier on the eye when the text is displayed in a sans serif typeface, such as Arial. For presentation-related content meant to be viewed on a computer screen, such as online courses, webinars, and podcasts, consider using a sans serif typeface in the design. The exception is for certain electronic documents (such as PDF files), where viewing can be *scaled or zoomed* to larger size, allowing for serif typefaces, similar to hardcopy print.

Using Capitalization Methods

Except for headings and titles, where there are few words, capitalization methods affect the learner when a number of sequential words, phrases, or labels appear in related context, such as in the *body* of a chart (bullet points, lists, statements, etc.) The use of "ALL CAPS," "Initial Caps," or "First caps" will affect consistency.

A series of all UPPERCASE letters makes the text look the same. Written languages thrive on *ascends* and *descends* as seen in the English letters like "b" and "g." These extenders give letters character, and inflection. Using ALL CAPS lacks differentiation and causes the eye to read the information again. If the words printed in all caps were read out loud, the sound would be monotone. By structuring text phrases similarly to the way we read (upper-case and lowercase), you can then use capitalization to place emphasis at par-ticular points on the visual. This helps learners differentiate between higher- and lower-priority information more easily.

In the application of uppercase and lowercase, capitalization choices are between the use of Initial Caps or First caps. *Initial Caps* is where the first letter (initial) of every major word is capitalized in a given line of text. The problem is that there is a lack of consistency on which words to initial cap. After all, what is a major word? Is it one with more than four letters? Is it one that is not a preposition? How do you decide? If you are not consistent, the learners will get distracted because reading several words that are shown with initial caps is not the norm, especially if the capitalization pattern is inconsistent.

First caps is where only the first letter of the first word in a text line is capitalized (other than proper nouns). This more natural reading pattern allows for a greater consistency and easier review of content, with less dis-traction for the learners.

Creating Emphasis

You can control eye movement by designing ways for the learners to immedi-ately know where to look when the visual is displayed. The title, heading, or headline of the displayed visual can be used effectively to guide the viewer to the most important area of the content. It is problematic if learners are searching through your displayed content, looking for something on the screen that remotely matches your words. When learners are confused or can-not grasp concepts immediately, receiver apprehension rises, attention span drops, and boredom sets in very quickly.[6] You can guide the eye to important elements by using words or graphics. Emphatic headings and well-placed arrows are both effective when designing guidance into visual content.

Headings can become *headlines*. If something is important, try to empha-size it in the title of the visual. You can't do this on every slide, but you can at least review all your headings and see where emphasis can be placed. Used wisely, emphasis that directs attention to important areas of a visual can affect both the physical and emotional reactions of the learners.

Some subjects are more challenging from a content perspective, considered *dry* by some presenters, requiring greater effort to maintain learner interest. A research presentation with intricate data will benefit from headings becoming headlines. Essentially, a portion of the data is extracted and highlighted in the heading to create emphasis. For example, a presentation on research regarding patient care may initially include a visual with the heading that says

"Results." This heading can be made more emphatic as a headline using the words "Patient Preferences and Expectations" to highlight a specific portion of the results. While there may be many results, this heading becomes the headline that brings the important point forward and prevents it from being embedded in the overall findings.

If the heading accentuates the learning process or contributes to the understanding of the topic, the memorizing ability of the learners can increase. For example the use of mnemonics can anchor learning points and help with recall. We can all remember the mnemonics we used in childhood, such as ROY G BIV representing the colors of the rainbow.

Directing the eye can be done graphically, as well. For example, using arrows as a design element can create the emphasis you need. Arrows not only show direction, but they can also indicate conflict, options, choices, and trends. Arrows with larger heads are easier to see from a distance. But be careful with arrows. Eye movement can easily be distracted when arrows point in too many directions on the same visual.

Structuring a Flow

When designing a presentation for the first time, or revamping an old one after a number of years, it is suggested you use an old-fashioned technique called pad and pencil. At the outset, write down exactly what you wish to accomplish in the time allotted for the topic. Lay out the lecture with a flow diagram covering what will be taught first, then what will be taught next, and so forth. This old-style process is time tested for effectively developing content, but it is something that many instructors, these days, fail to do.

With the introduction of PowerPoint and similar programs, people tend to jump right into the software, creating numerous slides, sometimes deciding on "two slides per minute" as a way of planning the time needed to create content. It is difficult to confine creativity to a predetermined number of slides per minute. However, when time is running out and the deadline for preparing content is approaching, the instructor compounds the process by copying and pasting slides from prior lectures into the current content. Then the effort is made to reshuffle things in the hopes of eventually creating a flowing logic. This is like organizing an already chaotic room versus starting with an empty space and deciding where the furniture will go. Rather than restructuring what exists, it is easier to build up from scratch.

When you shuffle things around, in your head it may feel organized, but when the learners hear the information they react as if it doesn't flow. As a result of poor planning, instructors end up jumping to different areas within the topic because there is no defined structure. The pad and pencil process allows you to structure a logical flow of ideas, limiting the content to higher priority material, before using any software application to design the content.

Creating Handouts

Handouts are support materials used to supplement presented content. In many cases, these materials are provided in hardcopy print format or offered as stored files on some intranet, Internet, or other accessible file server or computer system. In the academic environment, an interactive course management system (such as Blackboard) offers teachers a virtual learning environment for posting presentations, electronic documents, and other materials for review by learners. In other cases, handout materials, beyond textbooks, are printed in advance and offered immediately to learners in the classroom by instructors.

The biggest challenge in creating handouts is in deciding what information will be given to supplement the learning. From a design perspective, handout materials should *not* simply be a copy of a presentation, whether the handout is in print or in electronic form. In fact, the handout should look *different* from the presentation, containing more details and more information than the visuals displayed.

Format Considerations

A well-designed presentation is a combination of support images and spoken words that complement one another. Visuals with less information shift the focus to the presenter who provides the context and explanations necessary for learning. Other than having a video or audio recording of a presentation, a printed handout is not distributed with a presenter to explain the visual content. Therefore, a copy of the visual content alone is not effective for a learner at a later point. Handout materials should function independently of the instructor, and thus must be designed for *reading* rather than viewing. Handouts are different from the presentation in the same way a book is different from the movie.

If you choose to design your handouts as visuals (slides), you can increase the complexity of the content and add notes or other annotations to help clarify items. For example, if a visual contains four short bullet points, you may make a more complex version with more text and perhaps even sub-bullets to further explain the concepts. This "busy" version of the slide is the handout; the simple version is used in the presentation. If you don't wish to create two versions of the presentation, you might choose to create "speaker notes" for each visual and then print the images along with the supporting notes.

This allows you to add details that include references, explanations, and other information that may have been too detailed to fit on the slide itself.

The combination of visual and detail helps in the understanding of the content because the visual imagery on the handout, similar to the imagery shown during the presentation, sparks memory anchors in the learners, allowing for greater recall of key points or higher-priority information.[18]

Keep in mind that if the supporting notes are very extensive and there is already a textbook, article, or other available document that covers the same material you planned to include in the notes, just include a reference or offer a link to the material rather than reproducing or recreating it. This will save time and limit redundancy of information, especially for very data-intensive presentations. Those who present research usually provide many details on the visuals because someone in the audience may want to know each and every step, procedure, result, and conclusion. However, if the content is simplified using less cluttered visuals by highlighting key findings so that everyone understands the purpose, process, and outcomes, then the *manuscript* itself (or a reference/link to the publication) can be used as the handout. This will satisfy those desiring all the details and those wanting a general overview of the content.

Another option for handout materials is to create complete *narratives*. The narrative format is simply a document that summarizes the lecture, seminar, presentation, or discussion by highlighting key points and providing detailed explanations. Similar to the concept of "speaker notes," a narrative handout is written like a book, using full sentences, paragraphs, transitions, etc.

If you plan on having the learners take notes, then you can also consider *note-taking* handouts. These should include a combination of your visuals along with an area for note taking so that the learners can relate visual content to handwritten comments for later review. Software programs typically offer a print layout that includes three slides per page with adjacent lined boxes. While note taking is based on the learner's ability to focus on higher-priority concepts, the activity also promotes involvement in the topic.[19] From a teaching perspective, however, all content is visible on the handout. So, if you plan to reveal "surprising" information for a learning purpose or perhaps test the learners on content prior to showing the answers, the group will see the details ahead of time.

Print Meets Multimedia

As technology permeates the learning environment, handouts are now able to link the written word to a multimedia expression of animation, sound, or video. You may have noticed magazine ads, billboards, or other public signs that include a graphic filled with a black-and-white interlaced pattern of squares. The graphic is actually a two-dimensional barcode, more commonly known as a QR (quick response) code. The QR code contains a small amount of *data*, arranged as a collection of digital pixels, representing an Internet address (URL). The QR code can be accessed using a smart phone or similar device to display the linked multimedia content. Figure 4.2 is a depiction of a QR code, although this example is meant for illustrative purposes and is not linked to any website.

The purpose of a QR code is to link you to an interactive world that displays, demonstrates, or discusses details in a nonprint format that would otherwise have been left to the imagination. These QR codes can be strategically placed in handout documents to connect the reader to multimedia content, giving the handout greater utility. For example, a professor of biology creates a narrative handout to support a recent lecture on tropical plants and includes a QR code in the text that is a link to a short online video of a tour of the Amazon. Using a smart phone, a learner holds the phone over the QR code and uses the phone's camera and code reader application to capture the graphic, read the barcode data, and automatically open the link on the phone. The learner can now watch the video to get a more complete impression of the tropical plants discussed in the lecture.

As an instructor, think of how you can add this type of value to your teaching. Links to active Internet content can be embedded into printed support materials, manuals, and basically any place that can display a printed barcode. Free applications are available online to create the QR codes and access is convenient and easy. Smart phones are already equipped with applications (apps) that allow these codes to be read and instantly converted to a link that automatically connects to a website location that holds the related multimedia content. QR codes are allowing teachers to create a more interactive, rich learning experience, beyond the classroom, by linking printed materials to expanded visual expressions of relevant content.

Figure 4.2.   Sample (inactive) QR code used in print media to link to rich media content on a Web site

When content is designed efficiently for display and effectively for access to additional support, the learning is enhanced. Materials that include visual content, similar to the presentation, as well as detailed notes and references with possible links to expanded expressions, allow for less cluttered content design, more access to supporting notes, and a greater learning experience.

ADDITIONAL SENSE STIMULATION

> All our knowledge begins with the senses, proceeds then to the understanding, and ends with reason.
>
> —Immanuel Kant

We describe additional sense stimulation as a characteristic of one who appeals to multiple senses at the same time (using multimedia, interactive activities, etc.).[4] In a presentation, seminar, lecture, or discussion a number of "senses" can be affected, most notably the sense of *hearing*, because the instructor is speaking. Any movement or action on the part of the teacher or even on the visual support will affect the sense of *sight*. In fact, the two primary input modalities are hearing (auditory) and vision (visual). Auditory input includes narration, music, and sound effects. Visual input may be in varying formats, including text, pictures, diagrams, animation or video.[43]

At times, the sense of *touch* is used during interaction, such as passing a relevant object around. Some topics, such as science might include the sense of *smell* (chemicals) and others might include the sense of *taste* (culinary arts). The more senses that are stimulated in a session, the more memorable the experience.

Senses can also be described, simulated, or acted out to create the *impression* of the sense without the reality. For example, cooking shows teach the culinary art without the learner ever tasting or smelling the food, through the actions, words, and imagery used. Even though you cannot taste the food, your mouth still waters while looking at the image. This type of simulated sense stimulation is used more often than one might imagine and can additionally affect *feelings* or *emotions*. For example, during a medical presentation, visuals of amputees were displayed intentionally by the instructor, while prostheses were passed around the audience. The instructor combined the sense of touch, to evoke a corresponding feeling of empathy to create an impact. Incorporating additional sense stimulation requires more thought and careful planning to be used effectively. This effort leads to higher-level presenters who create uniquely memorable learning experiences.

Additional sense stimulation is not just related to the number of senses, but to the degree to which senses can be *heightened*. Technology can play a role in heightening the senses through the use of multimedia by incorporating audio, video, animation, or a combination of these. Hands-on activities, such as software applications, computer simulations, equipment operations, or any physical tasks that are used for learning can also heighten the senses. The use of an audience response system (ARS) or student response system (SRS) allows the use of input devices, commonly called *clickers* to induce real-time interaction while heightening the sense of touch through the activity.[44]

Group experiences in direct environments, such as clinical areas, archeological digs, or other on-site learning settings provide a greater sense of reality for the learner. For example, an art class visiting a museum to see paintings by impressionists has a heightened experience of additional sense stimulation from the direct environment than would have been possible with a presentation filled with images of paintings. When medical residents conduct rounds in a clinic, additional senses are stimulated simply because of the patient interactions in a live setting; something not present in a laboratory or lecture hall. When learners see an immediate application of content, their level of attention to the experience rises.

Whereas hands-on activities and group experiences are more traditional in the academic environment, the use of additional, more advanced technology, or *multimedia*, in the classroom allows for greater possibilities to enhance the learning. However, there is considerable debate in the literature as to the positive and negative effects of multimedia on comprehension, motivation, and student achievement. The challenge for many instructors is in the effective use of multiple presentation formats or multimedia to improve content without distracting from the intended message.[43] Yet, when used successfully, multimedia can motivate learners by simulating environments and offering expanded views of current topics.[45]

Incorporating Multimedia

Advances in technology and software applications allow instructors to design visual content to include multimedia in order to heighten the senses, beyond the delivery of the content. For example, playing a multimedia clip during your presentation may add the elements of animation, audio, and video to deliver a unique expression of an idea, concept, or process. The literature identifies the effects of multimedia as generating cognitive and emotional interest that provide a motivational quality to learning.[45] When students are more motivated, attention levels rise, leading to greater recall (working memory) of content.

In addition, the extent of learner control over aspects of multimedia, such as interactivity within learning modules, allows for a heightened sense or experience of content, especially when there is an ability to branch out, explore, investigate, and select portions of the content specific to understanding. An online course that includes interactive hyperlinks to different audio and visual cues allows learners to choose which areas to examine based on interest rather than preselected priority, as might have been the case in a lecture environment. Although such freedom may reduce the instructor's control as to how the material is taught (order, priority, etc.), the independent opportunity to experience the content, based on self-directed choices, supports the concept that learning is a shared responsibility.[13]

As an instructor, you can be sure that each year more of your students will have already experienced a wealth of technology in precollege classrooms. The International Society for Technology in Education (ISTE) is just one of the many associations for educators that promote efforts for the effective use of technology in PK–12 and teacher education. As more and more educators embrace technology in the classroom, the indication is that students exposed to multimedia during early education will expect similar design elements to appear in courses in a university setting. Therefore, it appears inevitable that college teachers need to seriously consider how courses are designed from the perspective of additional sense stimulation, especially in relation to technology and multimedia. It will become increasingly difficult for you to avoid the use of technology to enhance your content, especially when more and more of your learners are accustomed to multiple presentation formats (see "Communicating Electronically" in chapter 5, page 227).

However, while there appears to be a benefit to incorporating multimedia into the design of teaching materials, the components of multimedia (animation, audio, and video) can be very challenging and time consuming to create and *render*. Rendering is the process of turning the multimedia component into a useable form. Similar to how a document is *printed*, multimedia is rendered (digitally printed) to a file than can be used in a presentation. Before you spend countless hours creating a 15-second video clip, ask yourself if the multimedia event contributes significantly to the learning.

In addition to the time it takes to create multimedia events, existing computer/audio/visual equipment must be able to play the content without disruption. A poor visual display, a limited sound system, or a slow computer processor can degrade the multimedia to the point of distraction, negating the benefits of additional sense stimulation. In order to effectively support traditional lectures, presentations, or discussions with multimedia, the following offers insight into the nuances of using *animation*, *audio*, and *video* as part of the design process. By having a better understanding of the technical aspects, you can be better prepared to utilize elements that heighten the sense stimulation in the learning environment.

Animation

This effect is simply an object in *action*, either moving along a defined path or rotating in space. In our discussion of content design, we mentioned the distraction of animated text, and thus, text should never move. Objects, however, can be animated, especially if the animation aids in the teaching.

For example, a diagram with several sections can be split apart or brought together to show the relationship among the parts. Or a flowchart can have a moving arrow to demonstrate a defined path within a larger process. Or the same flowchart can be progressively animated for better explanation and visual clarity. However, multiple or excessive animations can be visually distracting and reduce the effect of your message.

Some animation, such as 3D modeling, can be very effective in showing multiple views or angles, sectional slices, wire-frame outlines, textured surfaces, and axis rotations that could not be possible in real situations. For example, a 3D image of a building, rotating slowly and then becoming transparent to reveal inner structural components can only be done using computer animation.

The learning curve for 3D modeling applications, or for other advanced animation software, can be quite steep, and many educators have limited time or resources to dedicate. In addition, compared to a PowerPoint slide, it takes a great deal of time to create and render short 3D animated clips, making this type of animation the most costly and the most demanding on computer processing speed. In some situations, predesigned animation clips for particular topics may be available, similar to clip art, which can be used in presentations without investing the time and effort to create the clips from scratch. Regardless of the length or complexity, the purpose of the animation should be to further explain the topic in order to advance the learning. But just showing special effects or using animation only for the sake of the animation has little value in teaching.

Audio

At times, you might want to add music or a sound effects at certain points in a presentation to provide additional sense stimulation or to heighten the experience. When audio is *continual*, such as instrumental music, it blends into the delivery. But if your topic is unrelated to the theme, tempo, or emotional significance of the music, then the background audio, with or without video, will not add value as different portions of the topic are introduced. This is why continual instrumental music in a one-hour lecture is rarely used. However, a short section of a presentation may include music to accompany a famous or historical biography, a poetic interpretation, a lighthearted anecdote, or some other unique moment where background audio may support the content effectively.

Intermittent or periodic sounds stand out and can be very effective or distracting. Intermittent sound in a presentation draws immediate attention, but if it is without logic or justification as to its added value, the sound can distract from the content. Unfortunately, some clip art includes embedded sounds that instructors use for no particular teaching purpose. Sounds that are directly linked to obvious visual cues are usually ineffective. To test the added-value effect of sound, mute the speakers and display your content to see if the intended message is clear without the sound. If it is, then don't add the sound effect.

Conversely, specific sound effects can be helpful in completing the context of a learning point. For example, a law professor is discussing a case related to a car accident that resulted from slippery road conditions. By comparing the sound of screeching tires on a dry surface versus the sound of tires sliding across a wet pavement the professor helps the learners evaluate the case from an additional perspective.

Keep in mind that any audio used in a learning session must be equally discernable by everyone listening. In the absence of overhead speakers or a distributed sound system, the attempt to play audio from a notebook computer or even from small external speakers may be problematic based on seating conditions and room size. It is best to test audio in the chosen setting to judge whether everyone will have the same experience.

Video

Additional sense stimulation occurs most notably when video is used in teaching. A video usually includes audio, such as music and voice-over narration, as well as live motion or animation. The combination of these elements enhances the *degree of reality* for learners and increases the attention to content.[45] Whereas sound and animation can be used as very quick "special effects" and possibly become distracting, video is more of a "production" that functions as a complete learning moment. A video "clip" is designed to make a statement either in support of existing content or to supplement learning. In fact, some video productions use such advanced computer-enhanced effects that they can simulate a real-life experience almost as if being in the live situation. Of course, advanced technology usually requires very current and quite often very expensive equipment. In the academic environment, budget constraints may limit the investment in state-of-the-art technology.

The multimedia issues with video usually involve *display*. Learner reaction to multimedia is highly dependent on the technology that delivers the experience.[43] Depending on the nature of the clip or the technical limitations of your computer, the video may not fill the screen or may not play smoothly. If the video is played "full-screen" and looks blurry or degraded, it is likely that it was created at a smaller size that cannot be enlarged without sacrificing quality. However, if playing the clip at the original size is visible from a distance, then you can still use it. To reduce file size, some clips are recorded at half the normal speed (frame rate). Usually, in short clips of less than 1 minute, this will not appear to be much of a problem. With longer clips, after some time, the video may begin to separate from the audio, causing a synchronization problem, most visible in the face, when the voice is heard but the mouth lags behind. Irrespective of incompatibility and technical issues, the best advice we can offer is to move on quickly and don't belabor the point or spend time trying to fix the problem. In most circumstances, your audience will not even know what you originally had embedded in your presentation. Find another venue for posting this added information, if necessary.

Another use of video to heighten the senses is live *streaming* video or video-on-demand (VoD), a continuous live feed usually done through a videoconferencing system, or over the Internet through webcams using online meeting applications such as Skype, WebEx, or GoToMeeting. In some learning environments these video interactions are similar to a news talk show format, where the image of a person at a remote site is displayed in the session. The ability for teachers to bring remote sites into the classroom alters the experience for learners by simulating access to distant parties. Keep in mind that because of heavy Internet traffic (many people online) the transmission of video over the Internet may degrade or get interrupted, causing the connection to display poorly and thus creating a negative effect on the learning. It is always advisable to test these connections ahead of time to make sure that the quality of the video and audio is sustainable without any technical issues. Lastly, always have a back-up plan.

Virtual reality technology is a more advanced type of an interactive video-based format where learners become *immersed* into the content. Gaming systems and other visual simulators of educational content can create an in-depth experience that stimulates all five senses, some real and some imagined, while allowing personal interaction in a virtual world. These *hi-tech, high-touch* systems are used in courses and programs where a real-life experience would be impossible.[46] For example, there are gaming applications available that target learning objectives through a gaming strategy. Software for patient examinations, where a simulated patient appears and the learner is able to dialogue and interact, eliciting symptoms and ultimately determining a diagnosis and a path of treatment, is one example. The experience heightens the senses to a much greater level, stimulating learner interest and allowing greater recall of high-priority information.

Regardless of how additional sense stimulation occurs, either through physical activities or multimedia design, the ability to enrich the learning experience supports effective teaching. As an instructor, you will be continually challenged to find ways to adapt content to meet the expectations of new learners. Your willingness to explore alternative methods for stimulating interest in content will lead to effective education and mutual satisfaction in the process.

ENVIRONMENT

> If a doctor, lawyer, or dentist had 40 people in his office at one time, all of whom had different needs, and some of whom didn't want to be there and were causing trouble, and the doctor, lawyer, or dentist, without assistance, had to treat them all with professional excellence for nine months, then he might have some conception of the classroom teacher's job.
>
> —Donald D. Quinn

The process skills that we have been discussing in this chapter deal mostly with content-related issues. Another integral part of the process is in managing the physical setting (learning space) that provides a *context* in which the content is offered.[47] We describe the skill of managing the *environment* as creating favorable conditions for presenting content.[4] However, the issues that may affect the learning atmosphere are not one-sided, as both teachers and students bear responsibility.

Various "classroom incivilities," such as distractions, interruptions, conflicts, and other disruptions correspond to student inattentiveness. In addition, studies show that these incivilities can be caused by or may result in the lack of teacher enthusiasm, clarity, organization, and responsiveness.[48, 49] If the surroundings are distracting, the ability for learners to concentrate is affected, despite the best efforts of even the most seasoned professor. In some cases, challenges are brought on by the institution, such as decisions affecting class size in terms of the number of students.[50, 51] It is apparent that the challenges of managing larger groups of learners are different because the presence of more people in a room can magnify the interaction among students to a disruptive level. To maintain an effective setting, the two most important considerations are *behavioral* and *conditional* with some issues that are more in your control than others.

Managing Behavioral Elements

Aspects of the environment that an instructor may control to a greater degree are behavioral in nature, such as time management, seating arrangements, disruptions, and so on. Studies that identify learner perceptions of teaching effectiveness include classroom management as part of the evaluation, including the ability to start and end in a timely manner.[4, 12, 52]

The proper management of "class time" by faculty appears to be highly significant to learners. Faculty administrative duties, meetings, or even the choice to answer questions at the end of a class, may affect classroom teaching time. Although these are common time-management issues, poor time management is often perceived by learners as not respecting the scheduling challenges students have throughout the day.[52] Other than acute awareness, there is no technique or suggested strategy to help you meet scheduled teaching time; however, it is important to understand that managing your available classroom time effectively leads to a more organized, comfortable learning atmosphere, thereby enhancing the educational experience.

Timeliness is not just a teacher's responsibility; in fact, for the learning environment to flourish, learners are equally responsible for punctuality. The disruption of students entering or leaving the room at random moments creates an unwanted distraction for those who want to concentrate on the topic. From a management perspective, the learning environment is your domain. You can establish guidelines, set ground rules, or define mutual expectations, and consequences at the outset. These can be outlined in the syllabus, or given as a verbal review on the first day of class to assure compliance in a collegial manner. In fact, in a *problem-based learning* scenario, student agreement to expectations is commonly termed a "contract."

Beyond tardiness, certain other learner behaviors may be distracting or annoying to both the teacher and the other students, making the learning environment uncomfortable. These include ringing cell phones, text messaging, web surfing, side conversations, sleeping (snoring), reading magazines, emotional outbursts, role playing (class clown, instigator, etc.), open conflicts (arguments), challenging authority, settling (packing or unpacking), walking in and out of the room, eating, personal relationships (flirting), inattentiveness, boredom, and sarcasm. Depending on the level of these distractions, the instructor may have to take appropriate action in order to eliminate the disruption.

The challenge is in the *strategy* used to manage the distraction in order maintain harmony in the environment. For example if the distraction is caused by *hostile* behavior, such as an open argument, a strong disagreement, or a challenge of authority, where others in the room feel the tension during the interaction, you may choose to deal with the issue by communicating with respect and understanding, using empathetic phrases such as "I understand your point," "I can clearly see your perspective," "It appears that we can agree to disagree on this" (see table 3.5 in the "Empathy" section of chapter 3, page 33). This type of open dialogue carries a warm tone, and appears empathetic, which may reduce the hostility to a degree.[53] However, the percentage of success in managing hostile conflict is significantly lower when an instructor chooses to address the issue "after class." This tactic does not reduce the tension that is still present during class, and may create more of a distraction as those involved in the conflict await the outcome of later confrontation.[53]

If the distraction is caused by *inattentive* behavior, such as boredom or apathy, the first step suggested is a self-assessment and reflection to see if the problem is related to your teaching methods (see "Beware of Boredom" in chapter 3, page 61). It may not be apparent, but simple involvement of the learners, perhaps through an activity or interactive discussion, can be the best remedy. Open dialogue and clear communication can stimulate thought and raise the level of attentiveness to the topic. However, singling out a student with a corrective, perhaps disparaging remark, such as "Well, if you were paying attention, you might have learned something!" would be less effective in engaging the student. In addition, this type of dialogue will affect the entire mood of the class.

At times, behavioral distraction may center on technology. For example, a ringing cell phone is an intermittent and unexpected sound that breaks the level of concentration to an existing discussion or visual activity.[54] From a cognitive perspective, the *ringing* is a temporary and minor interruption, as compared with an actual phone *conversation*, but serves as a distraction nonetheless. Moreover, when the ringing is recognizable (such as a popular song) the attention to the sound lingers. In addition, a ringing phone carries an implied sense of urgency, may signify emergency, or, in the case of antici-pation, the attention to learning drops for anyone who is expecting a call. As an instructor, you should consider a ringing cell phone as contributing the same level of distraction as someone entering the room unexpectedly, where attention would suddenly shift to the doorway. Although there may be times where cell phones can add to the learning environment, such as text polling, it may be better to request that all learners silence or set cell phones to vibrate (for emergency alerts) to reduce distraction.

ᨬ Heard It through the Grapevine ᨬ

It was right before Thanksgiving when I walked into a large lecture hall on campus, expecting the nearly 400 seats to be completely filled, as had always been customary for this particular talk. I normally have to wait several min-utes for everyone to settle. As I set up my computer for my presentation, I looked around and noticed about 50 students scattered throughout the audito-rium. I was perplexed as to why so few were attending this normally, very packed lecture.

I looked at the group and said "I appreciate the fact that you are here, but I am surprised that your classmates are not. Are the elevators not working? Is there a long line in the cafeteria? Have lots of people gone home for the holiday already?" One of the students responded, "A lot of students are pre-paring for finals and completing last-minute projects. They probably figured since there is no quiz planned for this lecture they could skip it."

I decided to add a caveat to the situation, "Well, coincidentally, I am planning to give a pop quiz today; and, as you know from our syllabus, your scores on this quiz will be part of your final grade."

Suddenly, the cell phones appeared, seemingly out of thin air, and each of the students began text messaging furiously. I had never observed such dexterity and determination. Within minutes, clusters of students were clamoring into the room, climbing over one another, filling the entire lecture hall to capacity.

While I was amazed at how quickly a few text messages could spread, I was even more impressed with the results. This technology-driven, socially networked generation gives new meaning to the word "connected."

I quickly remembered that I might have been partly at fault for the low attendance. Simply, there was a possibility that students did not give this lecture a priority. I gathered my thoughts and came up with a few strategies to immediately engage the crowd, while refraining from showing any disappointment to the newly arriving students.

Although I was internally offended, I looked at the bigger picture and knew that my goal had to remain being the *most* effective teacher I could be. My initial observation of the lack of students in the room immediately led to self-reflection and quick strategies to an engaging lecture. The lecture ended with a resounding applause!

━━∽∼∼∽━━

While not affecting the entire group, interactivity with technology can be more disruptive to an *individual* in the learning environment, as is commonly seen with text messaging, or computer access (surfing the web, social networking, gaming, writing reports, etc.). This is not to minimize the value of these communication devices. Studies suggest that more up-to-date, technology-oriented spaces facilitate learning more effectively.[46] However, access to an environment *outside* the classroom while supposedly being attentive to activity *inside* the classroom can shift one's focus to the external stimulus quite easily. As an instructor, you are likely to be able to notice the use of technology in the room, especially in the case of smart phones for text messaging or Internet access. Computers, however, may be serving the purpose of note taking; therefore, you will have to use your best judgment before deciding whether the computer activity is actually distracting the learner.

∼∽ A View of Technology ∽∼

In the spring of 2002, as department chair, I set myself the task of observing different faculty as they lectured. My goal was to take note of effective approaches to content in the hopes of improving the overall curriculum.

One of the classes of over 300 students was being held in a large auditorium. This was also one of the first lecture halls at our institution to be equipped with wireless communication to allow Internet access. At times, teachers would illustrate online research, download files, or gather other information electronically to enhance the learning.

When I arrived, I did not want to sit directly in front of the instructor, or even very close to the front, thinking I may become a distraction as an observer. Instead, I decided to sit in the back of the room, among the students, nearly in the last row. As I made my way up the aisle steps, I couldn't help but notice how many students had their laptop computers open, waiting for the class to begin. I passed row after row, computer after computer, impressed with the diligence of these modern-day electronic note takers. I finally took my seat, and had a great vantage point over the rows of all the students with a clear view of the instructor.

As the lecture progressed, from where I was seated, I could see many of the screens of the student laptops. I was very surprised at what I saw! Rather than using their computers to take notes, or review posted lecture materials, the students were engaged in a variety of other online activities: shopping for clothing, checking sports scores, playing video games, immersed in chat rooms, and visiting other nonrelated sites.

The instructor was completely unaware of this. I thought that perhaps the wireless access should be restricted to only the faculty, as a way of removing the distraction. What dawned on me was that there could be other factors compounding the problem: perhaps the students were simply not engaged enough to stay attentive to the topic, or maybe they were not clear about the expectations for class participation. What was I to do? Ultimately, the culmination of all our observations and our research led to the development of this book.

—◇◇◇—

Since the new generation of learners has grown up with the daily use of computers, their constant access to the Internet can be very challenging for instructors. The computer, as a resource, or as note-taking tool, may mask inappropriate uses. Because of this, many institutions establish acceptable behaviors that are described in the syllabus and discussed at the outset of each course. In reality, an individual's distraction is less of a problem in the learning environment than group disruptions. However, from a teaching perspective, all learners should stay focused on the topic, regardless of whether an individual's lack of attention affects others. Simultaneously, we focus our efforts on further developing faculty teaching effectiveness in order to help instructors better engage the learners. This combination allows us to partner with our students in the learning process.

Dealing with Conditions

In any teaching, presentation, seminar, lecture, or discussion, learners should be able to *see* and *hear* comfortably.[46] While all teachers and students desire a *comfortable* environment, the reality is that in many institutions, the learning spaces are less than ideal and not likely to change by individual influence. Teachers who understand and accept facility design limitations use their expertise to overcome these obstacles in order to make the educational experience as effective as possible (see "Classroom Climate and Conditions" in chapter 3, page 74).

A teacher should always assess the environment and may have to make minor adjustments to make the space more conducive to learning. This could be as simple as rearranging chairs in a room, moving lecterns and projection screens to create better sightlines, and adjusting microphones and lights. The objective is to make the learning space comfortable for the given activity. Just as a concert hall affects those listening to the music, the setting or location where the learning takes place directly affects learners involved in the session.[46]

A common distraction is the surrounding sound. If there is a noticeable pattern and a recurring problem can be determined, you may be able to adjust your teaching accordingly. For example, noise from busy hallways can be disruptive, especially at the very beginning or very end of each hour, when classes are changing. You can try to cover the highest-priority content when the noise is least distracting, leaving lower-priority tasks for less optimal times. Experienced faculty adapt to this recurring condition, using opening moments for taking attendance, setting up equipment, or writing notes on a board and then using closing moments for making brief announcements, collecting papers, or packing up equipment. With lower-priority items offered at busier (nosier) times, higher-priority content is delivered during quieter moments, allowing for increased attention (less distraction).

In general, if you can manage behavioral and conditional issues in an effort to create a comfortable learning environment, you will have an optimal atmosphere in which to achieve your objectives. Your flexibility and tolerability for these nuances will go a long way from further distracting you or your learners from content.

PROCESS — SUMMARY AND STRATEGY

Giving people a little more than they expect is a good way to get back a lot more than you'd expect.

—Robert Half

Table 4.6. Highlights of the process skills

Process Skill	Key Points
Content Organization applies real-world situations to simplify content	• Content organization is based on establishing structural clarity and a logical flow • Organization can be done by *"outlining-transitioning-comparing-summarizing"* • Deviations from the outline must be tied together at the end • Direct references, during class, should be concrete to focus group attention • General references, outside of class, can be abstract and can be used as a teaching tool • Concrete examples help to avoid generalizing • Real-world situations help link content to practical applications
Content Development develops a concise and clear message	• Content development should remain clear and concise • Multiple exposures and expressions (repetitions) reinforce concepts • Simplifying content helps avoid overwhelming the learners • Focusing on high-priority items helps fit content into the given time • The *before-during-after* strategy distributes content between *teacher time* and *learner time* • Stories should identify time, place and circumstance • The *Aha statement* (hook) encourages learner involvement • Story details help learners differentiate between what is important and what is not • Real-world analogies place content into context • Synthesis of information is the result of in-depth understanding

Table 4.6.   (Continued)

Process Skill	Key Points
Content Design creates support visuals that enhance the message without detracting from the delivery	• Technology (media format) affects design of teaching materials • Visibility and readability are critical to design • Cluttered or "busy" visuals distract the learner • Consistent (single) dark backgrounds with brighter foreground elements are easiest to read from a distance • Background color choices affect emotional responses to content • Geometric shapes guide the eye before text or data elements • Artwork (graphic images, photos, etc.) can enhance content, but distortions are distracting • *Builds* and *overlays* help reveal information in stages • Typefaces (fonts) affect reading speed and comprehension • Headings can become headlines to create emphasis • Handouts should combine visual content with detailed information
Additional Sense Stimulation appeals to multiple senses at the same time (using multimedia, interactive activities, etc.)	• Senses can be increased (number), described (simulated), or intensified (heightened) to stimulate learning • Group interactions, direct environments, and hands-on activities heighten sensory experience • Multimedia (animation, audio, and video) can generate cognitive and emotional interest in content • Animation can be used as an aid in describing complex processes • Continual audio blends into content if related to the topic • Video can simulate real-life situations for learners
Environment creates favorable conditions for presenting content	• A comfortable environment with minimal distraction enhances the learning experience • Poor time management by faculty negatively impacts learners • Tardiness on the part of learners is distracting to the entire group • Student behavioral distractions include text messaging, side conversations, open conflicts, sleeping, and inattentiveness • Open dialogue, during class, is effective in managing conflicts • Interaction or activity can be effective in reducing boredom • Physical conditions of the space should be assessed and controlled as much as possible

5

Performance

Good teaching is one-fourth preparation and three-fourths theatre.

—Gail Godwin

In the previous chapter we focused on the content. Bringing your content *to life* is expressed through the *performance* skills. Your delivery of information will affect a learner's ability to grasp concepts in the manner in which you intended. Any distractions in your style will reduce the effectiveness of the content, just as notes that are sung off-key will reduce the quality of the music. The melody of learning is played on an instrument called the instructor. At times, that instrument needs a bit of fine-tuning for the "performance" to improve.

The majority of the performance in communication is nonverbal, especially when there is an emotional connection to the content.[1] Quality content combined with effective performance allows learners to connect both logically and emotionally to a topic. The process of teaching is based on both form and function, logic and emotion, facts and feelings. From an educator's perspective, the emotional link to a learner is critical for an effective delivery of nearly every message. At times, the feelings are expressed through the body and the voice; seamlessly displayed, logically focused, and made highly interactive with thought-provoking discussion. The common thread in developing the performance skills is *delivery*. To better understand these skills, a learner's perspective is helpful. Table 5.1 outlines the positive and negative keywords expressed by learners relative to the performance skills.[2]

From a performance perspective, the skills are *visibly* expressive behaviors. It seems that students learn better when the instructor makes eye contact, uses well-timed gestures and movements, is clearly heard and understood, is comfortable with technology, and stays on the topic while welcoming interaction and discussion. The challenges for teachers involve the distractions that occur from excessive movements, vocal problems, and a seeming disregard for learning objectives and learner participation.

Table 5.1. Feedback on performance skills from both student and professional learners

Performance Skill	Feedback from Learners	
	Negative	*Positive*
Body Language Style	points at people, moves around too much, blocks view of the screen, shifts from side to side, turns away, never moves, distracting gestures	relaxed, poised, good posture, makes eye contact
Speaking Style	talks too fast, mumbles, says "um" too much, monotonous, soft voice, reads the slides, accent too heavy	easy to listen to, uses pauses, clear speech, understandable
Technology	laser pointer movement, intimidated with technology, too many technical problems, walks into the projector's light	handles glitches easily, uses a remote control
Focus	drifts from topic, off tangent	key issues, main ideas, sticks to the subject
Interaction	picks on people, ignores suggestions, does not welcome comments	handles tough questions, gets people involved, repeats responses, asks good questions, stimulates discussions

Conversely, the opportunities to enhance your delivery revolve around consistent actions and clear phrases that make learning more conversational and yet highly informative, while letting learners feel as if they are part of the experience, freely able to discuss, interact, and participate. As you minimize your challenges and maximize opportunities, you can continually focus on addressing the needs of your learners, based on their preferences.

There is a running thread or interconnection between the material being taught and the teaching of the material so that a seamless integration of the two provides a true learning experience. From an expression perspective, the performance skills described in this chapter focus on the teaching efforts needed to deliver the planned material effectively and efficiently. Although each of the skills plays a role in the delivery of information, preferences vary as to which elements have greater importance. Figure 5.1 illustrates the significance that student learners attach to each of the performance skills.

As you develop your effectiveness using the skills-assessment tools, any of your performance challenges should be addressed according to the significance noted in Figure 5.1, so that you can prioritize your efforts, based on learner preferences. For example, if you find that you are challenged in the areas of *speaking style* and *technology*, you should work on speaking style first because this is a more highly preferred skill as perceived by student learners.

The performance skills discussed in this chapter focus on the following sections: *body language style, speaking style, technology, focus,* and *interaction,* by offering perspectives, insights, references, and recommendations, to help you develop an effective delivery technique in order to bring content to life and improve your overall teaching effectiveness.

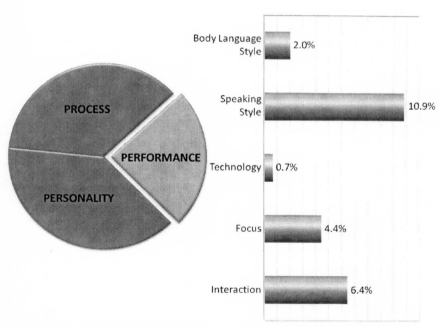

Figure 5.1.   Relative significance expressed by student learners for each of the Performance skills

BODY LANGUAGE STYLE

You teach and lead by who you are, sometimes by what you do, and seldom
by what you say.

—Russ Walden

Since the middle of the last century, learners have continually gathered more
and more information visually. From a television tube to YouTube, visual
stimulation is based on the concept of action. The *manner* in which information is offered is often more influential than the information itself. In many
cases, the visual expression of an idea is judged more on the "how" rather
than the "what." We describe *body language style* as a characteristic of one
who uses physical movements and gestures to support the presentation.[2] A
visual performance of content is the result of an overt action or some physical
movement that brings words to life. Surely your well-crafted message and
your masterfully designed slides deserve a quality performance in order to
create a three-dimensional view of content.

Depending on the situation, the way we communicate varies. Some studies suggest that 55 percent of everything you communicate is gathered from
what you look like when you speak; 38 percent from how you deliver the
information, and only 7 percent from what you actually say.[1] The studies
focused on prepared content and feelings and how those may be interpreted.
In the same way, the educational environment includes an emotional connection to content on the part of the instructor and the student. There is
also considerable debate in the literature as to the validity of these studies,
especially because many experiments conducted to determine results are
artificial or simulated.[3] In spontaneous conversation, such as open discussion, the verbal and nonverbal components of the content may not be as
skewed. However, when content is planned, organized, rehearsed, and
structured to meet an objective, the "spontaneity" is reduced and the nonverbal cues tend to dominate.[3] Some may argue that the verbal/nonverbal
percentages are different, but most agree that the delivery style of the
teacher can surely affect the interpretation of the message.[4]

ᨑ Little Things Mean a Lot ᨑ

In a recent seminar, I offered a perspective on the statistical measure that 93
percent of the prepared message is contained in the delivery, with only 7 percent gathered from content. Several people immediately concluded that "content is unimportant."

I was quick to point out that these particular statistics, when used in the context of a presentation, appear to suggest that the content is extremely important based on the available *margin for error*. If, in fact, only 7 percent of the communication is available for the content, then you have less room for mistakes. A typographical error on a slide is infinitely more obvious than a single "um" in the middle of an uttered phrase. A person can correct a misstated phrase by quickly rephrasing it. But a misspelled word on a slide cannot be justified with a claim that all the other words are spelled correctly, as if offering an amazing success rate.

I noted that to effectively communicate important information, quality supersedes quantity, which is why you need to choose the *right* content to occupy that seemingly elusive 7 percent slice of the pie. To balance the equation, if 93 percent of the communication is in the actual delivery, then the actions of the presenter are a critical part of the process, either reducing or optimizing the all-important 7 percent. In essence, delivery affects content, and content is extremely important.

⌇⌇⌇

The most visible catalyst for learning is a teacher. In the majority of learning environments, the instructor is in plain sight of the students as information is conveyed. Therefore, the manner in which the instructor communicates, the language of the body, is critical.[5, 6] Neurologically and biologically, the movement and actions of the body offer nonverbal cues and emotional connections.[7] The educational literature identifies visible nonverbal cues representing six universal emotions: *happiness*, *sadness*, *fear*, *surprise*, *anger*, and *disgust*.[7–9] A professor's actions may suggest any of these emotional states; and likewise, learners may exhibit similar expressions (especially in the face) in response to a professor's comments or actions.

Research indicates that happiness, sadness, and anger are most noticeable emotions in the body, followed by fear and surprise; with contempt (disgust) being the least visible in the body, evident mostly in the face.[9] Therefore, through visible actions, one or more of the six universal emotions may become evident in the learners, allowing a teacher to gauge the impact of the delivery. These nonverbal cues in communication work both ways, especially during moments of verbal interaction between teacher and student, even though during more natural conversations, such as discussion, the nonverbal cues are less dominant.[3]

In light of published research, from a body language perspective, an instructor can enhance the presentation of information by following a number of principles involving proximity, gestures and movement in order to add emotional context to expressed content.[4, 7–12]

Establish an Anchor

When presenting with visual support, it is best to set an anchor for the learners so they can watch you and reference your supporting slides simultaneously. The easiest way for viewers to observe a speaker along with supporting images is based on the *reading pattern*.[13] *Position your body* to the same side as the reading anchor in the language (i.e., left-to-right or right-to-left). For presentations in English (and many other languages), you should stand on the *left side* of the room—that is, the left side from the audience point of view. In such cases, the eye is less distracted if it sees the instructor speaking from the left, and then glances slightly to the right to connect to the content (left-to-right), before returning to view the teacher again.

If you stand on the opposite side of the room (the audience's right), the viewing pattern is reversed. As the learners look at you, and then begin to reference your slide content, they must navigate across the visual, backward through the text, just to find the anchor to begin reading. This extra step is a distraction. Listening is delayed and effectiveness is reduced. While the reading anchor is helpful, this is not to suggest that for languages written vertically you must stand on your head! The goal is to match the reading anchor when possible in order to make comparisons to content easier. If you are teaching without using supporting visual content, then as long as the learners can see and hear you, the position you take in the room will only matter to the extent of proximity or distance.[11]

Play an Angle

Depending on the room layout, the learners may only be able to see a portion of your body. For example, if you are on a stage or a raised platform in a large lecture hall, or if the seats are raked (where rows gradually rise higher from the front to the back), you will be more visible, especially if you are not standing behind a lectern. In other classroom or theatre-style seating arrangements, you may be standing on the same floor-level as the learners are seated. In those cases, perhaps only the upper portion of your body is clearly visible for the majority of the viewers, because others are seated in front of them. Still, in other cases, you may be standing behind a lectern, limiting the visibility of your full body, regardless of where anyone sits.

In some seminar or discussion environments, you may be seated and be less visible to the entire group, based on seating positions. When the instructor is more visible, more nonverbal information is conveyed through actions (gestures, movement, expressions, etc.). Such body language may suggest a positive or negative attitude on the part of the instructor, depending on how actions are perceived.[11]

The literature describes emotional body language (EBL) as the link between emotion and behavior, where specific actions convey meanings and feelings.[7] The concept of *immediacy* (directness, openness) is instrumental in how learners perceive teachers.[12] A more immediate instructor provides nonverbal cues such as smiling, gesturing, eye contact, and other expressions that enhance the learner's experience. While the face provides clear indications of emotions, classroom settings add the element of distance (proximity), which may limit the close observation of those facial expressions. Therefore, the visible parts of the body allow *posturing* to be used for emphasis in order to bridge the gap of proximity and make learners feel "closer" or more immediate to the teacher.[9]

When presenting, the positions of your *shoulders* enhance communication, because, regardless of the seating layout, or the presence of a lectern, everyone should be able to at least see your shoulders. The degree of directness or openness is based on the angle (orientation) of your body. Your shoulders control that angle. The more you turn away from the learners, the less open (positive) you appear, especially if your face is not visible.[9] If you find yourself staring at your content, with the front of your body not visible, and your face turned away for an extended period, then the effect of your communication will be lost. However, the more you turn away from displayed content (support visuals) the less likely the learners will be able to reference the information.

In order to strike a proper balance between supporting content and your audience, for most of your talk, you should be at a *45-degree angle* to the room itself. To create the angle, point your shoulders to the opposite corner of the room. This is a *rest* position of the body, which establishes a dual-relationship with the screen (content) and with the audience, especially when you need to gesture or move. Moreover, the rest position is a less direct orientation, allowing the body to choose moments of greater immediacy for emphatic effect.

When you square your shoulders to the back of the room, you move into a *power* position of the body, taking a more direct stance to the group.[1] It's a signal that the information being communicated is of greater importance or carries more emphasis. In addition, the directness of the body orientation adds to the immediacy of the communication.[10, 12] But don't stay in the power position too long or the effect will diminish. Emphatic moments should be used sparingly. You can vary the *rest* and *power* positions based on how you want to deliver the information at any point during a lecture, or while communicating interactively.[13] These two positions also keep you from turning away from the group for any extended period, while limiting your movements within the given space to only those areas that allow everyone a *frontal view* so that all of your facial expressions remain visible.[9]

Consider Proximity

The orientation of the body creates emphasis, while the action of the body creates effect. *Goal-oriented* actions of the body affect emotional responses in the viewer.[7] In other words, if you move toward or away from the group, the action adds meaning to the context or the situation.[9] If someone is running past you on the street, the movement suggests some sense of urgency. Actions of the body carry meaning. Movement becomes an object of attention. If your body is unusually still or rarely moves, the learners will find other objects for their attention. For example, if you are limited to speaking from behind a lectern, where you cannot move away from the structure (especially if tethered to the lectern by a microphone), then your body will remain fixed in one area and your movement will be extremely limited. When the action of your body is constrained, you may find students becoming restless or drifting into other activities, simply because there is little visible action of the body keeping their eyes attentive. With less visibility of the entire body, emotions are less likely to be attributed to related intentions.[8]

However, freedom of movement doesn't mean running back and forth, meandering aimlessly, or drifting from place to place for no apparent reason. Movement must be justified; that is, there has to be a logical reason for action or it is usually interpreted as a *distraction*. For example, if you walked across the room to pick up an object to display to the group, the reason for your action is clear. However, if you simply cross to the other side of the room, and continued speaking from the new area, there would be no apparent logic to the action, and therefore, no justification for such movement.

Depth Perception

Proximity is a measure of intention when it comes to body language. The level of familiarity rises when bodies move closer.[8] Instructors can vary the *depth* of movement in order to vary the level of familiarity or closeness with the group. Learners interpret action based on reference points or *boundaries*, which should be based on *depth*, not width. It is more effective to move closer or farther from the group than to move horizontally across the room. Reaction to body movement, toward or away, directly affects the emotional interpretation of such action when confined to a perceptible area.[8] Therefore, to use movement effectively, you should create a *limited area* of depth with perceived (but invisible) boundaries. When imaginary space is defined using reasonable boundaries, movement within the limited area will allow for consistency in action and thereby reduce distractions from haphazard activity.

Line of Sight

A common remark noted is a student's complaint that the instructor stands in front of the screen. When defining a space, consider an imaginary *geometric shape* that insures a clear line of sight to visual support elements. A limited boundary prevents you from blocking a learner's vision of the content. One such imaginary area is defined as the *Presenter's Triangle*™.[13, 14] Figure 5.2 illustrates how the area is defined in relation to the audience.

To create this triangle, draw an imaginary line from the person sitting to your far right to the left-edge of your screen. This is the long end of this triangle, an *angled wall* if you will. From each end of the imaginary line,

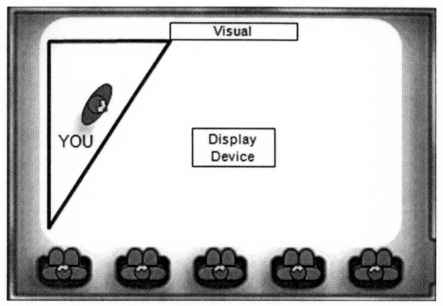

Figure 5.2. A top-down view of the *Presenter's Triangle* depicting the angled wall that creates a boundary in order to maintain a visible line of sight to the content

draw two lines meeting at a 90-degree angle to complete the shape behind you. This wraps you inside a large triangle. The angled-wall serves as your boundary in the defined space, preventing you from blocking the view of the screen when you speak. If you step through the imaginary wall, people on your right will not be able to see any displayed content. In addition, if you use the angled wall for navigation toward or away from the group, you will not drift into the far corner of the space.

Movement in a Defined Space

The *Presenter's Triangle* supports the issue of proximity. There are only three positions of the triangle that your body would occupy at any moment: the *front*, nearest the audience; the *middle*, where you should be most of the time; and the *back*, nearest the screen. Intentional movement adds value to content.[9] To engage learners with action, you need to change space in the triangle by moving to different positions periodically, but not constantly.

Because action is *readable*, movement can work in harmony with content. From a strategy perspective, choose the back of the triangle when the design of your supporting visual is complex, so that the audience can more easily compare what is on the screen to what is being said. Choose the front of the triangle when you want a closer connection with the audience, for more impact and personal interaction. When the body moves forward, the perceived attitude is interpreted as positive; conversely, when the body retreats for no apparent reason, the attitude is associated with withdrawal, a somewhat negative feeling.[11] To prevent this feeling, if you do move away from the audience, use a gesture toward a reference point behind you in order to give justification or a reason for the retreat.

⟿ Go Ahead and Back Up ⟿

As an instructor, you may be wondering how you would effectively use depth in movement, since at some point you would have to move away from the learners. Because visual support (slide content) is a part of the learning environment, any movement *away* from the group is interpreted as movement *toward* the content. Therefore the action is still judged as positive, even though the body is technically retreating.

However, to aid learners in making this positive association, you must *gesture to the screen* while moving backward, in order to create the visual justification for your withdrawal. In other words, the learners will accept your retreat because the gesture connects the action of your body to the content on the slide. It is as if you intended to move in the direction of the slide in order to collect the information needed to further explain your point or support the discussion.

In essence, the act of gesturing while the body moves away is not seen as withdrawal (retreat) from the group, but rather as movement *toward* the support content, thereby advancing the logic.

⚊⚍⚊

The relationship between movement and content is mutual. Decide where in the triangle you want to be when delivering certain content, and then check your visual design (simple or complex) to see if it supports your chosen spot in the triangle. For example, a "busy slide" exists in your lecture and it requires you to be in the back of the triangle for ease of comparison between body language and information. Yet, for greater impact, you prefer to be in the front of the triangle at that point in your topic. Consider redesigning the visual content (or adding a more simple slide) to seamlessly blend movement with supporting information.

It is natural to be able to move freely and talk simultaneously. But be aware that when the body moves while speaking, two "languages" are offered. This may be further compounded if learners are examining your slide content at the same time. Many professors have learned to avoid moving the body when making *specific* points; choosing instead to stay in one position, perhaps using gestures to direct attention to content (if needed). This limits the number of visual processes used by learners to interpret content.

The presence of lecterns in large classrooms and lecture halls can limit your visibility and effectiveness. Although lecterns serve a purpose from a materials perspective, that is a place to hold notes, computers, and other items, more effective speakers avoid standing behind lecterns. This is seen in more recent presidential debates such as the town hall meeting, where the candidates are completely visible, able to move freely, allowing the audience to emotionally connect to the content in greater depth.

⚊ Mastering the Lectern ⚍

Technically, you stand "on" a *podium* and stand "behind" a *lectern*. However, the terms are used interchangeably to describe the object employed by a speaker to read a speech, refer to notes, or rest a computer during a presentation or lecture. Although lecterns limit a more complete expression of body language, they are most often used when giving speeches. Without a lectern, you would look rather odd standing in front of a group, holding and reading several sheets of paper. The lectern supports the pages of the script while you deliver (read) the speech. Moreover, in a large group presentation, the lectern may be the only source for a microphone (if wireless microphones are unavailable).

The challenge with the lectern is that it usually covers 60 percent or more of your body and allows for little mobility. A recent trend has been the use of clear (see-though) lecterns to allow more visibility of the body, but movement is still restricted. Despite the limitations, there are ways that you can maintain a degree of effectiveness.

If possible, orient the lectern at a 45-degree angle to the room, matching the rest position of the body. From that angle, both your hands can rest on or touch the lectern. You can easily switch to a power position with just a turn of your upper body, leaving only your left hand resting on or touching the lectern.

If the lectern can't be angled but remains fixed and facing directly to the back wall (like a pulpit), you can still use the rest and power positions. While behind the lectern, take the rest position (45-degree angle). Only your right hand touches or rests on the lectern until you switch to the power position (by squaring-off to the back of the room), at which point both hands can rest on or touch the lectern.

Make sure the audience sees your hands as much as possible. If you hide your hands, the interpretation may be that you're hiding something, so try not to let your hands completely disappear for too long. If your wrists are higher than your elbows, you can still gesture to the audience or to the screen from behind the lectern. However, the lectern does create a visual frame of reference to height, and some people are at a disadvantage when trying to make gestures appear more natural. More modern lecterns offer elevation adjustments to compensate for height.

Even though you are somewhat trapped behind the lectern, the three positions of the triangle still exist, to allow for depth of movement. The middle of the triangle is when you're evenly balanced on both feet. The movement to the front or to the back happens by shifting your stance to one foot or the other.

These slight changes in body position may help to keep the audience looking at you from time to time. In light of the limitations the lectern places on the body, you can still effectively communicate through visible gestures, eye contact, and compelling content.

⚊⚊⚊

Lend a Hand

Just as the body can create emphasis and effect, the hands help clarify concepts, connect with learners, and construct visual relationships with content.

Verbal (vocal) expressions, when combined with supporting gestures add meaning to information, while increasing immediacy and augmenting the learning process.[12] Unfortunately, most presenters don't know what to do with their hands. When gestures are excessive, haphazard, disjointed, chaotic, uncoordinated, or disconnected from content, learners can be distracted in trying to connect nonverbal actions to the verbal phrases. For example, if you say the number "four," while showing *three* fingers, your listeners will have a disconnect between the verbal and nonverbal cues. Always keep in mind that learners will observe your gestures for congruity and consistency, trying to match your words to supporting actions.

ᨋ The Hands of Time ᨋ

One of the more common inconsistencies with respect to hand gestures involves the suggestion of a *timeline*. Many topics include references to stages, segments, steps, or other time-related sequences as part of some orderly process. The tendency is to visually describe time-related fragments sequentially, as they are likely to occur chronologically. Unfortunately, time-lines are often illustrated incorrectly, because you are facing a group whose perspective is the *opposite* of yours.

For example, suppose you use your hands to illustrate three stages of a process that advance over an imaginary timeline, from earlier (first) to later (last). The challenge with using gestures involves the *direction* of the progression. With languages that read left-to-right, a timeline follows the same pattern, left-to-right (past to future). Thus, you will likely use your *left hand* to position the first time segment to your left, adding the next stages progressively to your right, moving forward along *your* timeline, using *your* perspective.

The audience envisions their own timeline from *their* left to *their* right. Because you are *facing* the audience, the views are contrasting. To be consistent, you should use your *right hand* to identify the *earlier* moments on the timeline, and use the left hand to establish later stages.

The sequential references of a timeline must always match the audience perspective. This impression is also true with geography, where comparisons of west and east must be visually depicted according to how an audience would see the map.

ᨋ

Hand gestures can enhance communication or detract from the intended message.[15] Clarity in the body helps support clearness in the content. *Cohesive* gestures tend to identify concepts or items in space (as if placing a specific point "in the air") and allow learners to "see" what is being said.[16]

The term "virtual space" is used to describe the use of cohesive gestures to illustrate related thoughts in order to clarify content.[13] For example, a political science professor can visually establish *contrast* in American politics by lifting her right hand and holding it in the air to identify the Republicans and, at the same time, lifting her left hand to identify the Democrats. The two contrasting groups are momentarily floating in "virtual space," one on each side of the professor's body, clarifying to the learners that political parties are obviously "different." Be sure to remain consistent if you make multiple references to the items you placed in the air. Thus, if the professor uses the opposite hands for the political parties (Democrat, Republican) on a second reference, the learners will be confused, based on her earlier reference.

While virtual space can illuminate or demonstrate content more cohesively, in all cases, when you are completely in view of the audience, your hands should be visible at all times, never hidden in your pockets or behind your back. Hidden hands may suggest hidden agendas or lack of genuineness, limiting a more complete communication.[17] As an instructor, you should be aware of the different challenges and opportunities relative to gestures, including *energy*, *openness*, and *invitation*.

Energy

Gestures can help demonstrate concepts, and controlled animation of the hands can be effective to help illustrate points. However, too much liveliness in the hands will look distracting. The excess energy of *rhythmic* gestures that follow patterns of speech, but do not relate to content, can be confusing.[16] The term "conversational-izing" is described as moving the hands with the rhythm of speech, as if bouncing the gestures on every syllable.[14]

Gestures should freeze or stop moving to attach meaning to specified content and add congruence to speech.[18] For example, if you are using virtual space to depict two items (one issue with the right hand, and the other issue with the left hand), it is important to keep both hands extended, arms raised (wrists higher than elbows), holding the gestures relatively still, allowing time for the learners to connect the verbal cues (the two issues) with the non-verbal cues (the matching hand gestures). If your arms drop too quickly, or if your hands move excessively with your speaking pattern, learners will be less likely to register the impact of your gestures in relation to the concepts.

In essence, once you commit your gestures to spoken words, you need to let the actions pause or rest momentarily so that the listener is able to make a physical connection between spoken language and body language, anchoring your distinctions into memory.

Openness

The degree of openness in gestures affects the learners with respect to perceived attitude.[7] When the hands are apart, the body appears more "open" and less "defensive." When the hands are joined together, either in front of the body, or clasped behind the back, the degree of openness is reduced and the perceived attitude is more negative.[10] As a general rule, don't put your hands together for more than three seconds, as this will directly affect a number of body conditions, including vocal tone, energy, and the appearance of self-confidence.

Crossing the upper body with an arm to gesture or point to something will orient your body away, restrict your vocal tones by compressing your torso, and likely block your facial expressions if your arm is in front of your face. However, when the center of the body is unrestricted, that is, when nothing is blocking the front of the body, the highest degree of openness exists and the speaker looks more confident (less closed). If you are unsure as to what to do with your hands, just keep them to *your sides* when you are not gesturing, allowing you the greatest degree of openness with the body. Our observations directly linked learners' perception of self-confidence to this particular body gesture.

Invitation

The hands are very important communication tools, especially when *extending* or *lending a hand* to propose something of value. The opening of the arms is viewed as conveying warmth and empathy.[10] When the palm faces up as the arm extends out toward the audience, the "reaching out" gesture indicates approachability.[1, 7, 8, 15] Used mostly when interacting, the reaching out gesture visibly supports the proposal of value acting as an *invitation* to respond or to feel included.

For example, when you pose a question to a group, you are extending an invitation, seeking input in return. If you don't use your hands to include the group, the learners assume that the *last person* you look at is required to accept your invitation to answer. However, if you open your hands to the entire group, "reaching out" toward them, the gesture indicates an invitation to everyone to participate. The learners will realize that *anyone* in the group is allowed to respond. The opportunity for involvement is granted to the entire audience, not just to one person. This reaching-out gesture is also discussed in the "Interaction" section, later in this chapter.

Beyond interaction, the open-hand gesture implies a feeling of "attending to another's needs." It illustrates a "softness of action," representative of an embrace, akin to warmth, compassion, and affection. Likewise, when an open-hand gesture is used to direct attention to information, the invitation is extended toward content. Thus, a gesture with your left hand toward the screen, guides the eyes of the learners to specific points in your content, inviting a view of evidence to further explain a point.

Relax the Stance

When you are standing *evenly* balanced, with both your heels touching the floor at the same pressure, your chin *centered* on your body, gestures will appear rigid or unnatural. When the stance is even, gestures tend to move symmetrically, or the hands join together. Consider an "off-balance" stance, with the body anchored or shifted to one foot or the other and your chin aligned with one knee. This more *relaxed* posture allows your gestures to look more natural. Even when not gesturing, a relaxed stance suggests that you have control of the situation and you are perceived as being more confident.[8, 10] You don't want to look as if you are leaning to one side, or slouching, you just need to put slightly more pressure on one foot or the other, to anchor the body and create the relaxed stance. Avoid placing your hands in your pockets or on your hips which will give the impression of a more aggressive stance.

Make Eye Contact

Interpersonal communication is enhanced by eye contact. An infant will smile from watching the eyes of its mother. We speak to the eyes, not the ears, which is why communication is at its peak when people can look at one another. In fact, in one-to-one conversations, eye contact is a function of multiple elements of communication including closeness, specifics of conversation, degree of smiling, tone of voice, and more.[17] In a seminar or classroom setting, the instructor automatically scans the environment, followed by looking at the individuals repeatedly. The scanning of the individuals is known as frequent eye contact. It is not staring, but scanning.

In dealing with groups of people, as in a classroom lecture, the issues of proximity and distance will affect the impact of frequent eye contact. Interestingly, there is an equilibrium or balance that occurs in communication between proximity and eye contact. As proximity decreases, and people are nearer to one another, eye contact is reduced to compensate for the closeness and maintain the equilibrium.[19] For instance, in discussing a private matter with another person in a public place, you will stand relatively close to one another (so others cannot hear the discussion); and, each of you will make less eye contact with one another due to the closer proximity.

Understanding this relationship between distance and eye contact is especially helpful for the instructor in the classroom. As the size of your group increases, you should make *more* eye contact with those seated *farther* away, because your proximity to those seated closer requires less eye contact to preserve the balance. In some learning environments, others may be too far away to see your eyes. At greater distances, eye contact gradually disappears. This is why in presentations to very large groups *image magnification* is used, where the speaker is displayed on a large screen as the camera creates a closer view for those sitting farther away. Distance learning is enhanced by using a video camera, especially when the instructor makes periodic eye contact with the camera, as if looking into the eyes of the viewers.[13]

When teaching, you will find that there are two types of frequent eye contact, based on proximity. For smaller groups, *direct* eye contact occurs more often. For larger groups, *anchored* eye contact is used to create closeness.

Direct Eye Contact

Looking straight into the eyes of another person is considered *direct* eye contact. Direct eye contact is easier in a smaller group, simply because you have fewer faces to find. In a classroom of ten students it will be easy to look at every person in the room at one time or another during your discussion. Interestingly, in a one-to-one conversation, more eye contact is made by the listener than by the speaker.[11] This is obvious during a lecture, where the professor looks at different students periodically while speaking, but the students look only at the professor while listening.

Even with occasional glances to each learner in a small group, you may be uncomfortable making direct eye contact. If that is the case, you don't have to look directly into a person's eyes. Instead, you can look between the eyes, at the spot where the bridge of the nose meets the eyebrows. Or you can look at the whole head of the person as you speak. From a short distance, it will appear to the other person that you are making direct eye contact.

Anchored Eye Contact

In a larger audience, say fifty or more people, you can still make direct eye contact with several people, but probably not with everyone, mainly because of distance. While some people are uncomfortable with smaller groups and the higher degree of direct eye contact, others find larger groups intimidating because of the lack of direct eye contact. With more people in the room, you may find it challenging to manage the eyes of so many learners, especially because the *input* you receive from eye contact will need to be interpreted. Too much input can result in a feeling of being overwhelmed, intimidated, or distracted from concentrating on content or the discussion. To steer clear of this unsettling feeling, many teachers avoid eye contact by looking up into a corner of the room, looking down to the floor, or reading their notes, slides, or whiteboards.[17, 19] Yet, to remain focused on content, and appear closer to a large group, speakers use *anchored* eye contact.

For example, a large lecture hall is filled with hundreds of students as an anthropology professor begins his talk. During the presentation, his eyes occasionally leave the audience, for quick glances to visual support. After a brief look at a slide, the professor turns his head to the group again, but sees hundreds of eyes, causing distraction in thought as he tries to interpret the nonverbal input from so many people. To overcome this challenge, the professor initially identifies specific students in the group, perhaps five or six faces seated in different parts of the room. These are considered fixed visual cues or anchors. Then, after looking away momentarily, the professor can look back to the audience, find one of the faces, and make anchored eye contact with that one person, not the entire group. The concentration on content increases because the eye contact from one individual is easier to manage.

The anchors you select in the audience should be far enough apart so that it looks as if you are speaking to whole sections, even though your eyes are fixed on one person within that section. So, divide your audience into a few big areas and select one person from each section as your anchor. This strategy is especially helpful for those who feel uncomfortable speaking in front of larger groups. Anchored eye contact reduces the crowd to only a few people who happen to have a lot of other people sitting around them.

Regardless of the size of the group, the use of frequent eye contact, whether direct or anchored, allows an instructor to nonverbally connect to learners in a more positive manner, thereby increasing the effectiveness of teaching and enhancing the experience of learning.

Avoid Distractions

There are a variety of body language *distractions* such as moving frequently or being unsure of what to do with your hands. Many of these issues are caused by a variety of possibilities, most of which can be addressed with practice. Table 5.2 outlines some of the more common body language distractions, related causes, and suggestions for overcoming these challenges.

Since a great percentage of your delivery is nonverbal, the ability to control movements, gestures, and other expressions of the body is critical to the communication process. If you can remain consistent with actions, stay in a defined area, make eye contact with your learners, and avoid meaningless gestures, you will increase attention to the message within the material, especially since your physical delivery will appear seamless with your spoken words.

Table 5.2. Body language distractions, causes, and suggestions for improvement

Act Not to Distract		
Body Language Challenges	*Possible Causes*	*Ways to Eliminate the Distractions*
• wandering around in small areas or circles • walking aimlessly • moving frequently throughout the room • rocking back and forth, or side to side in one place	• processing new thoughts ("thinking on your feet") • lack of focus on topic • nervousness • full bladder • running out of time	• shift stance to one foot or the other and lock the upper muscles (quadriceps) of the anchoring leg • use only the positions of the Presenter's Triangle as stopping points • create interaction or discussion • review topic in advance
• moving your hands in the rhythm of your speech • moving one hand in small circles or haphazardly	• nervousness, anxiety • trying too hard to emphasize a point	• gesture to an individual or to the entire group • freeze or lock the hands on the first movement • keep hands at sides
• one or both hands in pockets • hands clasped behind back • hands clasped or held together in front of body	• possible hidden agenda or insincerity in delivery • protecting weaker part of body (stomach area) • unsure of specific content	• keep hands apart and visible at all times • gesture to an individual or to the entire group • keep front of body open
• turning away from the audience (possibly to read content)	• too focused on content • uncomfortable making eye contact • unsure of content, possibly unprepared	• create interaction or discussion • gesture to an individual or to the entire group • use PC as a prompter to glance at content • review content in advance • maintain 45-degree angle to group and screen • use anchored eye contact to target only a few individuals
• blocking the view of the screen or content	• unaware of sightlines • moving into light source to make specific references (pointing) to content	• stay within Presenter's Triangle • annotate content using graphics (arrows, circles, etc.) to draw attention to content items

SPEAKING STYLE

The right to speak must be earned by having something to say.

—Winston Churchill

Speaking Style is defined as a characteristic where one can be easily heard and understood while using proper inflection and tone when speaking.[2] If body language conveys the nonverbal cues, then the spoken language clearly expresses the verbal messages. While vocal clarity and volume are critical, there are many subtleties, nuances, intonations, inflections, and other deeper meanings in the spoken language that account for an instructor's speaking style. The connection of your learners to your speaking style is both physical and emotional, based not only on what the learners actually hear, but also on how they actually hear it.

As we noted earlier in our discussion of body language, six universal emotions are detectable nonverbally (happiness, sadness, fear, surprise, anger, and contempt) and these emotions can be determined from a person's voice.[20] In fact, the emotional context of the voice can be interpreted, even if the language is unknown, simply based on vocal tones.[21] If you are a professor who has multicultural learners, each student's ability to completely understand the fluency in your spoken words will vary. However, your voice will carry emotions that every learner will perceive similarly. If your voice sounds happy, you could be reciting a series of numbers and the emotion will be perceived in the same way, to everyone. To communicate emotions effectively with your speaking style, you need to control the *physical* attributes of your voice. Your unique vocal arrangement involves *proper breathing*, *verbal timing*, and *vocal inflections*, all of which can be enhanced to allow learners to listen more easily to the topic or to the discussion and connect emotionally to your teaching.

Finding Your Voice

The mechanics of a speaking voice include the *lungs* to control airflow and breathing in order to manage the length of phrases; the *larynx*, which determines vibrating frequency (high or low) in order to fine-tune pitch and tone (timbre); and the *articulators* (tongue, cheeks, palate, lips, etc.) used to vary volume, and enunciate the words. To maximize these components, it is important to understand how *physiology* plays a role. The literature is extensive on voice research, especially regarding vocal issues concerning men and women. It is widely recognized that male and female voices are physiologically different, and have different pitches, due to a variety of factors, most specifically related to the length of the vocal tract and the size of the vocal folds in the larynx. Basically, as air passes over the vocal folds, they vibrate (open and close) and the rate (frequency) of vibration results in vocal *pitch*.

A man tends to have a larger larynx, with larger vocal folds that generate lower-pitched tones enabling sound to project with more power and distance.[22] A female has a smaller larynx with smaller vocal folds that vibrate at higher frequencies.[23] The best comparison of a male and female voice is to think of the two parts of a loudspeaker where the woofer (man) carries the bass sound (lower frequency) over a larger surface and the tweeter (woman) carries the treble sound (higher frequency) across a smaller circle.[23] In addition, the shorter vocal tract in the female creates a more "breathy" sound, which adds another dimension to the tone.[24, 25] Physiologically, the female voice can be 25 percent more efficient than the male voice because of the ability to vary vocal processes in a smaller area at higher frequencies with softer tones.[23] However, vocal attributes are only favorable to those who understand how to use the voice effectively and who take advantage of the physiology where possible.

Proper Breathing

Learners have been quick to point out that one of the most distracting characteristics of a professor's voice is a monotone sound where the voice stays generally *flat* throughout the lecture.[2] Irrespective of gender differences, both men and women should understand the value of proper breathing in order to maximize the vocal components that contribute to effectiveness. At lower tones, men do not have many vocal variations but they have air flow power in the voice that ensures being heard at the back of the room.[24]

Unfortunately, having a greater supply of air that is unregulated may lead to other vocal challenges. For example, without variation in pitch, longer phrases delivered by males at a consistently lower frequency could produce a steady sound that is *monotone*. If you are a male instructor, consider some alternatives when speaking, such as using shorter phrases, and adding more pauses between phrases to release the stored air without saying any words. In addition, you may want to add more interaction to your lecture to encourage the sound of other voices in the room to break up any monotony that may occur in your vocal tone.

A woman typically has smaller vocal folds, and uses shorter breaths that cause the vocal tones to be softer. While she may not generate as much vocal power as a man, a woman's voice travels on a softer yet higher frequency, which can reach similar or greater distances than the loud lower tones usually associated with the male voice. However, acoustic features in the space such as high ceilings, carpeted floors, fabric-backed walls, or ambient noise will cause sound to dissipate, making volume more important than pitch. In those cases, the "breathy" female voice requires more air to sustain amplitude. Unfortunately, short intakes followed by quick bursts of air attempting to amplify the voice will result in loss of energy, mild fatigue, and strain. This is why, even in a smaller environment, women are encouraged to use a microphone.

Voice Projection

The most important component of vocal amplitude is air. With more air flow, vocal folds spread wider and close with more power. Think of clapping your hands. The wider the space between your hands, the louder the clap will sound. Voice gets volume from an adequate air supply. However, if you take air only into your lungs and not down into the lower abdomen, where the diaphragm contracts to allow more air to enter the body, you will quickly run out of air while speaking louder. By learning to use the diaphragm and the lower abdominal muscles (obliques) you can capture and control more air.[26] For example, simply saying the word "HA" automatically contracts the diaphragm to exhale the sound with relaxed muscle tension, projecting the sound efficiently.

In essence, the trained abdominal muscles help add resonance to the voice, creating changes in pitch and timbre, thereby increasing the spectrum of vocal tones, allowing you to say longer phrases at a consistently higher volume with less strain on the voice. Voice projection is especially important in the English language, where the emphasis or "point" is made at the end of a sentence, not at the beginning. Without enough air to support a longer phrase, the voice might trail off with insufficient volume, making the more important words difficult to hear or understand. Improper breathing can easily causes miscommunication. If a professor says, "Next Friday, everyone should get here on time because there will be a quiz," and trails off at the end of the phrase, students will only think they need to arrive on time, not having heard anything about a quiz. While there are breathing exercises that can enhance vocal power, technology may offer another solution by using microphones to amplify sound and allow the voice to be heard at greater distances.

Microphones

Regardless of how exceptionally you project your voice, a microphone can only add to your vocal quality, especially because you can vary the timbre in your voice with whispers and other softer sounds that would otherwise be inaudible. Many seasoned professors have learned the value of letting a microphone do the work of projecting sound, allowing the voice to retain its natural quality, conversational in many respects, and closest to the instructor's true speaking style. However, the amplified sound will also highlight minor distractions, especially for those who are less familiar with different types of audio technology. In most learning environments, there are basically two categories of microphones: those that are more *restrictive*, tethered to a lectern, attached to a mic stand, or handheld; and, those that are more *flexible*, wireless or corded, yet clipped to the clothing, allowing free movement of the hands and body.

When using a restrictive microphone, it is best to keep the mic lower than your face so that your expressions are visible. Moreover, from a vocal perspective, the clearest sound will emanate when the head is straight, or even slightly tilted (up, down, left, right) where the vocal tract is not hindered or compressed. It would be difficult to speak clearly if you shortened your esophagus by pressing your chin into your neck; or, if you elongated your neck by tilting your head far back as if looking at the ceiling. If the microphone is positioned too low, you may be closing your throat too much if your chin is forced lower to speak into the mic. It is better to stay back and keep your head straight as you talk "over" the top of the fixed microphone, rather than leaning into it. Even if you are holding a wireless handheld microphone (still considered restrictive because you must hold it one hand), it would be easier to maintain a clear speaking voice and keep a consistent level of sound if you rest the top of the microphone against your chin as you speak. This keeps the microphone in one place. Because many people use their hands when speaking, for emphasis, if the hand with the microphone moves around, then the voice will be intermittent and inaudible at times.

Flexible microphones not only allow you to move around, but the *lavaliere* (lapel) type feature also allows the microphone to clip conveniently to your clothing so your hands are free. Corded microphones are wired to an output system, and the long cord travels with you as you move. So, you will have to avoid accidentally tripping on the wire or getting tangled up by turning around completely. Wireless mics have two clip-on parts connected by a short wire. The lavaliere portion (the microphone itself) clips at the center of your body, and the battery pack (the transmitter) clips to your side. Although many wireless mics are designed to be hidden while still picking up sound from one or more directions, you may not be sure how a particular brand works. The default location is centered.

To position a mic, place your thumb at the center of your neck and rest your hand so that your palm is flat against your upper chest (similar to making a pledge). The point just below your hand, at the base of the pinky finger,

is usually an ideal level at which to clip the microphone. A microphone positioned too high or too low may sound distorted or muffled. Avoid clipping
the mic to a lapel or to one side of the body, because if you turn your head
away from the mic, your voice may not be heard as clearly. With wireless
mics, always make sure the batteries in the transmitter are fresh, especially
if you plan to use the microphone for an extended period (more than three
hours).

Finally, with all microphones, test the microphone before people enter the
room. Speak in your normal voice and ask any available technicians for assistance if microphone levels need adjustment. Check directly overhead from
where you may be standing for any loudspeakers in the ceiling that are active
because if you walk directly under a speaker with a microphone, you may get
unwanted feedback (a high-pitched frequency).

Vocal Power Training

Depending on your desire to become more effective though improved
vocal tones, there are several quick and effective breathing exercises that you
can do to help strengthen the resonance, tone, and volume of your voice.
These exercises involve correction of breathing rhythm and the development
of the abdominal muscles. In all such exercises, stand up, if possible, in order
to elongate the torso, and straighten the vocal tract for maximum air flow.

The easiest way to start developing the diaphragm muscle is to do the
"Hissing Balloon" exercise. Imagine your lower abdomen is a balloon that
needs to be filled with air. Take a deep breath and expand your stomach as
you take in the air, filling the balloon. Inhale through your nose, not your
mouth, to help target the air to the diaphragm, instead of the upper lungs. If
you do this correctly, you will see your stomach slightly bulge in all directions because the diaphragm muscle is flattening out to pull air down, like a
suction cup expanding as it fills. Now imagine making a tiny pinhole in the
balloon and slowly releasing the air using the letter "s" sound as in "ssss,"
keeping your teeth together, until all the air is gone. You will feel the tension
in your lower abdomen as you make the "ssss" sound, compressing the balloon (the inflated diaphragm) as the air escapes. Do a series of *five* intake/
release segments (take a deep breath, release the air, take another breath,
release the air, and so on, until you have done the balloon exercise five con-
secutive times). To check for proper muscle tension, poke your finger just
below your belly button as you release the air and you will feel the tightness.
Practice greater tension by forcing the "s" sound louder like "SSSS!!!"
Finally, practice short bursts as in "sss—sss—sss—sss" in order to feel the
diaphragm muscle contract repeatedly as you exhale to create the sounds.

"They Went Away" is a breathing exercise based on a graduated lengthening of sound through control of air flow. Say aloud the following phrase in one single breath: "One by one, they went away." Take another breath and say the same phrase again, but add to the numerical sequence, as in "One by one, and *two by two*, they went away." If you are able to say that last phrase in one breath, then continue graduating in sequence, with the next phrase: "One by one, and two by two, and *three by three*, they went away." You can see the pattern. The goal is to reach twelve (or higher), all in a single breath. To do this you will learn to inhale properly, dropping the diaphragm, expanding the lower abdominal muscles, to allow more air to enter the body, followed by contracting the muscles as you slowly exhale to push air over the vocal folds to sustain volume for a longer period.

A more advanced activity is a combination of breathing and phonetics designed to strengthen the abdominal muscles while fine-tuning the articulators (mouth, tongue, lips, etc.) for clear pronunciations. The "What a to-do" exercise covers the shaping of nearly every phonetic expression in the English language and is a great warm-up to use before a lengthy lecture where you plan on doing most of the talking. This sequence is purposely written in verse form and requires memorization to be most effective. The objective is to say the entire verse in one breath, pausing slightly on every comma and pausing longer at the end of each line, while clearly pronouncing every syllable, without clipping or cutting off any sounds.

> What a to-do, to die today, at a minute or two to two
> A thing distinctly hard to say, yet harder still to do
> For they'll beat a tattoo, at twenty to two
> A rah-tah-tah-tah-tah-tah-tah-tah-tah-too
> And the dragon will come, at the sound of a drum
> At a minute or two to two, today,
> At a minute or two to two.

The eleven beats on the fourth line should sound like "A-1-2-3—1-2-3—1-2-3-4." With practice, you will eventually be able manage enough air to say the entire verse, *twice*, in a single breath. In addition, the flow of sounds will expand and contract the lips to loosen the mouth muscles and make speech more fluid.

You can investigate more of these types of breathing exercises, many of them designed for singers or actors, if you want to increase your vocal range and maximize your voice projection, so that you don't sound monotone or inaudible. If you wish to do a series of planned exercises to build lower abdominal muscles, consider Pilates, which help build a solid core in the body using proper breathing techniques.

Verbal Timing

For a teacher, *verbal timing* is a matter of taking natural *pauses* in speech so that you can accomplish functional tasks such as transitioning between concepts, making eye contact, thinking, interacting, gesturing, and moving in a seamlessly smooth manner. One of the frustrations we often hear from students is that professors sound disconnected and disjointed when speaking, even though they are so well prepared. The issue is related to vocal delivery and not lack of preparation.

Verbal timing is a combination of "phrasing and pausing," where smooth and natural connecting phrases occur throughout concepts or across visual cues, such as between slides, while well-placed pauses help listeners digest content.[13] Breathing properly will help you deliver phrases that can be heard from a distance. But speaking style goes beyond the words that the learners hear. The pace of delivery (phrasing) compounded by the choice of words (fluency), creates varying levels of interest in the listener. *Phrasing* helps in the shaping of content into manageable "chunks" for learners to easily absorb as you speak. *Fluency* is the tone, wording, and level of sophistication in the content that advances knowledge. This section is especially important for those with accents.

Phrasing

Without a doubt, the teachers and presenters who appear smooth in their delivery have mastered the art of *phrasing*. In fact, we are often asked "If a person is an expert in the topic, what important verbal skill will make the content easier to understand?" The answer is transitioning between concepts using proper phrasing. The literature describes the use of verbal "chunks," which are small bits of related information that can be managed or learned. When these chunks are separated by *lead-in* phrases, which indicate changes in thought, topic, or content sections, learners are able to group the chunks into larger collections to eventually gain a more complete understanding of a topic.[15] For example, introductory phrases that may signify the beginning of a new topic (chunk) include "Today we will discuss . . . ," or "Next, we have this other case . . . ." Transitional phrases are used to connect smaller chunks (concepts) within a topic for verification, ("as a result, you might find . . ."), or for comparison ("on the other hand . . ."), or even to branch to a related subtopic ("in addition to this . . ."). Parenthetical phrases can be thought provoking ("What is interesting about this . . .").

When using speaker support material, such as an electronic presentation, *lead-in phrases* can help to create smooth and natural verbal transitions between slides. In web-based online teaching, archived podcasts, or other electronically delivered content where the instructor is not visible, such phrasing becomes even more important for listeners to be able to segment information. Table 5.3 lists several commonly used phrases that help learners organize chunks of knowledge into cohesive patterns.

When chunks are verbally signaled with appropriately chosen lead-in phrases, learners are better able to coordinate and "time" various actions such as taking notes, asking questions, and actively listening in order to process and manage information. However, when a large amount of content, containing many chunks of information, is read or narrated, without any smooth verbal transitions to connect the items, learners are unsure as to how to organize the content in a cohesive manner.[15] Students will find it difficult to follow the content, or may even be confused as to where the content belongs in a larger scheme. A professor delivering a presentation who narrates or reads each slide, line by line, word by word, is unlikely to have used transitional phrases to connect concepts. Moreover, because the students have learned to

Table 5.3. Lead-in phrases that help listeners receive and manage spoken content

Managing Expressions			
Lead-in Phrase	Type	Indication	Level
today, now, next, another	Introductory	Change	New topic
conversely, on the other hand, yet, but, however	Transitional comparison	Contrast	Same topic
moreover, in addition, and, furthermore, also, the following	Transitional branch	Cumulative	Subtopic
in fact, as a matter of fact, just to be sure, let me explain, to elaborate	Transitional bridge	Clarification	Same topic
from this, as a result, as indicated, as you can see, because, for this reason, this is why, this means	Transitional proof	Verification	Same topic
interestingly, curiously, surprisingly, what you may not know	Parenthetical branch	Stimulation	Subtopic
for example, for instance, suppose, case in point, taking a closer look	Illustrative	Instruction	Same topic
obviously, undoubtedly, of course, naturally, surely, apparently, merely, barely, evidently	Evaluative	Expertise	Same or subtopic
in summary, in conclusion, to wit, wrapping up, the bottom line, overall	Closing	Synopsis	Multiple topics

read by this point in their lives, the act of narrating the visible content is not educational.

Paraphrasing, however, is a more effective technique, because it allows the instructor to choose different words, beyond the visible content (slides), and select appropriate phrasing to advance the topic. The challenge for teachers is in using easy-to-understand phrases, expressions, and terminology that appear conversational, yet educational at the same time (see table 5.3).

Fluency

In social settings, conversational tone is not only acceptable, but demanded. However, in academic settings, the danger of *hyperfluency* lurks, because many professors believe that the "academic register" or educational discourse must be offered with a higher-level tone, replete with excessively long sentences, multiple prepositional phrases, parenthetical branching to subtopics, expert terminology, and other rhetoric that learners may find difficult to follow or comprehend.[27] Like the sentence you just read, the overabundance of spoken content leads to lengthy phrases without sufficient pauses to allow learners to digest, discuss or analyze offered information. As a result, there may be a perceived lack of clarity in the communication causing *receiver apprehension*, where learners feel like they are only hearing information, but not "getting" the essence of the knowledge.[28]

Interestingly, hyperfluency in instructors is often mimicked by students and may actually be helpful in building a learner's academic register so that he or she can effectively communicate in the classroom and in other perceived educational environments. In addition, students may begin to incorporate bits and pieces of elevated language in writing when it comes to academic papers and research.[27] Rather than discourage hyperfluency in students, it may be better to limit the process, allowing them to experiment with high-level phrases and terminology (although incorrect at times), even to the point of humorously imitating your linguistic collection of very big words so that they can raise their fluency in the topic and advance their academic register. But as an instructor, you have to strike a delicate balance between conversational and educational discourse because, after all, you are *teaching*, not preaching. You can't use lofty language or technical jargon so convoluted that learners are lost in your sesquipedalian sputtering speaking style! At the same time, you don't want to dumb down the language to the point where teaching is sacrificed and students are never challenged. The easiest way to guide students through your level of spoken expertise is to match fluency with *inflection*, where your speech is clear, understandable, free of distractions, and educationally engaging.

Vocal Inflections

It's not just what you say, but *how* you say it that makes a difference to the listener. The voice is an instrument of expression, playing a variety of intonations to orchestrate a finely tuned melody of content. *Inflections* are mannerisms in speech (modulation, emphasis, speed, etc.) that a speaker uses to engage listeners. In some cases, the inflections are part of the attributes or characteristics of a person's vocal delivery; in other cases, these mannerisms can be learned and developed to enhance the quality of speech. Certain inflections can make listeners more attentive including *geographical accent*, *juxtaposition*, and *triads*.

Geographical Accent

On numerous occasions, people have said to us, "I am worried about my accent." When asked to elaborate, they say that because of the way they sound, they fear that their learners may lose concentration on the subject, or won't pay attention. Depending on where you go in the world, your voice may sound different from the greater majority and people will say that you have an accent. A geographical accent is a characteristic pronunciation of words in a current language, based on a person's social background (*regional* accent) or as a result of phonetic habits developed in a native language (*foreign* accent). Typically, regional accents are noticed among those sharing the same language (usually the same country) and foreign accents are noticed among those with different languages (usually different countries). For example, a person native to France, speaking in French, will likely be identifiable to fellow native French speakers based on *regional* pronunciations. That is, the French dialect will carry an "accent" attributed to a region *within* the country (from the north, south, a specific city, etc.). Yet, *across* countries the accent is foreign. Thus, a person native to France, who speaks in English, will pronounce English words using phonetic habits from the French language. To someone who speaks English, those French-based pronunciations will be considered a *foreign* accent. The impact on teaching is related to how *familiar* the learners are to the accent and how easily can they get accustomed to nuances and phrasing so that comprehension is not affected.[29]

Regional accents sometimes carry more stigma or possible negative connotations as a result of regional rivalry (from sports, politics, culture, etc.) than because of the inflection itself. Conversely, foreign accents may carry more prominence or prestige, depending on the listener's appreciation. For example, some people enjoy a particular foreign accent from exposure to the culture thorough travel or through watching movies where a likeable character uses a specific inflection. Of course, foreign accents can be judged harshly at times, especially when cultural, political, or social issues affect a listener's feelings or attitudes, causing stereotyping and other judgmental responses.[29]

Nonetheless, even when listeners show a preference for native-language teachers (or those with similar accents) and rate these instructors more favorably, a strong foreign accent does not necessarily reduce the comprehensiveness associated with content. In fact, the literature suggests that *familiar* accented speech is easier to understand, and aids in comprehension.[29] Familiarity increases as learners hear the accented speech more often, especially in a multicultural environment, where native and nonnative speakers and *learners* coexist, making accented speech a common occurrence.

From a verbal timing perspective, accented phrases require more time to process than unaccented speech, which allows learners to focus more closely on the instructor's words and pronunciations.[30] This is not to suggest that you adopt an accent just to get learners to listen more closely to your words. However, you should not make vain attempts to discard your accent, or try to mask it in some way, unless you are mispronouncing words or using incorrect vocabulary in the nonnative language.

The real challenge with accent is speech *distortion*, where listeners are unable to correctly identify words and phrases because the accent is too strong or heavy, and more difficult to understand when speed of speech increases.[31] When word articulation and pronunciation sound unintelligible, a great amount of context will be literally "lost in translation," so to speak. When you are speaking it is difficult to hear yourself. To create a greater awareness of an accent issue, consider recording one of your lectures (in a classroom situation), and then listening to it. This task alone will help you to better understand your challenges. Table 5.4 can be used as a means of self-help for anyone with accent issues.

Juxtaposition

A unique inflection occurs when vocal emphasis is placed on a particular word in an unexpected way. The *juxtaposition* (placement) highlights the word in a distinctive manner. For example, the boldface text in the following sentence identifies the vocal emphasis. "I went to the big **game**." When speaking, some words receive greater vocal emphasis than others. In the English language, the tendency is to place emphasis on the noun (game) because the adjective (big) already contains a colorful description (modifier), so it doesn't seem to require any additional help from the voice. Moreover, the emphasis segregates "game" from other possible nouns such as "event" or "building," specifying a *logical connection* to the activity. However, by

Table 5.4. Self-help for people with geographical accents

Avoiding Language Barriers	
Accent Issue	*Action*
Unclear pronunciations	• Slow the speaking pace (speed) • Repeat key words and phrases • Use simple phrases and shorter sentences • Consider peer review/feedback to develop clarity
Cutting, clipping, or shortening words, or dropping syllables	• Close syllables at the ends of words • Develop vocal power (see "Vocal Power Training," page 206)
Fast-pace, garbled words	• Take more pauses at the ends of phrases • Create interaction (let others speak) • Give greater attention to "slide" simplicity to coincide with spoken words • Refrain from narrating content (reading slides)

juxtaposing the vocal weight to the adjective, the sentence would sound different, as in "I went to the **big** game." The unexpected emphasis is placed on the modifier (big), highlighting the value or critical nature of the game, making an *emotional connection* to the activity. When emphasizing nouns and verbs, the mind of the listener is attentive to logic. When juxtaposing the emphasis to adjectives, the heart of the listener is attentive to emotion. In a similar way, the juxtaposition of adverbs can be just as effective.

The use of the *split infinitive*, although discouraged by classical grammarians, can be an effective inflection for creating emphasis. Perhaps the most famous split infinitive is in the opening sequence of the television series *Star Trek* where part of the narration is "to boldly go where no man has gone before." The adverb "boldly" splits the infinitive "to go." Compare the following statements, noting the position of the adverb (in boldface text) in relation to the infinitive (in italics).

> "The button *is positioned* **conveniently** on the right side of the board."
> "The button *is* **conveniently** *positioned* on the right side of the board."

In the first sentence, the infinitive (*is positioned*) retains the true grammatical structure, with the adverb (**conveniently**) following the infinitive. The vocal emphasis focuses mainly on the button's actual location (the right side). In the second sentence, the adverb splits the infinitive and juxtaposes the phrase to focus more on the feeling of comfort, ease, and utility associated with the button's location.

Shifting the vocal emphasis to adjectives and adverbs may be challenging for native speakers, because the unusual inflection is not a natural speech pattern in the language, and therefore must be planned. Interestingly, nonnative speakers tend to have phonetic habits that may favor juxtaposition more naturally, and this adds to the likeability of particular accents in the voice. Whether you use this inflection intentionally or naturally, you can vary the vocal emphasis to create the desired effect with your learners.

Triads

A professor of fine arts makes a brief announcement as the class begins, "Today, we will be covering eleven different architectural approaches, each of which can be categorized into any one of seven master designs and grouped into four possible cultural expressions." The learners reluctantly brace for a lengthy note-taking session, wondering if they will be able to memorize the possible permutations that can be derived from such a collection of architectural styles. Perhaps the professor could have divided the content into manageable sections, such as *triads*, where related items are grouped into threes.

As an instructor, consider designing your lectures or assignments around the *rule of three*, where you have three main ideas or topics. Limit main topics to no more than three subtopics if possible. When giving quick examples, limit a series to three, such as, "As you can see, this has many different chemical properties, including X, Y, and Z," or "When you look at the case, the most important facts to consider are 1, 2, and 3." A finance professor may preview an upcoming assignment with: "In creating your report on monetary policy, consider the political climate, the concern of the banks, and the overall influence of the world markets." The triad helps the learner separate the items into manageable segments.

⩗ Three's Company ⩗

Speechwriters are famous for using triads or triplets, where the rhythmic pattern of the last item in the triad contains more syllables (beats) than the first two parts. For example, a politician might say: "We'll be more prosperous, we'll have lower taxes, and our children will have a future" (6 beats, 6 beats, 9 beats).

In some cases the triad is simply repetition, such as former British Prime Minister Tony Blair's "Education, Education, Education" or Martin Luther King's repetitive triad, with added beats before the last repetition: "Free at last! Free at last! Thank God Almighty, we are free at last!" Some triads are progressive in rhythm, such as the U.S. courtroom oath of "the truth, the whole truth, and nothing but the truth," with gradually increasing beats throughout the triad, making the progression somewhat predictable.

Popular references use triads. Many governments and religions are designed around three entities. Stories have a beginning, middle, and end. Children's stories use threes: three bears, three blind mice, and three little pigs. Movies gave us *The Three Musketeers*, *Three Coins in a Fountain*, and *The Three Faces of Eve*.

Comic strips generally use three panels, daily information is presented in a triad as "news, sports, and weather," and even humor is based on a "setup, setup, sting" pattern, with many jokes involving three characters or three situations, two of which are the same and the third containing the humor. The abundance of triads makes the use of such rhythm in speech very familiar to the listener.

—◇◇◇◇◇—

By occasionally adding triads to your lecturing, you can incorporate a rhythmic pattern of inflection that is noticeable, predictable, and pleasing to the ear. Triads are commonly advocated in writing, humor, and storytelling and are very effective in teaching by limiting content and making memorable associations. Using triads in teaching can be engaging, educational, and effective. Notice the use of the three operatives at the end of the prior sentence.

Um . . . Uh . . . Vocal Distractions

Whereas certain vocal inflections can be gratifying, there are also times where vocal distractions interrupt the rhythm of speech and may reduce the effectiveness of the content. Perhaps you are unable to say just the right thing at the right time, or you had something "at the tip" of your tongue, but couldn't quite get to the word. Maybe there were moments where you just hurried through content and were not really sure if you were clearly understood. There are so many reasons why hesitancy in speech occurs, especially in unplanned, unrehearsed, or unsuspecting moments. As an instructor, even though you have prepared the content, you still want the teaching to sound like a conversation or dialogue, as if being spoken naturally. When speech is spontaneously created, words are sometimes jumbled, garbled, or simply misused in the context of the given topic. While fluency promotes clarity, *disfluency* suspends the immediate connection to content, breaking up the listening pattern and possibly limiting comprehension. Such vocal distractions include *fillers*, *rapidity*, and *parenthetical intrusions*. Understanding and overcoming these distractions are critically important in optimizing clarity in speech.

Fillers

One of the most distracting elements in teaching is the use of *fillers* and, unfortunately, most people are unaware of the frequency at which these occur. The sounds we make in-between the words we say are commonly known as fillers.[32] In conversation and other unrehearsed speech, this type of disfluency is a frequent vocal disruption that occurs at a rate of 6 percent of the words spoken.[33] At times, fillers can occur when a speaker is trying to retrieve higher-level language or technical terms that are less often used in normal conversation. In some cases, the disruption occurs when describing pictures or scenes, where information is more vague or ambiguous. Unfortunately, any verbal hesitancy in speech can be interpreted as an uncertainty or lack of familiarity with content, which is why *silence* is the better filler when one is at a loss for words.

Some fillers are just added sounds such as "um," "uh," "er," or parenthetical inserts such as, "you know," "like," "again," "okay," "right," or emotional interjections such as "aha," "ah," "oops," "ugh," "wow." Fillers do not necessarily indicate a lack of knowledge, but they are usually vocal pauses inserted while retrieving knowledge. When speakers try to retrieve *less familiar* information, fillers such as *uh* and *um* are more likely to occur, and in some cases these verbal utterances are normal patterns in speech for the purpose of delay in order to keep from being interrupted or in order to find the best way of expressing information.[32]

However, the *length of the delay* following the filler, that is, the actual time it takes to retrieve information, can affect a listener's perception as to how familiar the speaker is with the content retrieved. For example, there is a difference between the *uh* and *um* fillers. The *uh* filler is typically a shorter, more temporary interruption, with a brief delay following the *uh*, suggesting that the speaker is familiar with the upcoming content, but is hesitant in forming the correct expression. The *um* filler tends to have a longer delay, suggesting that the speaker may be unsure and searching for possibly *unfamiliar* content. This hesitancy can happen when the upcoming content is highly technical or highly descriptive in nature and the speaker can't seem to find the right word or phrase or if the speaker is signaling a desire to not be interrupted during the pause. Coincidentally, in situations of suspicion or doubt, where skepticism exists for example, the longer delay following the "um" filler may suggest that upcoming content may be conjecture, guess-work, or possibly not the truth. In any case, whether *uh* or *um* is accidental or purposeful, the longer the delay or pause following the filler, as with "um," the more challenging for the learner in processing the continuity of content.[32]

At times, added sounds sometimes cause a *repetition* of the same word, such as "In the sixteenth . . . *uh* . . . sixteenth century." A repetition is easy for the listener because, in most cases, a key word is restated. Sometimes the filler is corrective in the middle of a word, such as "the financial *repor*—the financial *statement* . . . ." The immediate *repair* attempts to help the listener understand the intent of the message by clarifying the content. However, too many of these corrective statements will give the impression to the listener that the content is not prepared.

The filler may be a *false start*, such as, "When I look back, I *remem*—I never actually considered categorizing all the details." When words are truncated, or cutoff, the listener evaluates the initial part of the content (the false start) and compares it to the newer, more complete content to see if the information is the same or different.[33] The effect of an instructor's false start forces the learner to attempt to complete the instructor's thought, but there is little likelihood of the learner predicting the remainder of a cutoff phrase. Cutting-off sentences, or *clipping*, is more distracting when the focus on words is heightened, such as when body language is either limited (behind a lectern) or nonexistent (online webinar, podcast, voice conference, etc.).

When pauses are filled with sounds, such as "uh," or words are repeated or sentences restarted, learner comprehension can be adversely affected. At times, however, listeners may become more attentive to the word immediately following the filler.[33] A loss in comprehension is less if the word following the filler is predictable or familiar to the learners. This "expectancy" is usually the case for already-mentioned content. Examine the following sentences: "Water is a natural resource that can be managed. Many localities control the supply of . . . *uh* . . . water in an effective way." Note that the word "water," following the filler, has a prior context (in the first sentence) and its familiarity makes it predictable and thus logically expected.

If, however, you are not able to correct this disfluency, consider announcing a key word or phrase before elaborating on it. If learners hear the key word or phrase, prior to hearing the filler, then they may be able to ignore the filler when it occurs, or at least give it less weight as a distraction. However, there is no clear evidence that your learners will suddenly pay more attention to key points if you purposely precede words with fillers; therefore, we do not recommend using disfluency as a vocal strategy. Moreover, without your having previously mentioned the specific content, a purposely added filler will signify *new* content to the listener because the filled pause (*uh, um, er*, etc.) increases the expectancy that something new is about to be mentioned.[34]

This is more challenging to comprehension because expectancy is lower for a new word as it cannot be predicted with ease.

In reality, fillers are vocal evidence that you are thinking out loud. You're letting the audience hear your distraction as you search for the next word, or the ideal phrase. To counter this problem, consider using *silence* as a filler. A silent pause will give you time to find the right word or phrase and allow your learners to concentrate on your intended content more easily (see "Verbal Timing," page 208). Yet, if you find yourself using fillers frequently, you may be able to reduce the unconscious habit by using audible feedback to raise your awareness. Just as the eyes can observe a body language distraction, the ears can detect a vocal disruption. To help overcome a filler challenge, practice a presentation in front of a colleague. Have the person clap his or her hands, or snap their fingers, whenever you use a filler in your speech. Each time you hear the hands clapping or the fingers snapping, you will be conscious of the filler. Hearing an external sound associated with a verbal filler raises your awareness of the issue to help you minimize or possibly eliminate the distraction.

Rapidity

The act of getting up in front of people creates an altered sense of time, and some instructors sense that the spoken words are being phrased too slowly. As a result, the speed of speech increases. In conversation, listeners prefer more rapid speech, mainly to maximize the social time available for interaction. In learning situations, especially where processes, steps, or logical pathways are defined, listeners prefer moderate or a less rapid rate of speaking. Excess rapidity leads to reduced understanding. However, a moderate increase in speed may result in better comprehension for the listeners, while allowing teachers to cover slightly more material due to the faster pace.

With content familiarity and experience, there is evidence that faster speech suggests a professor who is knowledgeable, intelligent, and more of an expert, carrying a higher degree of credibility.[35] This is not always the case. While such perceptions are helpful in persuasive speech, a rapid delivery of content may hinder the learning of highly complex or technical information, such as process descriptions. Therefore, an effective strategy for a professor is to accelerate the rate of speech during argumentative discourse, philosophical discussions, and theoretical debates; but, consider a slower rate of speech when covering detailed processes, technical procedures, and other complex topics.

Interestingly, for more novice teachers where the learners sense the instructor is less familiar with the topic, the speed of speech may be interpreted as "rushing through" the content because of a perceived lack of expertise.

In these situations it is better to slow the rate of speech and take the time to explain content more thoroughly, even if the knowledge of the topic is sparse. Of course, the most important concern with rapidity is clarity. If the professor cannot be understood because the words are garbled, the issues of credibility, expertise, and knowledge are moot.

Parenthetical Intrusions

One of the most challenging aspects of vocal inflection—and there is evidence that instructors often drift from the topic, sometimes going off in an unknown direction—is the parenthetical intrusion. For example, the offset text in the previous sentence (—*and there is evidence . . . an unknown direction*—) is an example of such an intrusion. Additional spoken content that appears unrelated makes "getting to the point" more difficult.

⚞ Summer Daze ⚟

When I was a young boy, my family would spend the summers in a little house "out in the country," which was about an hour's drive from where we lived. The bungalow, as we called the place, was a small white house on top of a hill. There were neighboring homes with interesting neighbors, one of whom lived across the street. Mr. Longbine was a retired college professor who smoked a pipe and wore a big-brimmed hat. We used to call him Mr. "Long-time" because whenever he talked he spoke ever so slowly, taking forever to finish a sentence.

One morning, I was playing in front of the house, down at the bottom of the big hill. My mom and aunt were talking nearby, leaning against our white picket fence. I could see Mr. "Long-time" sauntering across the street, approaching my mom and aunt, greeting them by tipping his hat. He gets closer and begins to speak. "Good morning, ladies—and, may I say, what a fine morning it is—fine, in the sense of weather, not health—that is not to say that I don't wish good health for everyone—but it is just a beautiful day! I love the way the sun reflects—like a mirror, you know, along the lines of the old Victorian style mirrors—especially at this time of the morning—so reflective against the houses—your house in particular—which is what made me come over."

He leaned slightly on the fence, and used his pipe to help him gesture more emphatically, as he continued. "You see, as I looked from across the street, I could see your roof reflecting against the backdrop of the blue sky—that kind of blue that looks really blue, like a royal healthy blue, you know? Yet, the contrast to the blue sky was this dark gray, which at first I thought were clouds, thinking we haven't had rain in, what?—a few days, at least—I think it rained Wednesday, or maybe it was Tuesday—but it was more of a passing shower—not like some of the storms we get later in the summer—you have to pull the shutters closed for some of those storms, you know?"

As my mom and aunt stood there and listened, he casually bent down to tie his shoe and dust off some bits of grass from his trousers, stood up, stretched his back, and kept talking. "So anyway, I started thinking—if the dark gray clouds weren't bringing rain—I mean, with this being such a nice day and all—I kept staring over the top of your house and as I walked across the street and got closer—like I am now, standing right here and looking up—but I don't mean to sound like an alarmist or someone who worries a lot, because I am pretty even tempered. My wife says I am a bit of a worrier sometimes, and says I tend to jump to conclusions too quickly, and I suppose that maybe there's a bit of truth to that, but I don't think so. Yet, just to be sure, I came across the street and from this particular spot, it is very clear to me now that those gray clouds aren't really clouds at all—because they appear to be rising upward—not floating across the sky like you might expect—even if it isn't windy—and that being the case, I can safely say— actually, to be more exact,—I can definitely say—that without a doubt—your house is on fire."

He was still standing there, puffing on his pipe, leaning on the fence, as my mom and aunt frantically raced up the hill, attempting to douse the flames. Thankfully the damage was minimal, but it might have been avoided had Mr. "Long-time" made his point about ten minutes sooner.

≈∽∿∾≈

When speaking, instructors tend to insert extraneous comments or infor-mation within an existing line of logic, causing learners to keep track of mul-tiple independent thoughts while attempting to find a correlation.[27] A parenthetical intrusion is not a subset of the current discourse; rather, it is a completely separate statement requiring processing time by the listener. Notice the multiple parenthetical intrusions (shown in italics) in the following discourse spoken during a lecture by a law professor:

> "The majority of you—*I am assuming that everyone read the case, or should have—I know if you went online it can be downloaded—you need to be logged in, I think*—many of you can easily be swayed to the wrong side of the argument. It is obvious to anyone with knowledge of the situation—*and I am not suggesting that your opinions don't count—although there is a difference between opinion and con-jecture—I don't know if any of you watch Law and Order, but they do that all the time*—when you look at the facts, things are not what they seem."

The students are thinking, "And your point is?" The excerpt illustrates the lack of continuity in the logic because of the numerous branches to other pieces of nonessential information. If the parenthetical intrusions were eliminated, the professor would "get to the point" more quickly, much to the appreciation of the learners. Although you would not write in such a convoluted manner, speech is a spontaneous process and the editing is done vocally, without a chance to use the backspace or the delete key to clarify language. It is quite easy to drift to bits and pieces of parenthetical information before making your point. If you find yourself speaking with a number of diversions, consider focusing on a single target (point, objective, conclusion, etc.) and get to that destination in the most direct manner possible. The use of short phrases, single-word statements, or brief lists—and we don't want to belabor this point—it's not like we are purposely drifting—will reduce the use of parenthetical intrusions!

Overall, vocal inflections can be quite helpful to learners, especially when adding to the clarity of content. However, vocal distractions can significantly reduce comprehension and distract the listeners, undermining teaching effectiveness. As an instructor, try to develop a speaking style that favors your natural inflections and eliminates any distractions so that that the teaching and learning are harmonious.

TECHNOLOGY

> Technology is just a tool. In terms of getting the kids working together and motivating them, the teacher is the most important.

—Bill Gates

In terms of a skill, we describe *technology* as demonstrating familiarity with all equipment and other technical elements, such as multimedia.[2] Perhaps the most changeable aspect of education is the technology used to enhance learning. Interestingly, the underlying challenge for educators is in using that technology with ease and confidence. From a *process* perspective, it is important to understand the available range of technology that can be used in an academic environment. Of course, the mere presence of technology in the classroom does not guarantee that learning will improve.[36] However, from a *performance* perspective, it is important to know how to use technology in an effective manner to enhance the learning. It is not enough to simply know that a PC and a projector can be used to display content. You have to be able to seamlessly integrate the technology into your delivery. If you are uncomfortable using technology, or unfamiliar with the equipment, your effectiveness will suffer, especially because your learners are likely more technically proficient than you and will easily notice your challenges.

In many academic environments, student evaluations of teachers include a rating for the effective use of Audio-Visual (AV) materials.[18] In fact, while learners perceive technology to be beneficial for instructional clarity and content organization, instructors report that to use technology regularly they would need sufficient training and extra time for content preparation.[37] Moreover, many colleges and universities are slow to integrate the most current technology into the classroom setting, mostly for financial reasons. Yet the fact that technology is pervasive in the marketplace clearly compels educational institutions to continually restructure the learning environment to be more student-centered to match the current needs of a working society. The combination of instructors feeling unprepared and institutions being less than current makes the use of technology more of a challenge than an opportunity. Therefore, as an educator, you should continually become more familiar with relevant software and hardware systems that are designed to help you better communicate concepts and ideas.

Familiarity and Comfort

The educational literature is filled with books and articles outlining the continual struggles of teachers in embracing technology. Although Microsoft

PowerPoint is currently the most widely used software program for creating presentations, it is also the most widely abused software program for creating *poor* presentations.[38, 39] The problem, of course, is not the software application, but the application of the software. After all, citing PowerPoint as the design culprit is akin to blaming a keyboard for poor writing. The real issue is proficiency.

Reports indicate that college professors fear looking unprepared or less than competent in front of learners, especially when courses and materials have to be redesigned or repurposed to accommodate new classroom technology.[40] For example, a chemistry professor who has been comfortable writing formulas on a board is faced with the task of designing a slide presentation to support the lecture. The time needed to gain proficiency in using the graphics software program to design the course for electronic delivery and the effort required to become familiar with the AV equipment to deliver the content smoothly poses quite a challenge. The transition from chalkboards to keyboards is not that easy for every educator. Although the new technology is more welcomed by teachers who have entered the profession within the past ten years, many of the more seasoned professors have found the change more difficult to manage.[41]

The ever-changing sophistication of technological systems makes it difficult for us to offer advice on how to use specific equipment, as some technologies become obsolete, quickly displaced by something more advanced. However, the major categories of *displays* and *communication* allow for a general perspective. Some of the more popular audio-visual technologies in the classroom include: projectors, TV monitors, computers, interactive whiteboards, video conferencing systems, and microphones. Many of these are used in some combination, such as a computer with a projector along with a wireless microphone (for larger groups), a TV monitor with a video conferencing system, or an interactive whiteboard and a computer.

The easiest way to get comfortable using technology is to become familiar with it. If you have never used a VGA cable to connect a computer to a projector, then take the opportunity to get familiar with connections, settings, and other nuances of the equipment that might appear confusing if no one is available to help you. If part of your teaching includes distance learning or video conferencing, then make the effort to understand all aspects of the technology necessary to make the process of communicating seamless and free of technological distractions. If the academic environment allows Internet access in your classroom, then take the time to see what steps are necessary to connect to the web using the equipment in the room. Become familiar with cables, passwords, logon procedures, and other web-related requirements, just in case you lose your online connection and have to start again.

The last thing you want to do is waste the time of the learners while you make a vain attempt to figure out how to get a system to work. Not only will the learning be disrupted and the effort unproductive, but also you will feel less competent. In fact, professors with less technological proficiency may develop a fear of inadequacy, begin to lose self-confidence, and experience a loss of self-esteem.[40] Conversely, an instructor who uses technology effectively in the learning environment experiences an increase in confidence and enthusiasm.

While the educational institution is normally responsible for professional development and training, don't rely on a one-hour "lunch-'n'-learn" program for developing your technological prowess. The onus of learning new technology still rests with the individual instructor, so you will have to take it upon yourself to gain a greater level of expertise. Therefore, the more you practice with and use technology, the more accustomed to it you will get, and the more comfortable you will be in managing any glitches that might occur.

Projecting Confidence

The use of projectors to display information in a learning environment is not uncommon. From a delivery perspective, using a computer with an LCD projector to show slide presentations should appear seamless, but this is not always the case. Instructors who are less familiar with technology may be challenged by visual display issues such as navigation, sightlines, transitions, and readability from a distance (see "Technicalities of Reducing Clutter" in chapter 4, page 143). At times, professors may create distractions with projection technology that hinder learning. The main challenges include walking into the light source, overusing a laser pointer, and manually advancing slides.

Avoid the Light

Perhaps the most important issue to consider is whether learners have equal access to your displayed content. As discussed earlier in this chapter, the *Presenter's Triangle* is a self-imposed, imaginary boundary that helps maintain sightlines and hinders you from walking into the light source, or from stepping directly in front of the screen. If you happen to walk into the projector's light to reference something on the visual your body will become part of the reflective surface for content, causing a distraction. In some learning settings, projectors and screens are positioned higher to eliminate the possibility of a speaker walking in front of the displayed image, but some still choose to turn and point to the raised screen as if trying to identify some particular visual element. As noted in the "Content Design" section of chapter 4, slides that include annotations (circles, arrows, etc.) to highlight information are preferable to moving your body into the light or reaching to touch the screen to identify an item.

At times, instructors completely ignore the projector and stand directly in front of the display, as if in a spotlight. If you feel the need to move to an area in the room where your body may be in the light, some software programs, such as PowerPoint, allow you to temporarily blank the image by pressing the letter "B" on the keyboard (to display a black screen). Since black is the absence of light, it will not be noticed that you are in the light path of the projector. Pressing the letter "B" again or simply advancing the slideshow will restore the image.

Limit the Pointer

Some professors solve the problem of walking into the projector's light by using a laser pointer to direct attention to a specific area on a slide. If your visual content is properly developed, clearly organized, and well-designed, you should not have to use a laser pointer or any pointing device during the presentation. The pointer is typically a last-minute solution for a lack of forethought on how to display the content, emphasize with gestures, or accentuate with the voice. The fact that the pointer is in the hand of the speaker and readily available, makes its use spontaneous and often excessive.

There are several problems when using a laser pointer. One issue is that the pointer is difficult to keep steady, thus allowing the laser "dot" to shake or bounce. The erratic movement may be judged as haphazard and might suggest nervousness. Moreover, while moving the pointer, there is no visible *trail* that follows the moving dot along the outline of the intended shape. For example, if the pointer is moved in a circular pattern, the viewer must try to imagine the complete shape of a circle while concentrating on the referenced area. Compare that with incorporating a circle as a shape on the slide, effectively animated to delineate the area while remaining on the image as a continual reference.

The biggest challenge in using a laser pointer is that you have to spend time directing the pointer to a specific spot or general area on the image, causing you to reduce your interaction with the audience in order to look at the screen. Moreover, because the dot disappears each time you look back to the audience, the tendency is to repeat the pointing over and over each time you refer to the image—or you might continually point to the image and not look at the audience at all. Either way, the eye contact and attention is directed more at the content than it is to the learners.

It may be easier to simply use your voice to target specific areas and verbally guide the eye quickly through very complex information. You can say, "If you look at the center of the picture . . ." or "The object in the upper-right corner represents . . ." or "The second column in this table . . . ." You can even use hand gestures to direct attention, by lifting your hand to different heights, or by moving your hand closer to the image, without stepping into the light source or blocking the screen.

To be fair, we are not suggesting that you need to discard the laser pointer completely; rather, if you must use it, do so sparingly. However, in situations where content contains action, such as in a video clip, a laser pointer can be helpful in directing attention. Because the image is in motion, the pointer helps to steady the eye and focus on a specific area within the field of motion.

Get a Remote

If you find yourself touching the keyboard to advance the content of your presentation then you will appear out-of-touch with technology. Some may wonder if you change your TV channels manually at home! A remote control offers you incredible freedom of movement while allowing smooth transitions between slides. Because 98 percent of all electronic presentations are linear (forward or backward) a *two-button* remote control is all that is required to navigate through your content as you speak, allowing you to stay within the Presenter's Triangle and freeing you from touching or interacting with the computer.

Some remotes have an added button for a laser pointer, and some also have the capability to control the mouse pointer, as well. So, it's like having the left/right mouse buttons and the pointer all in your hand at the same time. The only thing to worry about is accidentally engaging and moving the mouse pointer while you present, creating an unintended pointing reference on the visual. Other remotes may offer additional features such as a countdown timer that makes the remote vibrate a few minutes before the time limit set for the talk.

Beyond slide navigation, a remote control allows you to stand at a fixed distance from the display equipment with the option of positioning your computer in front of you, yet at a reasonable distance so as not to block the front of your body. If you review figure 5.2, the *Presenter's Triangle*, earlier in this chapter, the area for the "display device" not only implies a place for a projector, but can also be the location for your computer. The simultaneous display of your content on your PC and on the projected image lets your computer function as a teleprompter so you do not have to continually look away, back toward the screen, when checking information.[13, 42] The viewing angle is perfect for the presenter who can glance momentarily toward the PC while appearing to make eye contact with a section of the audience. All in all, a remote is such a small piece of technology, at a reasonable cost, that allows for the seamless integration of software, hardware, and AV equipment.

Communicating Electronically

The communication aspect of technology involves a wide variety of possible media, ranging from interactive computer applications to sophisticated video conferencing systems. From a *process* perspective, we already discussed how the technology can be an additional source of stimulation for learners, allowing them to experience content in multiple formats and interact with others at remote distances (see "Multiple Expressions" in chapter 4, page 126). The communication of information includes a wide variety of formats including multimedia, video and web conferencing, satellite broadcasting, Internet radio, live video streaming, interactive whiteboards, and audience response systems. Some or all of these may be available to you as an instructor to enhance the learning experience (see "Incorporating Multimedia" in chapter 4, page 169). From a *performance* aspect, multiple forms of media must be managed effectively to appear integrated into the learning without distraction.

Multimedia

The use of animation, sound, and video can add to the learning experience, although many faculty are unsure as to how to use these elements effectively.[40] Learners prefer instructors who interact easily with technology.[2] To use multimedia successfully, make sure you practice with the special effects in advance.

⟿ Cell-less in Seattle ⟿

A science professor at a large university in the Northwest uses his desktop computer to create a very detailed animation of a cell splitting, along with arrows and lines to identify different cell components. He saves the entire animation as a "movie" and inserts the media object into his presentation as a *link*, meaning that the video is connected to the presentation, but not embedded into it. However, he does embed a sound file containing some classical music to play in background of the short movie clip. He copies the presentation to his notebook computer and proceeds to his class, which is held in one of the large lecture halls on campus.

Arriving a few minutes before the lecture, he connects his computer to the existing AV equipment and makes sure to plug the sound cable into his PC so the entire class will hear the music over the loudspeakers in the room. When the slide with the animated movie appears, only the music plays, but not the video. What happened?

When the professor copied the presentation from his desktop computer to his notebook computer, he inadvertently forgot to copy the video clip, which was only *linked* to the presentation and too large of a file to be embedded. The much smaller music file was able to be embedded into the presentation, which is why that part of the multimedia played.

Had the professor tested the media object after placing it on his notebook computer, he would have noticed the problem. The lesson is simple. Test all multimedia elements beforehand to make sure they will work as planned.

——∽∾——

Of all multimedia choices, *video with voice-over* is the most challenging to use in a live setting because the clip itself functions as a stand-alone presenter. As an instructor, if you are playing a clip that has voice-over narration, focus your attention on the video by watching the clip as if you are part of the audience. Do not turn toward the group while the video is playing, or the viewers will think you are going to make a comment, thereby interrupting the view of the video. However, if you do decide to interject comments during a voice-over video, practice with the clip and time your remarks so that they do not conflict with the narration. Or play the video without sound (mute the volume) and narrate the action yourself. While your words may not be as well scripted as the voice-over, your comments may provide a better context for the learning. As you make narrative comments, look directly at the video and talk louder because your face will be turned away from the group. The video clip has the focus, not you; therefore, you are allowed to talk without making eye contact with the learners. Preferably, the video clip should be short in duration. Keep in mind that you should practice the timing of your narration with the video in order for the delivery to appear smooth.

Distance Learning

Classroom environments are evolving to allow remote access to learning. Technology is giving space-challenged universities an opportunity to serve a greater community of students by expanding the reach of the traditional lecture hall.[43] At times, some or all of your learners may be in remote locations, observing your teaching over a video conference or possibly reviewing archived content in an electronic form, such as a podcast.

In situations where you need to communicate to remote learners, even if you have a live audience in the room, you must be able to engage the *remote* group as much as the on-site group. Learning objectives are best achieved through the active involvement of the participants, irrespective of where the participants are located, on-site or at a distance.[44] One way to make the remote group feel more actively involved is to interact more often with your live audience because they are the extension of the remote group. A television talk show is the best example of this situation. Imagine a talk show host with a live studio audience. When the host directs comments to the camera, the communication is directed to those watching from home, as well as to the live audience. Yet, the live studio audience provides immediate feedback, such as laughter or applause, acting as "surrogate representatives" of those watching from a distance. The live audience is actually part of the overall communication effort, thereby facilitating the active involvement of the remote audience, who continue to watch the show.

If you have a live group as you deliver content to learners at a distance (or even for later review), then include those in the room with you as part of the learning. Create "live" interaction so that remote learners feel the experience of being in the room. At the same time, engage the remote viewers by directing eye contact, gestures and other visible actions toward the camera as much as possible. In many distance-learning environments, the remote audiences can actively participate in the learning, being seen and heard by the on-site group as well. The challenge for the instructor is in involving and managing the two audiences, those near and those far, which may also require familiarity with the video technology. Yet the advantage of an expanded learning environment is in the fostering of education to a larger community, one that stimulates different opinions, attitudes, and applications of the original content.

In essence, distance learning solves the issues of time and space.[13] Without technology, an instructor would have to conduct multiple sessions in different places at different times to reach the same amount of learners.

Web Conferencing

A personalized, desktop-driven version of the structured video conference is called a *web conference*. This is a bridge between a conference call and a video conference, using telephone and computer technology, usually with an audience that is present and interactive, but all of whom are in remote locations, most likely at their desks. In most web conferences, material is presented using a computer to display the visual content (such as a PowerPoint presentation) and a separate telephone line is used for voice because phone quality through an Internet connection (VoIP or voice over Internet protocol) can be erratic and inconsistent due to varying transmission speeds.

While a web conference could also include a video window, where the instructor is visible through a web camera (webcam), the speed of the video may be slower than normal and, as a result, video is less effective in these sessions. Also, web conferencing is usually done from a desk, so the video window is likely to be a close-up of the speaker, a virtual "talking head" that adds little value in terms of body language to the delivery. Of course, the biggest communication hurdle in online learning is the lack of face-to-face interaction; but, learners do express satisfaction with the learning experience when a remote course is designed and delivered effectively using technology even though the "social aspect" of the traditional classroom is missing.[45]

Some web conferences have been termed *webcasts*, although a webcast is more often used for one-way, non-interactive *streaming video* such as you might find on a news network site (CNN, FOX, etc.). Rather than waiting for a timely TV show to be aired that may support the learning, instructors now provide students with links to supplemental webcasts that can be viewed at anytime, streamed directly to a computer.

Another type of web conference used in a learning context is a *webinar* which is a web-based seminar that might be conducted with an interactive audience or might be seen after the transmission time, as a downloadable recording. In some webinars, such as an online course, there is no voice-over. Instead, the topic is passively offered in a text-heavy slide format, peppered with a series of interactive questions and problems. Although some literature suggests that learners can achieve similar results with online sessions when involved in self-paced, task-oriented projects as compared to traditional teaching,[45] we believe the interactions among individuals will provide a more robust learning experience.

More common to university settings is the *podcast*. The term "podcasting" refers to using an Apple iPod (or equivalent) to store audio and/or video multimedia files for later playback and review on personal devices or through the Internet. While informative from a content perspective, a podcast is not interactive because it is a recording of an earlier event. For example, a lecture given to a group of students is recorded as a podcast, and contains the slides used in the lecture along with the professor's voice. Students can download the podcast onto a personal device, such as an iPod, for review of the content and to hear any comments or discussions that occurred during the live session. A podcast answers the question posed by a student who missed the lecture and asks, "What happened in class today?"

To be most effective with any type of web conferencing technology, keep in mind that the majority of the delivery is in the content design and the voice, with video being the least important element (and used infrequently in these settings). You should have uncluttered visual design and very clear speech. From a design perspective, although a web conference has each audience member sitting in front of his or her personal computer, don't make the content appear like a printed document, using a paper-white display and 12-point type as if the person is reading a book. Pretend it is a standard presentation to a live audience to create an effect similar to a live event.

During a podcast, from a vocal standpoint, consider identifying visual references by location or name. For example, just saying the phrase "If you look over here . . ." as you point to something on a slide, is obvious to the live audience, but will be challenging for someone only listening to the lecture as a podcast because the pointing action itself is not recorded, only voice and the slide content. Therefore, you will have to be more descriptive and say, "If you look at the larger rectangle on the right side of the image . . ." in order to guide the eye of the podcast listener to the particular element referenced on the visual. In fact, if you know that a lecture will be archived as a podcast, you can plan in advance to include geometric shapes and other annotations within the slide content to help a listener follow the topic more easily. With added annotations, your words can become even more descriptive by saying, "If you look at the larger rectangle on the right side of the image you will notice an arrow pointing to the exact area in question."

As an instructor who wishes to incorporate more current technology into the learning, the concept of communicating beyond the classroom will force you to be more specific, more design focused, and more aware of engaging not only those in front of you but also those at a distance or who may be learning at a later point in time without the benefit of seeing you.

Interactive Whiteboards

Another piece of technology that bridges the chalkboard and the keyboard is the *interactive whiteboard*, which is a large display connected to both a computer and a projector. Used in smaller group settings, the electronic board can simply function as a surface to display a projected image (presentation) or it can be used as a touch-screen with a special (digital) pen or just a finger to control software applications or to write notes. Unlike the traditional chalkboard or flipchart, the computer interface of the whiteboard allows anything written or drawn to be captured, saved, printed, e-mailed, or used in a manner similar to the way information on a computer might be used. This is helpful for those instructors who want to archive the interactivity and spontaneity associated with unplanned activities, such as discussions, explanations, demonstrations, and more.

To use a whiteboard effectively, consider the limitations imposed by having an interactive surface behind you. At times, you will have to turn away from the group, perhaps walk into the light source to touch an icon, block the view of content as you jot down ideas, and be less audible if you chose to speak while facing the board. To appear comfortable with the technology, first and foremost, try not to speak while actively using the electronic whiteboard. When your voice is directed toward a flat surface, especially from a short distance, the sound is muffled and less audible to those seated farther away. Treat writing and speaking separately. Accept the fact that the physical act of writing, drawing, or just touching the board to select icons is a "body language" and substitutes for spoken language until the action is finished. Too often instructors will rush the writing and speak quickly, not wanting to be turned away for too long. This faster pace leads to illegible handwriting; chaotic drawings; and softer, truncated vocal tones, making the learning more difficult. Interactive whiteboards require more time. To be more effective, write slowly and use large letters to make reading easier from a distance, and if you do find that you must speak while facing the whiteboard, speak loudly so that your voice "bounces" off the board and can be heard more easily throughout the room.

Audience Response Systems

As discussed in chapter 4, an audience response system (ARS) allows learners to use remote control input devices (clickers) to respond anonymously to displayed choice-based questions (see table 4.3 "Presentation Support Comparisons," in chapter 4, page 144). Regardless of the input device used to respond, your efforts will be more effective if you familiarize yourself with the technology. Practice displaying a question and using the remote device to choose an answer and then display the result. This process should work seamlessly so that you do not end up working through technical issues during your teaching time.

Audience response systems can take away from teaching time and may include some logistical or technical problems. If remote devices are to be distributed, assign each learner the responsibility of making sure the device is brought to class and that the remote has fresh batteries. In some ARS environments, a synchronizing of the student roster to the system is usually done in advance, where each learner must "register" the clicker so that later assessments will allow the instructor to match responses to the device assigned to the specific learner. Sometimes the registration process can become another task, as when a learner forgets to bring a clicker or for those times when the remote device stops working, thus preventing a learner from participating. From a class-size perspective, with larger groups, it may be difficult for you to distinguish whether the active participation is from understanding or from just pressing buttons.

Although the change of format from didactic lecture to more group participation is welcomed, there may be some other issues with an ARS. Some instructors report students bringing more than one remote to class to help another student appear interactive, especially when class participation or attendance is being monitored. In summary, we recommend an audience response system for its interactivity and the immediate feedback that it provides to the learners. We caution you against overuse and a reliance on the system for exams and quizzes.

Overall, you should become familiar with the equipment that is likely to be found in your environment. The most common technology that you will encounter in your lectures will be a computer and a projector. If you remember to use a remote control, stay out of the light source, and deliver the content with smooth transitions, the learning will be easier, the delivery less distracting, and the teaching more effective.

FOCUS

The main thing is that you keep the main thing the main thing.

—Albert Einstein

The effort required by learners to understand concepts is directly related to the effort needed from instructors to make the concepts understandable. This endeavor is a matter of *focus*, which we describe as an ability to generate recurring references to major points.[2] In any learning environment, the learner participates with the express purpose of reaching a goal or some *learning objective*. It is surely the desire of every instructor that every learner fully grasp the stated learning objectives. A professor's ability to stay focused on a set of limited learning objectives will help a learner grasp the material more easily.[6] Conversely, a teacher who continually drifts from the topic will produce confusion and disjointed connections to related concepts, thereby inhibiting learning.

Perhaps the greater challenges are in deciding how many learning objectives a particular topic may contain and how those goals are determined. There is no set limit to the number of learning objectives, but the choice will be affected by issues such as lecture time, subject complexity, and learner familiarity with the topic. In order for learners to grasp the material, without feeling overwhelmed, it is better to limit the number of objectives for a given topic. The learning objectives can be set *traditionally*, as part of a standard of teaching, where the goals are predetermined by the instructor, or the objectives may be derived using a *constructivist* approach, exemplified by problem-based learning (PBL), where goals are learner-determined in the context of the learning environment.[46-48]

Traditional Environments

In many educational institutions, the traditional approach is for an instructor to state the learning objectives of the entire program, the course of which is delivered in a series of topics over a specific length of time. Learners are typically given a course outline with the objectives clearly identified and arranged according to the instructional segments or sections. Many courses of study are instructionally designed around a standardized curriculum, with predetermined learning objectives created by instructors to accomplish educational outcomes or goals. Although each professor can design lectures and activities in his or her own manner, the overall effort must be focused on meeting the predetermined objectives.

For example, an engineering professor at a university may have a semester of sixteen weeks available to teach a course that meets three times each week, each session for one hour. The total of forty-eight clock hours will cover all of the learning objectives, with some objectives spanning multiple sessions and others attributed to perhaps a single lecture. Yet, to effectively teach the course and stay focused on the overall learning outcome, the instructor may have to incorporate multiple teaching methods to achieve different objectives, especially when some skills are easy to master and others more complex.[49]

Depending on the specific learning objective, one or more teaching methods could be used to create the optimal learning conditions necessary for achieving desired outcomes. Thus, if the objective in an accounting course is "to *define* current assets," then the teaching process might be to assign learners the task of memorizing the meaning of different accounting terms; or another technique could be to deliver an informative lecture that describes how the terms are used in financial reporting. These *passive* methods of task assignments or didactic lectures are used to achieve simple objectives. However, if the objective is "to *determine* the best inventory costing system given current financial conditions," then the teaching method could be to discuss and analyze different case studies to arrive at an efficient strategy. Irrespective of the course of study, *active* involvement of a discussion is necessary to accomplish a more complex objective. By choosing the appropriate teaching method, the instructor is able to focus more effectively on the specific learning objective.[49]

When the objectives are simple, such as defining, recalling, or describing concepts, more *passive* methods can be used. These include lecturing, showing a video, and assigning textbook reading. As the objectives become increasingly complex, such as analyzing, comparing, or strategizing, then more *active* methods are needed. These include research and writing activities, group discussions, and oral presentations. But don't look at learning objectives as having to be assigned one particular method or another; instead, consider combining methods where applicable to enhance the learning. Thus, if the objective is simple, you can still generate an interactive discussion. If the objective is complex, you can still deliver an informative lecture. The most important thing to keep in mind is that you should continually stay focused on the desired outcomes of the session, the topic, and the overall program.

If your approach to teaching is the traditional process of using preset or standardized learning objectives, then you will have a higher degree of control of the environment and, therefore, be more accountable for the learner's ability to replicate, communicate, and demonstrate learned concepts. As a result, if you significantly drift or digress from the topic your learners will struggle and outcomes may not be realized. One way to keep from digressing is to establish checkpoints or summary sections within the topic. This strategy is discussed in greater detail in "Content Organization" (see chapter 4, page 118).

Constructivist Settings

Traditionally, the instructor or a program creates the terms of learning (objectives, goals, and outcomes) and the learner is not vested in the development process. In fact, the learner may not accept wholeheartedly the objectives and may simply make the effort to show up to class, study, and pass the exam.[47] Some argue that in the traditional approach, although students are consuming knowledge, they may not be developing the expertise needed to apply such knowledge. In recent years, there has been much academic discussion on moving away from the frequently used teaching method of didactic lecturing and focusing more on highly interactive, small-group, problem-solving approaches to learning.

The *constructivist* philosophy supports a "learning by doing" process, where understanding stems from experience in a real-world environment, and where problems need to be solved while interacting with others who may offer alternative views and suggestions. Although traditional environments allow instructors greater control, in a constructivist setting, learners collaborate and take *ownership* of the educational experience by developing goals and objectives based on learner preferences. It follows that if learners are able to *actively participate* in the development of the learning objectives according to the goals that the learners prefer, and if those goals are consistent with those of the program, then both teachers and students would equally share the educational responsibility and achieve mutually desired outcomes.

In traditional environments, the main learning components of *theory*, *practice*, and *self-study* are generally separated into specific courses or activities to complete an overall program, whereas the constructive approach attempts to blend these three components, simultaneously, throughout a program.[48] From a teaching perspective, this combination is not easy to design, implement, manage, and assess.

As an instructor, you are faced with the odd notion of not doing any *teaching*; instead, you are *facilitating* learning by guiding students toward their own understanding of the concepts through a collage of active processes including discovery, practice, research, interaction, discussion, and problem solving. Although the *learning* objectives might be better described as *learner* objectives, the educational outcomes must still be realized.[46] In this respect, you need to use your professional expertise and experience to keep the learners from digressing from the topic, by pointing them in the right direction without leading them. It's as if you are a tour guide, but the group is walking in front of you, discovering the path on their own, yet, at the same time, knowing that you are right behind them, just in case they divert or drift too far.

Problem-Based Learning

One of the best academic models of facilitated instruction is *problem-based learning*, or **PBL**. Gaining popularity in the 1990s, and used mostly in medical education, PBL integrates theory and practice around problem-solving activities, with students actively collaborating in *small groups* to address real-world dilemmas. The course is designed around problems that require students to apply existing knowledge from multiple subjects and self-directed research, while developing, discussing, and testing different scenarios, outcomes, and facts to arrive at an acceptable solution. The process is exactly as would be the case in any real-world environment, but under controlled circumstances, because the learning is supervised, managed, and directed by a facilitating instructor who allows the students to "experience" and apply knowledge to a situation. In the absence of this instructor-led monitoring, learners would be left to their own devices, operate with limited organization skills, and likely function poorly as a cohesive team.[46] Yet teaching in this type of environment requires specific facilitation skills that are quite different from standard presentation skills used primarily in didactic lectures. Table 5.5

Table 5.5. Small-group facilitation strategies and tactics

Facilitating with Ease	
Strategy	Tactics
Advancement—the ability to keep the learning process moving forward toward a targeted conclusion where teacher guidance leads to learner consensus	• Set goals and objectives • Follow an agenda or outline • Clarify learning points • Summarize findings or results • Verbalize agreements
Flow—the effort to keep discussions focused and open to all participants and all ideas as instructor-led queries stimulate learner discoveries	• Listen to all ideas • Seek clarification of comments • Evaluate suggestions • Balance abstraction and specificity
Community—the task of handling the discussions, diversions, dominance, and other interactions related to group dynamics	• Monitor participation • Control the climate • Manage conflicts

outlines a number of facilitation skills that are useful in learner-centric small-group settings in order to maintain focus on the intended messages.

The merits of active learning associated with a constructivist philosophy, such as that used in problem-based learning, is a way of preparing students for the real world, although a number of challenges exist. Some of the obstacles include getting learners to buy into the process, keeping them motivated throughout, and developing facilitating expertise in the instructor community to develop a proficiency using a different method of teaching. The shift from the traditional approach of *presenting* information to a *guiding* of the learning process, with minimal interference, is not an easy adjustment for faculty, who need to be trained and supported in this endeavor.[46, 48]

Small-Group Discussions

When teaching takes place in discussion-oriented small-group environments, much of the talking is dialogue, not monologue, as is typical with lecturing. Interactivity occurs within the *entire* group, as learners ask and answer questions of not only the teacher, but also of one another with the intent of advancing the discussion. In order for interactivity to flourish without alienating learners, you need to monitor responses as you facilitate comments. You can be effective in managing group discussion by using specific positive or negative (yes-no) *lead-in* phrases to set or change the direction of interaction.[13, 42] Table 5.6 shows various combinations of commonly used lead-in responses that affect interactive discussion.

Lead-in responses can be used in a variety of ways. For example, if you hear a comment and decide to facilitate it by connecting what you heard to something previously mentioned, you might say "Yes, and that supports what we heard earlier." The lead-in of "*Yes, and* . . ." implies *commitment* by connecting the comment with that of another learner and possibly matching information taught earlier, as well. At times, your facilitation may be done

Table 5.6. Lead-in responses affecting interactive discussion

	Yes-No Matrix	
Lead-in Response	*Indication*	*Usage*
No, and . . .	Control	**State**—rules, policies, guidelines, principles
No, but . . .	Compromise	**Manage**—debates, discussions, alternatives
Yes, and . . .	Commitment	**Encourage**—agreements, support, collaboration
Yes, but . . .	Conflict	**Generate**—arguments, disagreements, distrust

with a slightly different phrase, where you might say, "No, and that is not in line with what the research suggests." The lead-in of *"No, and . . ."* implies *control* by stating evidence as to the validity or merit of the comment in relation to learning.

The most challenging lead-in phrase is one that begins with *"Yes, but . . ."* as this creates immediate *conflict*. You will find this lead-in used frequently, especially when ideas or suggestion are offered. For instance, suppose a student suggests a method for solving a problem and you say, "Yes, but that won't work." Your lead-in offers a positive "yes" immediately followed by a negative "but," creating a conflict of intention. How can you imply agreement along with disagreement at the same time? However, if you sincerely believe that the idea has *some* merit, then it is better to suggest a *compromise* or alternative by saying, "No, but in that regard here is what might work." The *"No, but . . ."* lead-in is effectively a negotiation of ideas that allows the discussion to move forward, whereas conflict keeps the discussion mired in argument until one side reluctantly gives in or concedes.

⤳ As the Teen Turns ⤳

The minute my son turned thirteen I looked at him and said, "Oh no! You're thirteen now. You are in *yes-but* mode!" He had this puzzled expression, unsure of what I meant.

I explained, saying, "That means for at least the next ten years, everything I say, every suggestion I make, every bit of advice I try to share, you will immediately respond with the words 'Yes, but . . .'—thereby completely negating all of my logic!"

He shook his head, rolled his eyes, and simply responded, "Yeah, but that's not true."

I rest my case!

⤳⤳

The words "yes, but" will always be conflicting, so try to avoid using this response and be sure to recognize when learners use such conflicting terms during dialogue in order to avoid petty arguments that stifle the discussion. As an instructor, you must effectively manage interactivity to support learning objectives in order to keep the group focused on the topic.

Handling Digression

Instructors sometimes use digression as a teaching technique to help learners see a bigger picture by discussing seemingly disparate concepts that are later shown to be related (see "An Expression of Digression" in chapter 4, page 136). In the absence of a planned strategy, you might find yourself drifting from the topic during a lecture or discussion, for a variety of reasons. You may be overexplaining a concept, telling an unrelated story, debating an irrelevant point, managing classroom distractions, dealing with off-topic questions, searching through teaching materials for trivial support data, or simply having your mind wander to other thoughts that are totally disconnected from the current content.

One way to overcome such diversions is to anchor major points or precepts to an overall or central *theme*, while making recurring references to the anchored elements. The theme is a running *thread* that connects every major point made during a lecture or discussion. Suppose the overall theme of a lecture is to have the learners understand *how the stock market works*. If you are about to tell a story about how you were once stuck in traffic on a visit to the New York Stock Exchange, then check the story against the theme ("how the stock market works"), you will quickly see that telling the story would only digress from the topic because the function of the stock market is unrelated to the building's geographical location or to the related traffic conditions in the area. In the same way, if a student asks a question about why Switzerland has not changed its currency to the Euro, you would realize the question is not directly related to the overall theme of how the stock market works. Unless you are able to link the answer to the overall theme, you may need to defer the answer to a later time, perhaps after class. While this may not satisfy the learner's immediate need for information, your effort to stay focused will ultimately benefit the entire group. This effort is not easy, especially because the nature of group interaction and discussion invariably leads to digression when individual expressions and opinions arise.

Attending to your overall theme can only be functional if there are recurring references to major points. Using the earlier example of "how the stock market works," if you establish the concepts of "demand," "trading," "trends," and "fluctuation," then these can become *memory anchors* that can be referenced multiple times throughout the lecture and discussion. Recurring references to key learning points help you to focus on the overall learning objective, reducing the chances of digressing or drifting from the topic.

Whether your teaching activity is in a traditional environment or in a constructivist setting, the ability to maintain a steady focus on the learning objectives is crucial to achieving educational outcomes. To actively engage learners, the elements of discussion, analysis, debate and other group dynamics must be managed in relation to an overall theme. It is through collective collaboration that learners and instructors maintain a healthy dialogue of concepts and ideas with less likelihood of digression from educational goals and a greater focus on group interaction.

INTERACTION

Teachers who cannot keep students involved and excited for several hours in
the classroom should not be there.

—John Roueche

We describe *interaction* as a characteristic of one who establishes a connection with learners through questions, comments, and other participation.[2]
From a performance perspective this is a *proactive* skill because the instructor
initiates the interaction (see also "Stimulating the Interaction" in chapter 3,
page 97). A professor should stimulate learners to respond by *inviting* interaction (proactive) and encourage students to participate by *looking* approachable (reactive).

The educational literature is filled with references to learner-centric activities, such as interaction, as contributing to teaching effectiveness.[5, 6, 50, 51] It
behooves instructors to seriously consider involving students in the educational process, rather than simply narrating content in lectures, seminars, or
presentations. From our own research, the feedback we received from a number of students and professionals indicates a consensus that favors involvement, where learners welcome the opportunity to express opinions, answer
questions, and participate actively in discussions.[2]

Invariably, in nearly every college classroom, the majority of the talking is
done by the teacher.[52] In fact, using a coding instrument to analyze teaching,
a *two-thirds rule* appears to be nested in teacher behavior; that is, two-thirds
of all classroom time is spent talking; two-thirds of that talking time is the
instructor speaking; and two-thirds of the instructor's speech is in the form
of lecture, directions, or other student-directed comments.[53] In other words,
teachers verbally dominate the classroom. This is not surprising considering
that content is prepared by the instructor and taught to the students, mostly
in the form of lecture.

One would expect the teacher to dominate the process, especially when
communicating in a very *direct* manner through lecturing. However, it has
been shown that *indirect* actions can initiate responses, such as when a professor asks questions, reiterates something a student has mentioned, or builds
on student ideas.[54] Teacher-student interaction has been shown to motivate
learners to explore a topic more thoroughly.[55] In fact, learners may be
inspired to initiate additional interaction, such as expanding on a discussion
point, or offering additional comments, thereby enriching the classroom
experience, such as in constructivist settings like problem-based learning
(PBL) and small-group discussion-based seminars. The "two-thirds rule" of

teacher verbal dominance does not apply in these highly interactive situations because the instructor is a facilitator.

When students feel free to raise their hands, ask questions, make comments, and interact when ready, learning outcomes are more positive. This involvement should never be discouraged. Regardless of the venue, from a small seminar to a large lecture hall, if learners are asking questions it means that they are listening and thinking. A professor should embrace interaction as a learning tool and not treat it as a disruption. Think about it; if you are never interrupted, then perhaps no one is listening. Interaction is a clear measure of engagement, especially because reactions from learners are visibly expressed.[7-9]

The literature identifies interaction as a two-part process: getting participation and then handling the response or contribution of the participant.[53] The offer made by an instructor to learners to actively participate is based on the both verbal and visual evidence. What you say and how you say it are related. Initial interaction is usually done by *invitation*. The "invitation" is usually in the form of a question, typically tied to the immediate topic. The learner, by accepting the invite, typically provides a response. Provided that the question is *open-ended* and does not lead to judgment if incorrect, this give and take—invitation and acceptance—is how teachers involve students in the learning process. But, beyond the question-and-answer format, interaction can include various types of invitations, such as comments, directions, suggestions, and other forms of participation that actively involve the learners.

For the most part, the interaction is prompted by the instructor, although students can extend invites, as well, by asking questions or making off-hand comments, especially as they become more at ease with the instructor and the rest of the class. However, learners need to be *invited* to participate based on the teacher's ability to visibly offer or verbally indicate the opportunity for interaction.

Asking Questions and Managing Responses

The effective use of questions helps learners understand the material in a more collaborative manner. As a result, you will find that class participation rises, and students soon feel empowered not only to respond, but also to stimulate additional interaction by posing questions, comments, thoughts, and ideas. This type of active involvement creates a rich experience for your learners. Just be sure to limit yourself to *one* question at a time. Some instructors ask a series of related questions before a learner has a chance to respond to even one. This is done sometimes in order to clarify or further simplify the question. It is difficult for a listener to manage multiple moments of inquiry.

For example, a biology professor asks a student, "How many cells does this organism contain? Do you think the cells are healthy? What would happen if one of the cells contained a virus?" It will be challenging for the student to easily respond to the three separate questions contained in the professor's inquiry. As a rule, let the question mark be the barrier to your potential barrage. In other words, stop speaking immediately after the first question of a potential series. This strategy will force you to ask more pointed questions while allowing learners to respond more accurately, without the added effort of trying to manage multiple queries. As an instructor, you need to control the interaction by understanding various techniques regarding different kinds of questions and expected responses.

Using Open-Ended Questions

You can stimulate interaction through the types of questions you ask. The more closed your question, the more limited the response. Evidence suggests that *narrow* questions allow for one correct answer while *open* questions have many answers and usually invite opinion or commentary.[53] You can make your questions *proactive* (open-ended) instead of *indicative* (leading) or *reactive* (closed).

For example, a professor asks a student "What do you think?" This *open-ended* question allows the student to respond in a narrative manner, providing mostly an opinion. But compare that with the professor adding more information to the question, "I believe the choice is risky, but what do you think?" This is a leading or *indicative* question because it suggests the instructor's preference, and may make the student change the response to agree with that preference. Finally, contrast those two kinds of questions with the professor asking, "I believe the choice is risky. Do you agree?" This type of question is *reactive* or closed, allowing only a yes or no response. In addition, the question is indicative of the teacher's preference and will likely lead the student to answer "yes" to agree with the knowledgeable authority. To stimulate interaction, elicit ideas, and engage learners in discussion, instructors should ask open-ended questions and then manage the responses to fit with key learning objectives.

Intentionally Asking Simple Questions

Accepted by learners as a knowledgeable authority, an instructor can quite easily complicate the learning process by asking difficult questions. This is not to suggest that a professor avoid challenging students with thought-provoking problems, but where interaction is desired, success breeds confidence in students and encourages greater involvement.

Students should be given the chance to get some questions correct, thereby increasing their willingness to interact. A more confident learner feels his or her comments and questions will be looked upon more favorably by the instructor and by fellow classmates.[52] Many professors opt to create a positive climate for interaction by making the *first question* asked of students a truly *opinion-based* question. Such an open-ended question cannot be answered incorrectly. By allowing the student to give an opinion, the response is less difficult to express. Such questions usually begin with "how do you feel about . . ." or "what do you think . . ." to allow the learner to give a true opinion.

Throughout a lecture, instructors also make use of closed (reactive) questions to periodically test or gauge the level of understanding of the learners. These short-answer questions should be simple enough to understand, while allowing students to share in the responsibility of learning, especially because there is only one correct answer to each question. If the instructor has built a level of trust, then students will respond to closed questions, even if the possibility exists of giving a wrong answer, as long as the student is not made to feel ashamed of failure. To diminish a learner's fear of being wrong in front of others, audience response systems allow anonymous responses to closed questions (true-false, multiple choice, etc.) which still creates an interactive environment in which the instructor can use the feedback. For optimal effectiveness, tie all questions and interactions to key learning objectives.

Polling and Discussion Questions

To boost confidence in students so that they participate more freely without fear of criticism or disapproval, you should initially seek *volunteers* rather than make arbitrary selections. One way to identify volunteers is through a *polling* question. This usually begins with the phrase, "How many of you . . ." or, more simply, by beginning the question with the word "who." The result of the polling will be the visibly raised hands of those who feel confident in responding.

The *discussion* question is the follow-on to the polling question, directed at the student that you selected from among those who voluntarily responded to the polling question. The discussion question should be open-ended, preferably based on opinion, allowing the student to express the answer in a manner that is most comfortable for the student, based on the depth of their knowledge of the topic.

Using a polling question can also help you identify those most interested in interaction. If the first question of your lecture, seminar, or presentation is a very *general* polling question, where nearly everyone could respond, take a mental note of who raises a hand *first* in the group. This learner is the one with the most energy, the one most willing to participate, and the one who can serve as your volunteer at a later point should you decide to arbitrarily select someone for interaction without polling.

As a rule, we suggest that whenever you use a polling question, have an immediate discussion question ready for a selected volunteer. It is important for students to feel that any response to your initiated offer is an opportunity to contribute to the learning. If students raise their hands, it is your responsibility to follow through with the interaction by selecting someone and offering that person a chance to speak. For example, if you ask, "Who watched the president speak last night?" and, after a show of hands, you continue with the lecture, those students that raised their hands will wonder if they contributed any value by responding. It is not enough to simply *use* interaction; rather, you must *make use* of the interaction in a way that advances learning.

Foreshadowing

As a lecture unfolds, instructors should keep track of all interactions, as some early comments may apply at later points during the session. The literature describes this activity as the ability to "inventory ideas."[53] This allows an instructor to make better use of learner contributions after responses have been given. But what if your learners have not contributed any ideas to your inventory? You can purposely induce useable comments using a technique called *foreshadowing*. The process is simple. You invite interaction by posing a question that allows for a number of different responses, some of which you know will apply to later learning points in the discussion. When one of those points is brought out, you refer back to the earlier contributed response, as if it were the catalyst for the current part of the discussion.

For example, a speech communications professor is lecturing on the skills of public speaking. He polls the students to see who has seen distractions or bad habits in a speaker. From those responding, the professor selects several students, each of whom mentions different distractions including: clicking a pen, playing with coins in a pocket, rocking back and forth, reading the slides, saying the word "um" too often, and so forth. The professor mentally creates an "inventory" of the ideas offered by the learners. He also knows the exact part of the lecture where each response connects, but he waits to use the comments in context with a learning point. So, perhaps fifteen minutes later, he sees an opportunity to connect one of the ideas in the inventory and says, "When it comes to movement, the body can cause problems. As Judy mentioned earlier, rocking back and forth is very distracting."

The foreshadowing technique associated with the open-ended question allowed for multiple responses to be cataloged and used later. The professor incorporates a response (contribution) at the appropriate point (context) to support the topic, while giving credit to the student (recognition) for having added value to the learning (shared responsibility). Foreshadowing is a very high-level skill that allows you to preplan interaction so that student participation is perceived to be driving the learning through active involvement.

Repeating and Paraphrasing

Envision, if you will, a large lecture hall with 350 students seated in the cascading rows of a university amphitheatre. A student in the second row raises her hand to pose a question. The professor reaches out toward the student, extending the invitation to participate, and the student proceeds to ask the question. The professor responds by saying, "Yes, exactly! In fact, *that* will be on the exam!" Any student who is not within earshot of the question will be wondering, *"What? What will be on the test? What did she ask?"* This is not an uncommon occurrence in the college classroom, especially when groups are larger in number.

Unless you are absolutely sure that everyone in the room has heard the question or comment, you should repeat the response so that all the learners can place your subsequent reply in the context of the dialogue that initiated it. In order for everyone to benefit from a comment or question, you can choose to repeat it or paraphrase it, depending on the length or complexity of the statement.

An economics professor is giving a seminar to large group of students in a lecture hall. He is focusing on the fluctuations of the U.S. dollar in the current economy. One of the students asks the professor, "Why does the dollar fluctuate?" The professor can simply reiterate or repeat the question by saying, "The question is, 'Why does the dollar fluctuate?'" and then he can continue to give the answer. The entire group hears the question exactly as it was asked, followed by hearing the professor's answer. In a variation of the same reiteration, the professor might have included the student's question as part of a statement, saying more concisely, "The reason the dollar fluctuates is . . ." and continuing with the answer. In either case, the original question is restated, because it was short enough and simple enough to repeat.

Paraphrasing may be required if the question is long or complex. Using the same scenario, suppose the student asks the question differently, saying to the economics professor, "I was watching a press conference on the news last night and the secretary of the Treasury kept saying that our dollar is not as strong as it used to be and that it can be worth more one day and less the next day, depending on different things, so I am a little confused about what causes this. Can you explain it?" Such a lengthy question will be difficult to repeat word for word, so the professor can choose to paraphrase the question by saying, "The question relates to comments made by the secretary of the Treasury as to how the dollar fluctuates. This fits perfectly with our discussion. I agree that the fluctuating dollar is a concept that can be somewhat confusing, so let me explain." Notice that the teacher has an opportunity to rephrase the original question in a way that fits into the current topic, which is focused on the fluctuation of the dollar, even though the student did not actually utter the exact phrase "fluctuation of the dollar" in the question.

Paraphrasing slightly alters the original comment or question and restates it using the *preferred* context of the instructor. Interestingly, in this example, the professor purposely skipped the point about the strength of the dollar but could save that part of the question for later use if needed. Students participate more if their ideas or opinions are deemed to be useful and the literature appears to support the efforts of a teacher who can *inventory* student comments for further development.[53] Moreover, because the instructor is seen as an authority, the act of repeating or paraphrasing a student-initiated question, comment, or opinion gives *recognition* to that student and tends to validate the contribution, encouraging others to consider adding similar value to the learning to receive the same recognition. The recognition is for the value of the interaction and not necessarily for the comment itself.

Giving Dignity

Interaction can be challenging for both a teacher and a student. As you elicit responses, you will, at times, receive an *incorrect* answer to a closed (narrow) question. Managing this moment is critical, and we suggest you consider the concept of giving dignity for a wrong answer.

Let's use a simple example from early education. A grade school teacher asks a young student, "What is 7 times 5?" If the student replies "30," not only might there be some giggling from other students, but the teacher may also compound the problem by saying "No" or "Wrong" and move on to someone else. There is no dignity left for the student who failed to answer correctly. This child may even grow up detesting math. But, a true "expert" finds the right *question* to a wrong *answer*, and uses the question as a response to the answer.

In this example of "What is 7 times 5?" the seemingly wrong reply of "30" is really a *correct* answer—but, to a *different* question (as in "What is 6 times 5?"). The teacher offers the different question as a response, saying,

"Actually, 30 is 6 times 5." The student may feel that something about the wrong answer was still correct. There is more dignity in this approach.

To bring this into higher education, learners have a fear of criticism from teachers, as well as a fear of disapproval from peers (classmates) in the event that a contribution is looked upon unfavorably. In a lecture, seminar, or presentation, you may find that a learner who responds incorrectly to your question will feel awkward or embarrassed at being wrong.

You can alleviate the uncomfortable feeling by finding the logic behind the incorrect response, and then using that logic in a positive manner. As you hear the inaccuracy, ask yourself, "What question leads to *that* answer?" If you discover it, and then offer the question as the response, you will reduce the feeling of failure by giving dignity for a wrong answer while adding value to the learning environment by offering additional information.

Using Automated Responses

To mitigate the fear of disapproval for an incorrect answer, some large lecture halls are equipped with an audience response system (ARS), which allows all students to respond to closed questions, especially multiple choice. Using interactive handheld devices, referred to by some as "clickers," learners make selections, choices are tabulated, and charts are displayed (projected) for all to see. Students can become more engaged and involved in the learning, as they participate as a group and run relatively no risk of failure for an incorrect response.[56]

In the absence of a built-in response system, if Internet access is available from your classroom location, you can conduct similar group interaction automatically. Several websites currently offer instant "polling" via cell phones, where participants can text-message choices and the results are automatically updated and simultaneously displayed within the current slide presentation while the "votes" are being cast. As an instructor, you can use anonymous interactive technology to check the learning level of the class, especially if two or three simple questions are posed near the end of a lesson to see how much the class retained. However, these questions have to be planned ahead of time.

⤳ Three Little "Es" ⤳

Have you ever been asked a question and you did not know the answer? Whether this happens to you in a lecture or discussion, the feeling of not being able to respond immediately can be frustrating, especially because learners accept you as an authority of knowledge.

It is not uncommon for teachers to "not know" something, regardless of the level of expertise. If you don't know the answer, you can simply admit to it and offer to investigate the issue at a later point. However, many instructors prefer to use the "I'll look into that later" option as a last resort.

Initially, if stumped, you could choose to investigate the issue by soliciting *more information* from the learner in order to stimulate your memory. To do this, simply reply to the question with *another question*, using one of the three "E" words: *explain, elaborate, example.* You might say: "Would you *explain* that?" or "Can you *elaborate*?" or "Could you give me an *example*?"

Any of these phrases will expand the dialogue as the student provides more information to *clarify* the original question. The additional clues will narrow the range of possible answers. As the student provides more details, the chances of enlightenment rise, and one of those clues might trigger your memory enough for you to address the question sufficiently.

It is quite possible that the "E" word strategy may *not* jog your memory, even after the learner clarifies the question with more details. However, from a student perspective, the brief interactive dialogue will give the appearance that you genuinely sought to answer the question by seeking additional information.

—◇◇◇—

Inviting Interaction

The words you use to initiate responses go hand-in-hand with how you look when the invitation is worded. Of course, interaction is not as easy as it appears, especially because "how it appears" makes all the difference. There are several challenges to initiating and sustaining interaction, mostly centered on action and appearance. As mentioned in the *Body Language Style* section of this chapter, the action of the body provides visual support for the intention of the invitation.[17] The learners need to know who is included in the invitation before any acceptance can take place.

If you do not "demonstrate" your intention to have students interact, if you do not provide a visible appearance of an invitation to participate, then you may find limited acceptance, because your students will not be sure if your invitation is meant for everyone or just a few or perhaps just one person. In essence, the actions of your body clarify the intentions in your mind.

The nonverbal communication surrounding the invitation to interact involves an *including* gesture, where the hands are used to create a connection with the learners. The *reaching-out* gesture is when the palm of your hand faces up as your arm extends out to the audience. The palm of the hand represents sincerity (honesty, openness) in the body, nonverbally signaling an invitation that appears friendly, approachable, receptive, and warm.[1, 7, 8, 13]

In many cultures, a more formal reaching-out action is done with a handshake, where an extended arm and open hand (exposed palm) offer a greeting, a parting, or signify an agreement. In a lecture, you can "shake hands" with the entire group by using a reaching-out gesture, as a way of greeting learners, parting from them, or bringing them into agreement. The body language of reaching out, extending the arms and opening the hands, serves as a visual cue for the learners that you appear receptive to participation, welcoming the interaction. This gesture should be done without any movement of the fingers that might be seen as a rush to get answers.

Let's examine a real-world scenario. A fine arts professor has his *hands in his pockets* as he lectures. He looks out at the students and asks "Who can name the type of column design used by the Romans?" Nearly every student immediately looks down, to avoid being chosen. The professor unknowingly *disinvited* the students from participation with his body language. He gave them a signal to *not* interact. One student later said, "I realize that eye contact with this professor is the only way to get selected, so I chose to look down." Apparently, so did all the other students. When we interviewed teachers as to why they refrain from interaction, the common responses included: "I stand there, waiting for some answers, and no one gives any!" Or "Interaction takes too much of my time."

So, let's reflect back. We have all experienced the unpleasant "called-on" moment in school where the teacher simply selected the participant. In fact, we held back, hoping not to be "picked on." As soon as we saw the teacher establish eye contact with another student, we felt relieved! Definitive eye contact at a moment of inviting or seeking interaction is perceived to be very intimidating, as we have all experienced it. Our fine arts professor with his hands in his pockets scans the room and stops. At that exact moment, the student in his line of sight feels "picked on." This common "dis-invitation" with poor body language, even with good questioning, is the reason why your students don't interact in class. Further, to address the issue of "insufficient time" for interaction, the answer is very simple: always link interaction to the learning objectives and it becomes an integral part of the process.

To correctly invite everyone, extend your arms to the *width* of the group, your left hand gesturing to the person to your far left, and your right hand gesturing to the person to your far right. The width or "spread" of the gestures is only as wide as to include the people sitting to opposite sides. You need only extend your arms out *slightly*, in a relaxed manner, reaching out so that everyone understands that your question is directed to the *entire group* and not just to one section or one person.

Similar to an "embrace," the width of your gestures shows how many are embraced by the action. This language of your body nonverbally invites any-one within the connected span of your gestures to participate. It's as if you drew an imaginary "arc" from the tips of your fingers on each hand, encom-passing the group in a circle, so that anyone sitting within this arc is invited to interact. Don't drop your hands too quickly or the effect will be lost. If you only use one hand, then only those people to whom you gesture toward will feel included, and the rest of the group will wait. Moreover, if you make *no* gesture at all, the group will assume that the last person that you looked at *must* respond, because only your eyes made the selection, similar to the earlier example of the fine arts professor. This doesn't mean that by simply extending your arms to the group that you automatically will have every hand in the air ready to accept every invitation to interact. But the action will sig-nify to the class that you are purposely including everyone in the room and not just one individual.

≈≈ It's Always about *YOU* ≈≈

The *reaching-out* gesture is used not only during interaction, but throughout a lecture, seminar, presentation, or discussion, especially when connected to the word *you*. For example, a professor asks, "How would *you* handle this situation?" The word "you" in that sentence is contingent upon the nature of the reaching-out gesture. There is a big difference if an open palm gesture is directed at one individual (meaning only one person is expect to offer a response) or if both hands open to the entire group (meaning everyone is invited).

From a consistency perspective, try to match verbal and nonverbal cues by reaching out to the group on the all-inclusive *you*. While this does not have to happen every time the word *you* is uttered, the vocal reference combined with the body language enhances or emphasizes the connection. This seem-ingly simple action is highly effective in stimulating interaction by making you appear more friendly and approachable.

≈≈≈

The reaching-out gesture of extending the arms to embrace the group clearly invites the entire group to participate. However, you must *hold* your gestures, sustaining the action throughout the length of your invitation, *until you receive response*. If the question is to the group, then acceptance occurs when you choose from those who volunteered to respond (likely by raising a hand). If you were interacting with only one person, then you would keep your arm extended throughout your question until the other person begins to speak or react, which is the moment of acceptance. Although this "holding" of the gesture may feel unnatural, it will only be a matter of seconds before reaction occurs. Gestures take time to be processed by the viewer.

Many professors take too long to get to the point of the invitation. As a result, the tendency is to make a quick gesture to the group, then release it, and continue with a long-winded series of statements, before inviting participation. For example, a managerial psychology instructor already understands the value of extending her arms to the group to appear inclusive when inviting interaction. Unfortunately, she only shows the reaching-out gesture momentarily as she asks, "How many of you—and perhaps you may have to think about this for a moment, and you'll probably be discussing it after class, as well—how many of you would allow a person to continue working as a bank teller—and let's say that individual has been working over five years—would you let the person continue, knowing that two coworkers suspected that person of stealing?"

The challenge for this teacher is in the length of time it takes her to extend the invitation. She may have initially extended her arms to the group, but after the first few words she likely tired of the gesture, dropped her arms to her sides and began adding more and more details until finally arriving at the actual question. If you find yourself asking lengthy questions, mostly filled with extraneous details (see "Parenthetical Intrusions" in this chapter, page 219), then you need to either limit the excess banter or mention all of the finer details *before* creating the interaction. In other words, try to *time* the inviting action (body language) as closely as possible to the invitation (spoken language) so that the gesture stays visible and is held long enough for the acceptance to take place.

Using the same example, the professor could have said "You may have to put on your thinking caps for this one, and you'll probably talk about this after class, as well. A bank teller, who has been working for five years is suspected of stealing by two coworkers." She then uses the *reaching-out* gesture here to invite interaction and continues, "How many of you would allow the suspected person to keep working?" By placing the physical action of *reaching out* nearer to the question, the gesture can be suspended or held open throughout the entire invitation.

You will likely find that it is quite uncomfortable to keep your arms extended for a long period of time. Therefore, holding a gesture open will ensure that your question remains short and to the point. Lackadaisical, "as-if-I-care" actions, such as flinging your arm quickly or pointing your finger at someone, have negative or punitive connotations and should be avoided.[13] The context behind "extending an invitation" means exactly that—a visibly pleasant action that prompts acceptance. Upon that acceptance, it is the responsibility of the instructor to direct the interactive process in a manner that supports the learning activity.

Overall, the most important issues related to interaction are in the discourse and the delivery. The words you use to invite conversation, the way you handle responses, and the complimentary physical actions you use to support the interaction all serve to involve learners in the education process as active participants. Interaction, when done effectively, has a direct link to a professor's likability. As an instructor, your skill in fostering an interactive learning environment will lead to greater effectiveness in teaching.

PERFORMANCE — SUMMARY AND STRATEGY

Tell me and I forget.
Show me and I remember.
Involve me and I understand.

—Chinese proverb

Table 5.7. Highlights of the performance skills

Performance Skill	Key Points
Body Language Style uses physical movements and gestures to support the presentation	• Positioning the body to the same side as the reading anchor in the language is effective • The angling of the shoulders is used to create impact and emphasis • The *Presenter's Triangle* is a defined area that allows depth of movement while respecting lines of sight to content • Gestures help clarify concepts by constructing visual relationships with content • When hands stay apart and remain visible, the degree of *openness* is greater, reflecting higher self-confidence • The *reaching-out* gesture (opening the hand) creates an invitation for learners to respond or react • When shifting the stance to one foot or the other, the relaxed posture implies confidence • Frequent eye contact, *direct* or *anchored*, allows for emotional connections with learners
Speaking Style can be easily heard and understood while using proper inflection and tone when speaking	• Proper breathing, verbal timing, and vocal inflection affect listening and comprehension • The male voice features lower pitch and higher volume, but lacks variance in tone, which can sound monotone during longer phrases • The female voice features higher pitch, melodic resonance, but the softness in tone variation requires more control of breathing for volume (loudness) • Narration of content, such as reading the slides, causes a flat tone of voice • Voice projection is enhanced through breathing exercises or microphones to equalize spoken content in a large room • Wireless lavaliere microphones are the least restrictive, but most sensitive to distracting sounds (such as scratching from clothing, or high-pitched feedback) • Lead-in phrases indicate changes in thought, topic, or content sections

Table 5.7.   (Continued)

Performance Skill	*Key Points*
Speaking Style can be easily heard and understood while using proper inflection and tone when speaking (continued)	• Hyperfluency is using overly high-academic or technical language that reduces comprehension and causes learner apprehension • *Juxtaposition* is a unique vocal emphasis placed on a particular word in an unexpected way • Using triads (*rule of three*) helps learners separate items into manageable segments • *Fillers* (um, uh, er) are a type of verbal hesitancy that can be interpreted as unfamiliarity or lack of knowledge • Speed of speech (*rapidity*) is content-dependent, faster during general conversation and slower during detailed instruction • *Parenthetical intrusions* are extraneous comments or diversions within a spoken phrase, which distract learners
Technology demonstrates familiarity with all equipment and other technical elements, such as multimedia	• Learners easily perceive an instructor's lack of comfort or familiarity with technology • Teachers fear looking incompetent, unprepared, or technologically challenged • Software proficiency is required to create, update, or redesign presentations to incorporate advanced multimedia elements (animation, sound, video, etc.) • Walking into the light source (such as standing in front of the screen) is a distraction that suggests unfamiliarity with equipment • A laser pointer is often overused, whereas predesigned, on-screen annotations (circles, arrows, etc.) are visually more effective in directing attention to content • A remote control seamlessly advances visual content from a fixed distance • In distance learning, the remote learners must stay actively involved • Web-conferencing and podcasts call for uncluttered visual design and very clear speech • Interactive whiteboards require legibility and limited speaking while writing • Using an audience response system (ARS) increases interactivity, offers immediate feedback on learned material, but can be difficult to manage with larger groups

Table 5.7. (Continued)

Performance Skill	Key Points
Focus generates recurring references to major points	• Learning objectives are critical in defining course expectations and requirements • Traditional approach pre-sets the objectives, constructivist approach allows learners to set the objectives • Passive teaching methods, such as assignments or lectures are used for simple objectives; active involvement, such as discussion, is useful for complex objectives • In constructivist settings, such as problem-based learning, the teacher is a facilitator • Lead-in phrases can support ideas or create conflict in facilitated dialogue • Anchoring major points to a central theme while using *recurring references* prevents digression from the topic
Interaction establishes a connection with learners through questions, comments and other participation	• *Open-ended* questions allow for elaboration and may stimulate further discussion • A series of multiple questions phrased as a single inquiry will confuse learners • Intentionally asking simple questions increases interaction and reduces apprehension • *Polling* questions elicit volunteers who can then be asked follow-up *discussion* questions • *Foreshadowing* is preplanned interaction that generates ideas that will be applied at later points to connect concepts to contributed learner responses • Repeating or *paraphrasing* learner comments gives recognition and validates participation • Giving dignity is finding the right question to a wrong answer • Interaction must be invited using a *reaching-out* gesture to express the request. • Gestures that lead to interaction should be held or sustained until a response begins

ASSESSMENTS

Test fast, fail fast, adjust fast.

—Tom Peters

6

Skills Assessment Tools

> Teaching is the only major occupation of man for which we have not yet
> developed tools that make an average person capable of competence and per-
> formance. In teaching we rely on the "naturals," the ones who somehow
> know how to teach.
>
> —Peter F. Drucker

While high-level skills are a natural talent for some, continuous self-
evaluation and self-reflection will allow those not so endowed to develop proficiency and look like a "natural." The assessment process is simple. Following the completion of a course or program, learner preferences on evaluation
forms are typically measured in general categories, ranging from content to
delivery, with the collected ratings tabulated and statistics generated. Whenever assessments are done by a group, such as with student evaluations, the
aggregated total of all individual ratings should be combined to provide a
measure of an instructor's "performance." Although student evaluations of
teachers are considered reliable and helpful, many instructors interpret the
results pessimistically, as if the glass is half-empty, judging anything less
than stellar ratings as evidence of learner dissatisfaction and therefore, poor
performance.[1] It appears that these "group feedback" instruments *generally*
rate performance, but do not readily suggest methods for improvement, other
than what can be construed from specific comments made by individual
learners. This is why our self-assessment targets *specific* skills, based on
learner preferences, so that you can focus directly on particular areas for self-
improvement.

Applying Science in Design

The work toward creating these assessment tools began with evaluating classroom teaching effectiveness using medical and dental students and professionals, and was later expanded to include other diverse professions.

Although our initial study of learner preferences led to the emergence of the twenty-one skills covered in the prior three chapters, our expanded findings allowed us to fine-tune each of the skills using hundreds of additional learner responses from which to filter. After years of surveys, comments, collected data, interviews, and observations, we developed a series of assessment tools to measure the effectiveness of a teacher.

Based on our findings, and supported by a vast body of research, our assessment tools were created according to guidelines for an effective "Scholarship Model."[2-4] We expanded the scope of these assessment tools for use in different presentation situations, including lectures, webinars, and speech-only situations. Further, we enhanced the scholarship by making the assessment tools public, expecting peer review and critique, while offering an opportunity for other scholars to use and develop these instruments.[5, 6] To broaden that access, the assessments were repurposed into *electronic interactive* formats to analyze input and provide instantaneous feedback with weighted numerical scores, along with highlighted areas for improvement.[7] The assessment tools are limited in scope and not designed to be a summation of a teacher's total efforts. However, these forms can be augmented with other student evaluations to get a more complete assessment of a teacher.

Forms of Measurement

The Skills Assessment form refines our original and expanded filtered list of positive and negative keywords about "teaching effectiveness" into easy-to-understand descriptive statements called *challenges* and *opportunities*. The checkbox-style evaluation form lists a total of forty challenges and forty opportunities spread across the twenty-one skill areas. Each of the eighty independent elements is *weighted* differently, based on the learner preferences noted in our research findings.

Three *versions* of our skills assessment have been developed to address specific learning conditions relevant to the teaching situation. The *Standard Evaluation* measures all eighty independent elements listed on the form. This is the most commonly used assessment for those who can be seen while presenting and who have supporting slides to enhance the content. Your classroom lecture would be typical of this scenario.

To allow evaluation in other learning contexts, we designed *subsets* of the Standard Evaluation. For example, in a voice-over setting, such as a webinar, conducted without a web camera, where the learners cannot see the teacher, the *Webinar Evaluation* is appropriate. Of the eighty independent elements from the Standard Evaluation, a number of selections are masked (grayed-out), including all of the body language style elements, since these items cannot be observed by the learners. Table 6.1 identifies the purpose and use of

Table 6.1. Assessment form choices based on the learning conditions

Choosing the Correct Assessment Form	
Learning Conditions	*Recommended Evaluation*
Lectures, presentations, or seminars, where you can be seen and you also have accompanying "slides"	STANDARD
Lectures or speeches, where you can be seen but you do not have accompanying "slides" (such as in keynote addresses and broadcasts)	SPEECH-ONLY
Lectures where you cannot be seen, only heard, and you have accompanying "slides" (such as in webinars, iTunes, podcasts, and other voice-over sessions or procedures)	WEBINAR

each of the three different assessment formats, Standard, Speech-Only, and Webinar, and when to choose the appropriate evaluation form, based on the relevant learning conditions.[7]

Assess Yourself

The easiest way to get a profile of your skills is to do a self-assessment. Figures 6.1a, 6.1b, and 6.1c show the three-part Standard Evaluation, covering the challenges and opportunities associated with the twenty-one skill categories.

The three-page assessment is easy to use. In addition to entering your *name*, an optional four-digit *Speaker ID number* allows for anonymous identification when sharing results among a group of teachers. The *date* helps keep track of the original observation, which is useful if the evaluation is initially completed on paper (as it appears in this book) and then later entered into the electronic format, freely available online,[7] to perform the numerical analysis.

Each assessment is divided into three areas: *Personality* (Fig. 6.1a), *Process* (Fig. 6.1b), and *Performance* (Fig 6.1c). Checkboxes are used to select elements within each of the skill categories. Inadequacies are described as *challenges*. Strengths are described as *opportunities*.

Frequently observed elements, even if conflicting, should be marked. It is quite possible for you to have challenges and opportunities within the same skill category or in different skill categories. For example, in the skill of *Happiness*, you might check the box "Smiles"; but in the *Energy* skill, you might

NAME		STANDARD EVALUATION

Speaker ID # [ ][ ][ ][ ]   Date [   ]

STANDARD EVALUATION

Evaluation of a presenter who can be seen, and who has accompanying "slides" (such as in a PowerPoint lecture or seminar).

PERSONALITY		
General Description	**Challenge**	**Opportunity**
1. Caring Is viewed by the audience as genuine and sincere	☐ Is sarcastic; has an "attitude" ☐ Finds fault ☐ Makes negative comments	☐ Is encouraging ☐ Gives positive reinforcement
2. Empathy Sees and understands from the perspective of the audience	☐ Does not share any personal experiences	☐ Recalls experiences that match audience's current feelings
3. Happiness Evidently enjoys giving the presentation	☐ Shows anger or disappointment	☐ Smiles ☐ Incorporates humor
4. Energy Demonstrates a liveliness in sharing knowledge	☐ Looks "too" serious ☐ Looks tired	☐ Keeps audiences engaged, awake and attentive
5. Passion Believes in what he/she is presenting	☐ Apologizes for the presentation or topic	☐ Enjoys the topic
6. Motivation Instills a sense of enthusiasm	☐ Creates boredom	☐ Generates a positive reaction
7. Expertise Logically explains or simplifies the materials	☐ Does not try to simplify complex topics (is "too" knowledgeable)	☐ The presentation can be followed by a non-expert ☐ Knows the audience
8. Inspiration Audience feels encouraged to incorporate learned concepts	---	☐ The audience responds with good comments and positive feedback
9. Self-Confidence Appears prepared and in control of presentation or discussion, regardless of the audience size, level of expertise, or rank	☐ Visibly expresses nervousness ☐ Intimidated by the audience	☐ Comfortable with the act of presenting
10. Approachable Appears friendly and receptive to comments and interaction	☐ Interrupts audience interaction	☐ Encourages audience participation and comments ☐ Audience feels they can ask any question
11. Personal Appearance Looks and behaves professionally	☐ Appearance is distracting ☐ Uses inappropriate language or humor	☐ Dresses appropriately

Figure 6.1a.   Page 1 of the print version of Standard Evaluation, covering the Personality skills

Speaker ID # [ ][ ][ ][ ]   Date: [   ]

PROCESS		
General Description	**Challenge**	**Opportunity**
12. Content Organization Applies concepts using real-world situations to simplify content	☐ Makes abstract references ☐ Content and related visual elements are disorganized	☐ Breaks up the topic into a few subsets or sections ☐ Incorporates concrete examples
13. Content Development Develops a concise and clear message	☐ Tries to cover too much material in the given time	☐ Uses stories or analogies to enhance content
14. Content Design Creates support visuals that enhance the message without detracting from the delivery	☐ Has cluttered or busy slides ☐ Uses moving or animated text lines ☐ Does excessive animation of objects ☐ Has bullets that are full sentences or that wrap to multiple lines	☐ Has content that is readable from a distance ☐ Uses dark backgrounds, with lighter text and images ☐ Supports main points with an appropriate visual ☐ Creates proper contrast among visual elements
15. Additional Sense Stimulation Appeals to multiple senses at the same time (using multimedia, interactive activities, etc.)	☐ Has inaudible or unclear sound ☐ Projects a poor visual display that is difficult to see	☐ Uses additional or enhanced sense stimulation
16. Environment Creates favorable conditions for presenting content	----	☐ Organizes the room for optimal viewing and comfort

Figure 6.1b.   Page 2 of the print version of Standard Evaluation, covering the Process skills

Speaker ID #				Date:		STANDARD EVALUATION

PERFORMANCE		
General Description	**Challenge**	**Opportunity**
17. Body Language Style Uses physical movements and gestures to support the presentation	☐ Wanders or moves around too much ☐ Body is unusually still or rarely moves ☐ Turns body away from the audience ☐ Crosses body with either arm ☐ Puts hands together while speaking ☐ Uses excessive or meaningless gestures ☐ Blocks audience's view of screen	☐ Takes a relaxed stance ☐ Presents from the reading-anchor side (left side, if in English) ☐ Stands at an angle (45-degrees) ☐ Keeps hands at sides when not gesturing ☐ Keeps hands visible at all times ☐ Makes eye contact with the audience
18. Speaking Style Can be easily heard and understood while using proper inflection and tone when speaking	☐ Speaks too quickly ☐ Uses a flat or soft tone of voice ☐ Narrates or reads the slides ☐ Uses filler words (such as: umm, err, okay, right, etc.)	☐ Voice is audible (uses microphone where appropriate) ☐ Uses pauses and silence ☐ Smooth and natural verbal transitions between slides
19. Technology Demonstrates familiarity with all equipment and other technical elements (such as multimedia)	☐ Does not handle technology glitches well ☐ Walks into the projector's light	☐ Interacts easily with technology ☐ Uses a remote control to advance slides
20. Focus Generates recurring references to major points	☐ Digresses or drifts from the topic	☐ Focuses on limited learning objectives
21. Interaction Establishes a connection with the audience through questions, comments and other participation	☐ Does not extend arms or hold gestures open to initiate interaction ☐ Does not welcome comments or questions	☐ Reaches out (opens hands) to the audience ☐ Repeats the question or the comment as a part of the response ☐ Uses "open-ended" questions ☐ Intentionally asks simple questions

Figure 6.1c.   Page 3 of the print version of Standard Evaluation, covering the Performance skills

check the challenge of "Looks too serious." Your reasoning for what appears to be a conflict between the statements may be that you feel that you do exhibit both of these characteristics on a regular basis. Some skill categories might not be observed or are not applicable in a particular presentation. In such situations, the related checkboxes should be left unchecked.

Although the *printed* evaluation form does not offer measured levels of effectiveness, it allows you to track your progress from previously filled assessments. Making side-by-side comparisons provides evidence as to which challenges you have overcome and which opportunities you still need to consider. In order to obtain measureable results, you will need to *analyze* your assessment by entering your selections into the *electronic* version of the form.

Interactive Electronic Assessments

The interactive electronic assessment tools are freely downloadable from the MedEdPORTAL website, a resource of the Association of American Medical Colleges (AAMC).[7] MedEdPORTAL is a peer-reviewed publication service and repository for medical and oral health teaching materials, assessment tools, and faculty development resources. The MedEdPORTAL site is not restricted to medical institutions. Therefore, any individual or organization can register (create a free account with no obligation) and have access to the educational materials. Many of these resources are not specific to medicine, such as our Skills Assessment tools, which are designed to measure the level of effectiveness of a presenter (who may be a teacher, trainer, speaker, etc.). Figure 6.2 outlines the process of converting a printed assessment to the electronic format for analysis using the available online tools.

While the MedEdPORTAL Web site includes all three assessments (Standard, Speech-Only, and Webinar), our electronic *standard* evaluation is also accessible from our publisher's Web site (for a free download, visit: www.rowmanlittlefield.com/isbn/1442208929). The electronic tools are designed to be user friendly, providing immediate feedback and a measurable pathway to self-improvement. Similar to filling in the three-page printed form, you make selections on appropriate skills. When using the interactive assessment, as you make selections (check boxes), the automatic link to the research data is activated and the resulting measurements are instantly calculated showing your numerical value. A *blank* checkbox (unchecked) has no effect on the final analysis. Additionally, the *results* page includes a *skills grid* identifying (highlighting) challenged skill areas in need of attention. Along with the skills grid, analytical data is compiled from the elements selected on the form, weighted according to learner preferences.

Understanding the Electronic Analysis

Figure 6.3 shows a sample of the results page from a filled electronic assessment, depicting the skills grid and the analysis data.

At the bottom of the results page you will see the calculations for the *level of effectiveness* with a student learner, with a professional learner, and with a

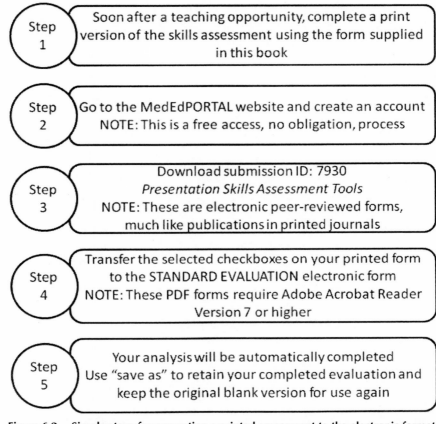

Step 1 Soon after a teaching opportunity, complete a print version of the skills assessment using the form supplied in this book

Step 2 Go to the MedEdPORTAL website and create an account
NOTE: This is a free access, no obligation, process

Step 3 Download submission ID: 7930
Presentation Skills Assessment Tools
NOTE: These are electronic peer-reviewed forms, much like publications in printed journals

Step 4 Transfer the selected checkboxes on your printed form to the STANDARD EVALUATION electronic form
NOTE: These PDF forms require Adobe Acrobat Reader Version 7 or higher

Step 5 Your analysis will be automatically completed
Use "save as" to retain your completed evaluation and keep the original blank version for use again

Figure 6.2. Simple steps for converting a printed assessment to the electronic format for analysis

group comprising both, as well as a relative *consistency deviation* and an overall *Speaker Index.*

As shown in Figure 6.3, the skills grid lists the twenty-one skills in the order appearing on the three-page assessment, separated by columns according to learner-type—students (S), professionals (P), and the mix of both (S/P). If a skill category has been observed to be more of a challenge, part or all of the related row will be *highlighted* based on the learner-type that perceives the skill as challenged. In the sample grid illustrated, the skills of *empathy* and *body language style* are highlighted in all three learner columns. The implied *recommendation* is that attention be given to the observations noted in those skill categories to see how the challenges may be addressed. The skills grid is a

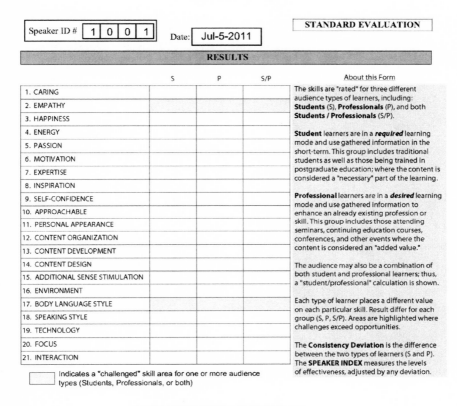

Figure 6.3. Sample electronic skills assessment analysis results page with skill grid and calculations

visual indicator of suggested priority areas for improvement. To optimize skills, the goal is to eliminate challenges and to take advantage of opportunities.

Table 6.2 describes the terms used on the results page of the electronic assessment. In our experience we have found that *high* efficiency speakers are those that have a consistency deviation of 3 percent or less and an overall Speaker Index of 80 or greater. These levels would be excellent targets to

Table 6.2.   Terminology used on the results page of the electronic skills assessment

Term	Definition
Student	Student learners are in a *required* learning mode and use the gathered information in the short term. Traditional "students" fall into this category, as well as anyone being trained in postgraduate education. The content taught to this group is typically considered to be a "necessary" component of their learning.
Professional	Professional learners are in a *desired* learning mode and use the gathered information to enhance an already existing profession or skill. Professional learners include those attending seminars, conferences, continuing education courses, and other events where the content is considered to be an "added value."
Level of Effectiveness	For each learner type (students and professionals), this is a numerical score of your effectiveness. For example, only use the value for student learners if you are in classroom teaching.
Consistency Deviation	This numerical value shows the extent to which you *vary* across different groups (students, professionals, and a mix of both). The lower the deviation, the more consistent you are with different learners. Your goal should be to have no deviation (a value of zero).
Speaker Index	This value takes into account your effectiveness as well as your consistency. This index should be used for teachers who have multiple groups of learners.

pursue, although unlikely to achieve prior to fully developing your skills. However, once you attain these levels, maintain your consistency as you continually self-reflect and self-improve.

Understanding Learners

The electronic assessment measures effectiveness levels for different audience types or "learners." Our research findings suggest that learners listen with a specific appreciation for particular characteristics in a teacher.[8] Some learners attach greater significance to one skill versus another, and the analysis indicates the extent to which "student learners" and "professional learners" perceive a presentation differently. Therefore, an instructor can appeal to students by focusing on those characteristics most preferred by student learners. The same instructor, in a different setting, should focus on different skills when faced with an audience of non-students, such as professional learners. For presentations to be more effective, it is important to know the type of learner (students, professionals, or a mix of both) and the related preferences.

An audience member may fit the profile of a "student learner" or a "professional learner" at different times, depending on the nature of the learning. For example, a trained surgeon attending a mandatory continuing education course in updates on Occupational Safety and Health Association (OSHA) regulations will perceive the information as a student learner. The same surgeon attending a seminar on the latest developments in his subspecialty may listen as a professional learner. You may find that some of your audiences are a mix of learner types and you will need to be equally effective with everyone in the group. As you use this book to develop your skills to be more effective, your consistency deviation score will keep getting lower, preferably to zero, allowing you to be more effective with *any type* of learner.

Applying the Results

To maximize the utility of these assessments, examine the particular level of effectiveness that most closely matches your audience (student learners, professional learners, or both). This measurement is the best indicator of how you are perceived by that type of audience. Thus, if you mostly present to student learners, look at those comparisons more closely, rather than at the overall speaker index, as an indicator of your effectiveness. The Speaker Index measures your effectiveness across all audience types and is useful for those who present to a variety of groups. Think of your Speaker Index as the extent to which you use your skills as a communicator to satisfy any type of learner in any learning environment.

When there is difficulty in gaining access to a computer to input the observations into the electronic version of the form, it is suggested that a blank assessment form be printed and the entries then be made by hand. All fields on the electronic assessment are purposely left empty, including the date field, so that the forms can be printed and duplicated for multiple uses. At a later point, manually completed forms can be input electronically for the automatic analysis to be computed (see Figure 6.3).

To become familiar with the assessment criteria, review the entire form prior to giving your presentation (if a self-evaluation) or share the form with the person you are observing (if a peer evaluation) prior to their presentation.

This process allows you or the person observed an opportunity to start incorporating the skills that learners perceive to be effective. It is suggested that these forms be used as complements to other evaluation methods.[9] The feedback can assist with faculty development, improve general presentation/teaching skills, and provide input regarding online teaching.

Audience Evaluation Tools

Earlier in this chapter we discussed the student evaluations as a commonly used and reliable form of feedback, even though results from such assessments are more wide-ranging in scope. At the same time, it is not likely that the detailed skills assessment tools illustrated in this book can be used efficiently with large groups, as the evaluation effort may too time consuming to track numerous observations related to twenty-one skill categories and eighty independent elements. However, the ability to filter group feedback through the same research criteria as is used for individual assessments can create a harmony of perspectives in evaluating effectiveness. In that regard, we have designed a *learner version* of the skills assessment that can be used by a group to evaluate a teacher, collectively combining the input to arrive at a "group index" or cumulative measurement of effectiveness from an audience perspective.

The *SPICE Model*™ measures a collection of skills, grouped into areas that can then be targeted for improvement.[10] Using a 5-point scale, from a low of 1 to high of 5, a learner uses the SPICE Model (or similar format) to rate the observed skills of a teacher in each of five distinct categories: *Speech*, *Presence*, *Interaction*, *Clarity*, and *Expertise* (SPICE). Figure 6.4 shows the components of the SPICE Model evaluation form indicating how similar evaluations may be worded to cover a group of skill categories.

Table 6.3 identifies the specific skills that collectively contribute to each of the SPICE Model groupings.

The SPICE Model COLLECTOR

As a complement to the SPICE Model, in order to measure gathered responses, we designed the *SPICE Model Collector*™. This is an electronic input form that analyzes group evaluations based on the same learner preferences used with our individual skills assessment tools.[11] For your convenience, the SPICE Model Collector is accessible online (for a free download, visit: www.rowmanlittlefield.com/isbn/1442208929). Feedback from multiple evaluations is aggregated and then analyzed to measure effectiveness across different learner types, arriving at an overall Speaker Index. The

Please evaluate the following items, using the rating scale shown, from LOWEST (1) to HIGHEST (5)

Speech Can be clearly heard and easily understood, using pauses and inflection to vary pace and tone	○ 1 ○ 2 ○ 3 ○ 4 ○ 5 Low————————————High
Presence Appears energetic and in control of the presentation, effectively using gestures and movement to enhance concepts	○ 1 ○ 2 ○ 3 ○ 4 ○ 5 Low————————————High
Interaction Encourages participation, asks questions, and appears receptive to comments or suggestions	○ 1 ○ 2 ○ 3 ○ 4 ○ 5 Low————————————High
Clarity Presents an organized, clear message, using concrete examples, supported by uncluttered, easy-to-read slides	○ 1 ○ 2 ○ 3 ○ 4 ○ 5 Low————————————High
Expertise Logically explains and simplifies the content while meeting stated learning objectives	○ 1 ○ 2 ○ 3 ○ 4 ○ 5 Low————————————High

Figure 6.4. The SPICE Model™, showing the grouped skill categories and relative rating scale

Table 6.3. SPICE Model™ general groupings derived from individual skill categories

Spice Model Groupings	*Skill Categories*
Speech Can be clearly heard and easily understood, using pauses and inflection to vary pace and tone	Speaking Style
Presence Appears energetic and in control of the presentation, effectively using gestures and movement to enhance concepts	Happiness Energy Self-Confidence Body Language Style
Interaction Encourages participation, asks questions, and appears receptive to comments or suggestions	Caring Empathy Approachable Interaction
Clarity Presents an organized, clear message using concrete examples, supported by uncluttered, easy-to-read slides	Content Organization Content Development Content Design
Expertise Logically explains and simplifies the content while meeting stated learning objectives	Expertise Focus

SPICE Model Collector results are highly consistent with our individual skills assessment analysis discussed earlier; measuring 90 percent of the preferences identified in the more comprehensive assessment tools.

Figure 6.5 shows a *collective* analysis of twenty-five evaluations for a "sample" teacher. In this sample SPICE Model Collector analysis, the teacher appears to be more effective in using the skills preferred by

Speaker Evaluation

Speaker | Sample Teacher

Program | Sample Course

DATE | July 5, 2011

Please enter the total responses for each rating level (1-5) within each skill category.

Skill	1	2	3	4	5	AVG
Speech — Can be clearly heard and easily understood, using pauses and inflection to vary pace and tone	0	2	14	8	1	3.32
Presence — Appears energetic and in control of the presentation, effectively using gestures and movement to enhance concepts	0	3	9	9	4	3.56
Interaction — Encourages participation, asks questions, and appears receptive to comments or suggestions	0	0	7	10	8	4.04
Clarity — Presents an organized, clear message, using concrete examples, supported by uncluttered, easy-to-read slides	3	9	12	1	0	2.44
Expertise — Logically explains and simplifies the content while meeting stated learning objectives	0	0	8	11	6	3.92

Students	Professionals	Students & Professionals	Consistency Deviation	Speaker Index
65%	71%	68%	6%	**64**
Learners				

SPEECH	PRESENCE	INTERACTION	CLARITY	EXPERTISE
Points 16.6	Points 17.8	Points 20.2	Points 12.2	Points 19.6
Responses 25	Responses 25	Responses 25	Responses 25	Responses 25

Figure 6.5.   Sample of the SPICE Model Collector™ showing the analysis of multiple evaluations

professional learners (71 percent), as opposed to those of student learners (65 percent). As an instructor, the appeal to student learner preferences is critical. Looking more closely at the sample analysis, the teacher averaged 2.44 out of 5 in the area of Clarity. This SPICE Model category is a measure of several *process* skills including: *Content Organization, Content Development*, and *Content Design* (see table 6.3). The process skills are the ones more preferred by student learners. The teacher now has a general impression as to which group of skills needs to be addressed in order to improve. However, there is no clear indication as to which elements within each specific skill should be targeted. In other words, the group results, gathered and reported on the SPICE Model Collector, provide a *general guideline* toward areas of improvement, whereas the individual Skills Assessment targets *specific skill elements* that can be acted upon to continually improve.

Using Existing Evaluation Forms

Regardless of how evaluation data from individuals is gathered, a group analysis allows a teacher to see collective ratings to help identify general areas for improvement in subsequent teaching. For those who already use group feedback forms, such as student evaluations, it is likely that many of the groupings shown in the SPICE model are currently assessed on your existing forms, although the wording may be different. In some cases, simply adding one more items to an existing evaluation would cover all five of the categories noted in the SPICE model. Therefore, current evaluation criteria from an institution's assessment form that closely matches the categories noted in the SPICE Model can be aggregated and input into the SPICE Model Collector form to perform an analysis.

For example, suppose your current student evaluation contains fifteen teacher attributes to assess skills related to course content, teaching, interaction, and so on. When you compare the elements on your existing form with that of the SPICE Model categories (see figure 6.4) you notice that many of the attributes match. For those matching items, the existing evaluation results can be used as input to the SPICE Model Collector to measure your effectiveness in terms of the researched learner preferences. This is a convenient way to allow existing student feedback from standard institution forms to be measured in the same way as our skills assessment tools.

The SPICE Model Collector allows input for up to 1,000 evaluations and the electronic form automatically analyzes the learner responses, calculating an average score in each category, along with a summary of total responses. All results are tabulated according the same peer-reviewed published data on learner preferences that we use to measure effectiveness with our individual skills assessment tools. The fact that results are based on research findings reduces bias and subjectivity when calculating levels of effectiveness.

Regardless of how the evaluation data from individuals is gathered, the group analysis allows a teacher to see collective ratings to help identify generalized areas for improvement in subsequent teaching. Although the results from the group analysis cannot target specific areas for improvement, only generalized categories, it is in your best interests to experience *multiple forms of feedback* based on learner preferences. The combination of these perspectives paints a complete picture of your skills.

Toward Triangulation

Teaching effectiveness can be assessed using diverse evaluation strategies including student evaluations, peer reviews, and self-assessments, the combination of which is referred to as *triangulation*.[9, 12–17] Multiple perspectives allow an instructor to understand how skills are evaluated and where improvements can be made.

As part of faculty development, you can use the individual Skill Assessment to perform several self-evaluations. At the same time, one or two of your colleagues can conduct peer reviews of your skills using the same individual assessment tool. Finally, the SPICE Model can be used by your learners to do a group evaluation of your performance. You can then compare the results of this triangulation using all three assessments (student, peer, self) to see a more complete picture of your effectiveness.

If you use the suggested assessments, before and after reading this book, you will identify your challenges and maximize your opportunities in every teaching forum. As a result of your efforts to continually improve, you will ultimately become a more effective teacher!

Track Your Progress

Table 6.4 is a blank progress chart that can be used to keep a record of your self-assessments. The comparisons will help you monitor your progress toward improving your effectiveness. Use the calculated results from each of your electronic individual skills assessments to record the analysis data in the boxes provided, which are arranged similar to the calculations shown at the bottom of the sample results page in figure 6.2.

Table 6.4. Progress chart for tracking assessment results

Date of Assessment	Effectiveness Levels with Learners			Overall Results	
	Students	*Professionals*	*Students & Professionals*	*Consistency Deviation*	*Speaker Index*

It is never too late to be what you might have been.

—George Eliot

References

CHAPTER 1

1. Jahangiri L, Mucciolo TW. Characteristics of effective classroom teachers as identified by students and professionals: A qualitative study. *Journal of Dental Education* 2008:72(4):484–93.

2. Berliner DC. Learning about and learning from expert teachers. *International Journal of Educational Research* 2001:35(5):463–82.

3. Berk RA. Survey of 12 strategies to measure teaching effectiveness. *International Journal of Teaching and Learning in Higher Education* 2005:17(1):48–62.

4. Jahangiri L, Mucciolo TW, Choi M, Spielman AI. Assessment of teaching effectiveness in US dental schools and the value of triangulation. *Journal of Dental Education* 2008:72(6):707–18.

5. Abrami PC, d'Apollonia S, Cohen PA. Validity of student ratings of instruction: What we know and what we do not. *Journal of Educational Psychology* 1990:82(2): 219–31.

6. Aleamoni LM. Student rating myths versus research facts from 1924 to 1998. *Journal of Personnel Evaluation in Education* 1999:13(2):153–66.

7. Cashin WE. Student ratings of teaching: Uses and misuses. In: Associates PS, ed., *Changing practices in evaluating teaching: A practical guide to improved faculty performance and promotion/tenure decisions.* Bolton, MA: Anker, 1999:25–44.

8. d'Apollonia S, Abrami PC. Navigating student ratings of instruction. *American Psychologist* 1997:52(11):1198–208.

9. Eiszler CF. College students' evaluations of teaching and grade inflation. *Research in Higher Education* 2002:43(4):483–501.

10. Emery CR, Kramer TR, Tian RG. Return to academic standards: a critique of student evaluations of teaching effectiveness. *Quality Assurance in Education* 2003:11(1):37–46.

11. Greenwald AG. Validity concerns and usefulness of student ratings of instruction. *American Psychologist* 1997:52(11):1182–86.

12. Greimel-Fuhrmann B, Geyer A. Students' Evaluation of Teachers and Instructional Quality—Analysis of Relevant Factors Based on Empirical Evaluation Research. *Assessment & Evaluation in Higher Education* 2003:28(3):229–38.

13. Havelka D, Neal CS, Beasley F. Student evaluation of teaching effectiveness: What criteria are most important. Paper presented at the annual Lilly Conference of College Teaching, Miami University, Oxford, OH, 2003.

14. Howard GS, Conway CG, Maxwell SE. Construct validity of measures of college teaching effectiveness. *Journal of Educational Psychology* 1985:77(2):187–96.

15. Lewis KG. *Techniques and strategies for interpreting student evaluations.* San Francisco: Jossey-Bass, 2001.

16. Millea M, Grimes PW. Grade expectations and student evaluation of teaching. *College Student Journal* 2002:36(4):582–90.

17. Read WJ, Rama DV, Raghunandan K. The relationship between student evaluations of teaching and faculty evaluations. *Journal of Education for Business* 2001:76(4): 189–92.

18. Shevlin M, Banyard P, Davies M, Griffiths M. The validity of student evaluation of teaching in higher education: Love me, love my lectures? *Assessment & Evaluation in Higher Education* 2000:25(4):397–405.

19. Sojka J, Gupta A, Deeter-Schmelz D. Student and faculty perceptions of student evaluations of teaching: A study of similarities and differences. *College Teaching* 2002: 50(2):44–49.

20. Sproule R. The underdetermination of instructor performance by data from the student evaluation of teaching. *Economics of Education Review* 2002:21(3):287–94.

21. Theall M, Abrami PC, Mets LA. *The student ratings debate: Are they valid? How can we best use them?* San Francisco: Jossey-Bass, 2001.

22. Trinkaus J. Students' course and faculty evaluations: An informal look. *Psychological Reports* 2002:91(3, Pt 1):988.

23. Wachtel HK. Student evaluation of college teaching effectiveness: A brief review. *Assessment & Evaluation in Higher Education* 1998:23(2):191–212.

24. Seldin P. Self-evaluation: What works? What doesn't? In: Seldin PA, ed., *Changing practices in evaluating teaching.* Bolton, MA: Anker Pub. Co., 1999:97–113.

25. Berk RA, Naumann PL, Appling SE. Beyond student ratings: Peer observation of classroom and clinical teaching. *International Journal of Nursing Education Scholarship* 2004:1(1):1–26.

26. Cederblom D, Lounsbury JW. An investigation of user acceptance of peer evaluations. *Personnel Psychology* 1980:33(3):567–79.

27. Doyle KO, Crichton LI. Student, peer, and self evaluations of college instructors. *Journal of Educational Psychology* 1978:70(5):815–26.

28. Goldstein J. Making sense of distributed leadership: The case of peer assistance and review. *Educational Evaluation and Policy Analysis* 2004:26(2):173–97.

29. Irby D. Evaluating instructional scholarship in medicine. *Journal of the American Podiatric Medical Association* 1993:83(6):332–37.

30. Love KG. Comparison of peer assessment methods: Reliability, validity, friendship bias, and user reaction. *Journal of Applied Psychology* 1981:66(4):451–57.

31. Lee GC, Wu C-C. Enhancing the teaching experience of pre-service teachers through the use of videos in web-based computer-mediated communication (CMC). *Innovations in Education and Teaching International* 2006:43(4):369–80.

32. Milman NB. Web-based digital teaching portfolios: Fostering reflection and technology competence in preservice teacher education students. *Journal of Technology and Teacher Education* 2005:13(3):373.

33. Beck RJ, Livne NL, Bear SL. Teachers' self-assessment of the effects of formative and summative electronic portfolios on professional development. *European Journal of Teacher Education* 2005:28(3):221–44.

34. Centra JA. Self-ratings of college teachers: A comparison with student ratings. *Journal of Educational Measurement* 1973:10(4):287–95.

35. Leggett M, Bunker A. Teaching portfolios and university culture. *Journal of Further and Higher Education* 2006:30(3):269–82.

36. Ross JA, Bruce CD. Teacher self-assessment: A mechanism for facilitating professional growth. *Teaching & Teacher Education* 2007:23(2):146–59.

37. Cosh J. Peer observation in higher education: A reflective approach. *Innovations in Education and Teaching International* 1998:35(2):171–76.

38. Tucker PD, Stronge JH, Gareis CR. *Handbook on teacher portfolios for evaluation and professional development.* Larchmont, NY: Eye on Education, 2002.

39. Ambady N, Rosenthal R. Half a minute: Predicting teacher evaluations from thin slices of nonverbal behavior and physical attractiveness. *Journal of Personality and Social Psychology* 1993: 64(3):431–41.

40. Felton J, Mitchell J, Stinson M. Web-based student evaluations of professors: The relations between perceived quality, easiness and sexiness. *Assessment & Evaluation in Higher Education* 2004:29(1):91–108.

41. McCroskey JC, Richmond VP. Increasing teacher influence through immediacy. In: *Power in the classroom: Communication, control, and concern.* Hillsdale, NJ: Erlbaum, 1992:101–20.

42. Onwuegbuzie AJ, Witcher AE, Collins KMT, Filer JD, Weidmaier CD, Moore CW. Students' perceptions of characteristics of effective college teachers: A validity study of a teaching evaluation form using a mixed-methods analysis. *American Educational Research Journal* 2007:44(1):113.

43. Riniolo TC, Johnson KC, Sherman TR, Misso JA. Hot or not: Do professors perceived as physically attractive receive higher student evaluations? *The Journal of General Psychology* 2006:133(1):19–35.

44. Schaeffer G, Epting K, Zinn T, Buskist W. Student and faculty perceptions of effective teaching: A successful replication. *Teaching of Psychology* 2003:30(2):133–36.

45. Gurung RAR, Vespia K. Topical articles: Looking good, teaching well? Linking liking, looks, and learning. *Teaching of Psychology* 2007:34(1):6.

CHAPTER 2

1. Shannon CE. A mathematical theory of communication. *The Bell System Technical Journal* 1948:27:379-423, 623–56.

2. Jahangiri L, Mucciolo TW. Characteristics of effective classroom teachers as identified by students and professionals: A qualitative study. *Journal of Dental Education* 2008:72(4):484–93.

3. Crumbley L, Henry B, Kratchman S. Students' perceptions of the teaching of college teaching. *Quality Assurance in Education* 2001:9(4):197–207.

4. Greimel-Fuhrmann B, Geyer A. Students' evaluation of teachers and instructional quality: Analysis of relevant factors based on empirical evaluation research. *Assessment & Evaluation in Higher Education* 2003:28(3):229–38.

5. Kane R, Sandretto S, Heath C. An investigation into excellent tertiary teaching: Emphasising reflective practice. *Higher Education* 2004:47(3):283–310.

6. Okpala CO, Ellis R. The perceptions of college students on teacher quality: A focus on teacher qualifications. *Education* 2005:126(2):374–83.

7. Onwuegbuzie AJ, Witcher AE, Collins KMT, Filer JD, Weidmaier CD, Moore CW. Students' perceptions of characteristics of effective college teachers: A validity study of a teaching evaluation form using a mixed-methods analysis. *American Educational Research Journal* 2007:44(1):113.

8. Schaeffer G, Epting K, Zinn T, Buskist W. Student and faculty perceptions of effective teaching: A successful replication. *Teaching of Psychology* 2003:30(2):133–36.

9. Sheehan EP, Duprey T. Student evaluations of university teaching. *Journal of Instructional Psychology* 1999:26(3):1–7.

10. Spencer KJ, Schmelkin LP. Student perspectives on teaching and its evaluation. *Assessment & Evaluation in Higher Education* 2002:27(5):397–409.

11. Witcher AE, Onwuegbuzie AJ, Minor LC. Characteristics of effective teachers: Perceptions of preservice teachers. *Research in the Schools* 2001:8(2):45–57.

12. Bryant J, Comisky PW, Crane JS, Zillmann D. Relationship between college teachers' use of humor in the classroom and students' evaluations of their teachers. *Journal of Educational Psychology* 1980:72(4):511–19.

13. Doutrich D, Hoeskel R, Wykoff L, Thiele J. Teaching teachers to teach with technology. *Journal of Continuing Education in Nursing* 2005:36(1):25–31.

14. Gordon HRD, Yocke R. Relationship between personality characteristics and observable teaching effectiveness of selected beginning career and technical education teachers. *Journal of Vocational and Technical Education* 1999:16(1):47–66.

15. Hulsmeyer BS, Bowling AK. Evaluating colleagues' classroom teaching effectiveness. *Nurse Educator* 1986:11(5):19–23.

16. Salles J, Baranauskas MCC, Bigonha RS. Towards a communication model applied to the interface design process. *Knowledge-Based Systems* 2001:14(8):455–59.

17. Webster J, Hackley P. Teaching effectiveness in technology-mediated distance learning. *Academy of Management Journal* 1997:40(6):1282–309.

18. Ambady N, Rosenthal R. Half a minute: Predicting teacher evaluations from thin slices of nonverbal behavior and physical attractiveness. *Journal of Personality and Social Psychology* 1993:64(3):431–41.

19. Caso L, Maricchiolo F, Bonaiuto M, Vrij A, Mann S. The impact of deception and suspicion on different hand movements. *Journal of Nonverbal Behavior* 2006:30(1):1–19.

20. Coulson M. Attributing emotion to static body postures: Recognition accuracy, confusions, and viewpoint dependence. *Journal of Nonverbal Behavior* 2004:28(2):117–39.

21. Rammstedt B, John OP. Measuring personality in one minute or less: A 10-item short version of the Big Five Inventory in English and German. *Journal of Research in Personality* 2007:41(1):203–12.

22. Rosip JC, Hall JA. Knowledge of nonverbal cues, gender, and nonverbal decoding accuracy. *Journal of Nonverbal Behavior* 2004:28(4):267–86.

23. Babad E, Avni-Babad D, Rosenthal R. Teachers' brief nonverbal behaviors in defined instructional situations can predict students' evaluations. *Journal of Educational Psychology* 2003:95(3):553–62.

24. Skiba DJ. Got large lecture hall classes? Use clickers. *Nursing Education Perspectives* 2006:27(5):278–80.

25. Jahangiri L, Mucciolo TW. Presentation skills assessment tools. MedEdPORTAL (AAMC), 2010. Available at: https://www.mededportal.org/publication/7930.

CHAPTER 3

1. Jahangiri L, Mucciolo TW. Characteristics of effective classroom teachers as identified by students and professionals: A qualitative study. *Journal of Dental Education* 2008:72(4):484–93.

2. Greimel-Fuhrmann B, Geyer A. Students' evaluation of teachers and instructional quality: Analysis of relevant factors based on empirical evaluation research. *Assessment & Evaluation in Higher Education* 2003:28(3):229–38.

3. Onwuegbuzie AJ, Witcher AE, Collins KMT, Filer JD, Weidmaier CD, Moore CW. Students' perceptions of characteristics of effective college teachers: A validity study of a teaching evaluation form using a mixed-methods analysis. *American Educational Research Journal* 2007:44(1):113.

4. Teven JJ, McCroskey JC. The relationship of perceived teacher caring with student learning and teacher evaluation. *Communication Education* 1997:46(1):1–9.

5. Teven JJ. Teacher caring and classroom behavior: Relationships with student affect and perceptions of teacher competence and trustworthiness. *Communication Quarterly* 2007:55(4):433–50.

6. Finn AN, Schrodt P, Witt PL, Elledge N, Jernberg KA, Larson LM. A meta-analytical review of teacher credibility and its associations with teacher behaviors and student outcomes. *Communication Education* 2009:58(4):516–37.

7. Mehrabian A. Significance of posture and position in the communication of attitude and status relationships. *Psychological Bulletin* 1969:71(5):359.

8. Burnett PC, Mandel V. Praise and feedback in the primary classroom: Teachers' and students' perspectives. *Australian Journal of Educational & Developmental Psychology* 2010:10:145–54.

9. Dweck CS. The perils and promises of praise. *Educational Leadership* 2007:65(2):34–39.

10. Maag JW. Rewarded by punishment: Reflections on the disuse of positive reinforcement in schools. *Exceptional Children* 2001:67(2):173–86.

11. Cole D. Constructive criticism: The role of student-faculty interactions on African American and Hispanic students' educational gains. *Journal of College Student Development* 2008:49(6):587–605.

12. Banfield S, Richmond V, McCroskey J. The effect of teacher misbehaviors on teacher credibility and affect for the teacher. *Communication Education* 2006:55(1):63–72.

13. Chesebro JL, McCroskey JC. The relationship of teacher clarity and immediacy with student state receiver apprehension, affect, and cognitive learning. *Communication Education* 2001:50(1):59–68.

14. Weaver RR, Qi J. Classroom organization and participation: college students' perceptions. *Journal of Higher Education* 2005:76(5):570–601.

15. Fritschner LM. Inside the undergraduate college classroom: Faculty and students differ on the meaning of student participation. *Journal of Higher Education* 2000:71(3):342–62.

16. Cornelius-White J. Learner-centered teacher-student relationships are effective: A meta-analysis. *Review of Educational Research* 2007:77(1):113–43.

17. Kusto AR, Afful SE, Mattingly BA. Students' perceptions of and preferences for professors. *New School Psychology Bulletin* 2010:8(1):47–55.

18. McAllister G. The role of empathy in teaching culturally diverse students. *Journal of Teacher Education* 2002:53(5):433.

19. Ambady N, Rosenthal R. Half a minute: Predicting teacher evaluations from thin slices of nonverbal behavior and physical attractiveness. *Journal of Personality and Social Psychology* 1993:64(3):431–41.

20. Bryant J, Comisky PW, Crane JS, Zillmann D. Relationship between college teachers' use of humor in the classroom and students' evaluations of their teachers. *Journal of Educational Psychology* 1980:72(4):511–19.

21. Coulson M. Attributing emotion to static body postures: Recognition accuracy, confusions, and viewpoint dependence. *Journal of Nonverbal Behavior* 2004:28(2):117–39.

22. Kane R, Sandretto S, Heath C. An investigation into excellent tertiary teaching: Emphasising reflective practice. *Higher Education* 2004:47(3):283–310.

23. Rosip JC, Hall JA. Knowledge of nonverbal cues, gender, and nonverbal decoding accuracy. *Journal of Nonverbal Behavior* 2004:28(4):267–86.

24. Levy JB. As a last resort, ask the students: What they say makes someone an effective law teacher. *Maine Law Review* 2006:58(1):50–98.

25. Siegel DJ. *The developing mind: How relationships and the brain interact to shape who we are.* New York: The Guilford Press, 1999.

26. Sylwester R. *A biological brain in a cultural classroom: Enhancing cognitive and social development through collaborative classroom management.* Thousand Oaks, CA: Corwin Press, 2003.

27. De Gelder B. Towards the neurobiology of emotional body language. *Nature Reviews Neuroscience* 2006:7(3):242–49.

28. Meijer M. The contribution of general features of body movement to the attribution of emotions. *Journal of Nonverbal Behavior* 1989:13(4):247–68.

29. Murray HG. Research on low-inference teaching behaviors: An update. In: Perry RP, Smart JC eds., *The scholarship of teaching and learning in higher education: an evidence-based perspective.* Dordrecht, The Netherlands: Springer, 2007:184.

30. Murray HG. Teaching effectiveness in higher education. In: Smart JC, ed., *Higher education: Handbook of theory and research.* Vol. 7. New York: Agathon Press, 1991:135–72.

31. Goleman D. *Emotional intelligence.* New York: Bantam Books, 1995.

32. Hopkins WS. Philosophies of human nature and nonverbal communication patterns (doctoral dissertation, Oklahoma State University, 1973). *Dissertation Abstracts International* 1974:34:6517A. (University Microfilms No. 74-8048).

33. Berk RA. Student ratings of 10 strategies for using humor in college teaching. *Journal on Excellence in College Teaching* 1996:7(3):71–92.

34. Garner RL. Humor in pedagogy: How ha-ha can lead to aha! *College Teaching* 2006:54(1):177–80.

35. Kher N, Molstad S, Donahue R. Using humor in the college classroom to enhance teaching effectiveness in "dread courses." *College Student Journal* 1999:33(3):400–406.

36. Schmidt SR. Effects of humor on sentence memory. *Journal of Experimental Psychology* 1994:20(4):953–67.

37. Feldman KA. Effective college teaching from the students' and faculty's view: Matched or mismatched priorities? *Research in Higher Education* 1988:28(4):291–329.

38. Kunter M, Tsai YM, Klusmann U, Brunner M, Krauss S, Baumert J. Students' and mathematics teachers' perceptions of teacher enthusiasm and instruction. Learning and Instruction 2008:18(5):468–82.

39. Zhang Q, Sapp DA. The effect of perceived teacher burnout on credibility. *Communication Research Reports* 2009:26(1):87–90.

40. Teven JJ. Teacher temperament: Correlates with teacher caring, burnout, and organizational outcomes. *Communication Education* 2007:56(3):382–400.

41. McCroskey JC, Richmond VP. Increasing teacher influence through immediacy. In: *Power in the classroom: Communication, control, and concern.* Hillsdale, NJ: Erlbaum, 1992:101–20.

42. Carbonneau N, Vallerand RJ, Fernet C, Guay F. The role of passion for teaching in intrapersonal and interpersonal outcomes. *Journal of Educational Psychology* 2008: 100(4):977–87.

43. McCroskey JC, Holdridge W, Toomb JK. An instrument for measuring the source credibility of basic speech communication instructors. *Communication Education* 1974:23(1):26–33.

44. Berliner DC. Learning about and learning from expert teachers. *International Journal of Educational Research* 2001:35(5):463–82.

45. Gurung RAR, Vespia K. Topical articles: Looking good, teaching well? Linking liking, looks, and learning. *Teaching of Psychology* 2007:34(1):6.

46. Frymier AB. Affinity-seeking in the classroom: Which strategies are associated with liking of the teacher? Paper presented at the Speech Communication Association 78th Annual Meeting. Chicago, IL, 1992.

47. David AP. Examining the relationship of personality and burnout in college students: The role of academic motivation. *Educational Measurement and Evaluation Review* 2010:1:90–104.

48. Pintrich PR. A motivational science perspective on the role of student motivation in learning and teaching contexts. *Journal of Educational Psychology* 2003:95(4):667–86.

49. Yoshida M, Tanaka M, Mizuno K, Ishii A, Nozaki K, Urakawa A, Cho Y, Kataoka Y, Watanabe Y. Factors influencing the academic motivation of individual college students. *International Journal of Neuroscience* 2008:118(10):1400–1411.

50. Deci EL, Ryan RM. *Intrinsic motivation and self-determination in human behavior.* New York: Plenum, 1985.

51. Hamilton Richard J, Jean A. Intrinsic enjoyment and boredom coping scales: Validation with personality, evoked potential and attention measures. *Personality and Individual Differences* 1984:5(2):183–93.

52. Vallerand RJ. On the assessment of intrinsic, extrinsic, and amotivation in education: Evidence on the concurrent and construct validity of the academic motivation scale. *Educational and Psychological Measurement* 1993:53(1):159–72.

53. Conrad P. It's boring: Notes on the meanings of boredom in everyday life. *Qualitative Sociology* 1997:20(4):465–75.

54. Feldman KA. Identifying exemplary teachers and teaching: Evidence from student ratings. In: Perry RP, Smart JC eds., *The scholarship of teaching and learning in higher education: An evidence-based perspective.* Dordrecht, The Netherlands: Springer, 2007: 93–143.

55. Bereiter C, Scardamalia M. *Surpassing ourselves: An inquiry into the nature and implications of expertise.* Chicago: Open Court Publishing Co., 1993.

56. Borko H, Livingston C. Cognition and improvisation: Differences in mathematics instruction by expert and novice teachers. *American Educational Research Journal* 1989:26(4):473–98.

57. Ericsson K, Charness N, Feltovich P, Hoffman R. *The Cambridge handbook of expertise and expert performance.* Cambridge: Cambridge University Press, 2006.

58. Ericsson KA, Charness N. Expert performance. *American Psychologist* 1994: 49(8):725–47.

59. Mylopoulos M, Regehr G. Cognitive metaphors of expertise and knowledge: prospects and limitations for medical education. *Medical Education* 2007:41(12):1159–65.

60. Sternberg RJ. Abilities are forms of developing expertise. *Educational Researcher* 1998:27(3):11.

61. Westerman DA. Expert and novice teacher decision making. *Journal of Teacher Education* 1991:42(4):292–305.

62. Herling RW. Operational definitions of expertise and competence. *Advances in Developing Human Resources* 2000:2(1):8–21.

63. Lampert M, Clark CM. Expert knowledge and expert thinking in teaching: A response to Floden and Klinzing. *Educational Researcher* 1990:19(5):21–23, 42.

64. Lee GC, Wu C-C. Enhancing the teaching experience of pre-service teachers through the use of videos in web-based computer-mediated communication (CMC). *Innovations in Education and Teaching International* 2006:43(4):369–80.

65. *Harvard Magazine.* Talking teaching and learning. *Harvard Magazine* 2011: March–April:42–49.

66. Hendricson WD, Andrieu SC, Chadwick DG, Chmar JE, Cole JR, George MC, Glickman GN, Glover JF, Goldberg JS, Haden NK. Educational strategies associated with development of problem-solving, critical thinking, and self-directed learning. *Journal of Dental Education* 2006:70(9):925.

67. Livingston C, Borko H. Expert-novice differences in teaching: A cognitive analysis and implications for teacher education. *Journal of Teacher Education* 1989:40(4):36–42.

68. Darby A. Teachers' emotions in the reconstruction of professional self-understanding. *Teaching and Teacher Education* 2008:24(5):1160–72.

69. Aleamoni LM, Hexner PZ. A review of the research on student evaluation and a report on the effect of different sets of instructions on student course and instructor evaluation. *Instructional Science* 1980:9(1):67–84.

70. Centra JA. Student ratings of instruction and their relationship to student learning. *American Educational Research Journal* 1977:14(1):17–24.

71. Cohen PA. Student ratings of instruction and student achievement: A meta-analysis of multisection validity studies. *Review of Educational Research* 1981:51(3):281–309.

72. Marsh HW. The validity of students' evaluations: Classroom evaluations of instructors independently nominated as best and worst teachers by graduating seniors. *American Educational Research Journal* 1977:14(4):441–47.

73. McKeachie WJ. Research on college teaching: The historical background. *Journal of Educational Psychology* 1990:82(2):189–200.

74. Jahangiri L, Mucciolo TW, Choi M, Spielman AI. Assessment of teaching effectiveness in US dental schools and the value of triangulation. *Journal of Dental Education* 2008:72(6):707–18.

75. Kouzes JM, Posner BZ. *The leadership challenge*. San Francisco: Jossey-Bass, 2003.

76. Boyd BL. Using a case study to develop the transformational teaching theory. *Journal of Leadership Education* 2009:7(3):50–59.

77. Gunther M, Evans G, Mefford L, Coe TR. The relationship between leadership styles and empathy among student nurses. *Nursing Outlook* 2007:55(4):196–201.

78. Bass BM, Avolio BJ. *Improving organizational effectiveness through transformational leadership*. Thousand Oaks, CA: Sage Publications, 1994.

79. Cohen NH. The principles of adult mentoring scale. *New Directions for Adult and Continuing Education* 1995:66:15–32.

80. Crisp G, Cruz I. Mentoring college students: A critical review of the literature between 1990 and 2007. *Research in Higher Education* 2009:50(6):525–45.

81. Bar-On R. The Bar-On model of emotional-social intelligence (ESI). *Psicothema* 2006:18(Suppl.):13–25.

82. Ruscio AM, Brown TA, Chiu WT, Sareen J, Stein MB, Kessler RC. Social fears and social phobia in the USA: Results from the National Comorbidity Survey Replication. *Psychological Medicine* 2008:38(1):15–28.

83. Hofmann SG, Ehlers A, Roth WT. Conditioning theory: A model for the etiology of public speaking anxiety? *Behaviour Research and Therapy* 1995:33(5):567–71.

84. Stein MB, Walker JR, Forde DR. Public-speaking fears in a community sample: Prevalence, impact on functioning, and diagnostic classification. *Archives of General Psychiatry* 1996:53(2):169–74.

85. Rutledge PA, Mucciolo T, Bajaj G. *Special edition using Microsoft Office PowerPoint 2007*. Indianapolis, IN: Que Publishing, 2007.

86. Rutledge PA, Mucciolo T, Grey J. *Special edition using Microsoft Office PowerPoint 2003*. Indianapolis, IN: Que Publishing, 2003.

87. White KA. Self-Confidence: A Concept Analysis. *Nursing Forum* 2009:44(2):103–14.

88. Karp DA, Yoels WC. The college classroom: Some observations on the meanings of student participation. *Sociology and Social Research* 1976:60(4):421–39.

89. Gorham J, Christophel DM. Students' perceptions of teacher behaviors as motivating and demotivating factors in college classes. *Communication Quarterly* 1992:40(3):239–52.

90. Flanders NA. *Basic teaching skills derived from a model of speaking and listening*. Teacher Education Division Publication Series. Report A72-19. San Francisco, CA: Far West Lab. for Educational Research and Development, 1972.

91. d'Apollonia S, Abrami PC. Navigating student ratings of instruction. *American Psychologist* 1997:52(11):1198–208.

92. Felton J, Mitchell J, Stinson M. Web-based student evaluations of professors: The relations between perceived quality, easiness and sexiness. *Assessment & Evaluation in Higher Education* 2004:29(1):91–108.

93. Riniolo TC, Johnson KC, Sherman TR, Misso JA. Hot or not: Do professors perceived as physically attractive receive higher student evaluations? *Journal of General Psychology* 2006:133(1):19–35.

94. Schaeffer G, Epting K, Zinn T, Buskist W. Student and faculty perceptions of effective teaching: A successful replication. *Teaching of Psychology* 2003:30(2):133–36.

95. McCroskey JC. The affinity-seeking of classroom teachers. *Communication Research Reports* 1986:3(3):158–67.

96. Coladarci T, Kornfield I. RateMyProfessors. com versus formal in-class student evaluations of teaching. *Practical Assessment, Research & Evaluation* 2007:12(6):1–15.

97. Rudd NA, Lennon SJ. Body image: Linking aesthetics and social psychology of appearance. *Clothing and Textiles Research Journal* 2001:19(3):120.

98. Albanese MA. The validity of lecturer ratings by students and trained observers. *Academic Medicine* 1991:66(1):26–28.

99. Kearney P, Plax TG, Hays ER, Ivey MJ. College teacher misbehaviors: What students don't like about what teachers say and do. *Communication Quarterly* 1991: 39(4):309–24.

100. Snetsinger W, Grabowski B. Use of humorous visuals to enhance computer-based instruction. 1993. Available at: http://www.eric.ed.gov/PDFS/ED370580.pdf

CHAPTER 4

1. Schonwetter DJ. An empirical comparison of two effective college teaching behaviors: Expressiveness and organization. Paper presented at the Annual Meeting of the American Educational Research Association. San Diego, CA, 1995:65.

2. Cohen PA. Student ratings of instruction and student achievement: A meta-analysis of multisection validity studies. *Review of Educational Research* 1981:51(3):281–309.

3. Feldman KA. The association between student ratings of specific instructional dimensions and student achievement: Refining and extending the synthesis of data from multisection validity studies. *Research in Higher Education* 1989:30(6):583–645.

4. Jahangiri L, Mucciolo TW. Characteristics of effective classroom teachers as identified by students and professionals: A qualitative study. *Journal of Dental Education* 2008:72(4):484–93.

5. Land ML. Vagueness and clarity in the classroom. In: Husen T, Postlethwaite TN, eds., *International Encyclopedia of Education: Research and Studies*. New York: Pergamon, 1985.

6. Chesebro JL, McCroskey JC. The relationship of teacher clarity and immediacy with student state receiver apprehension, affect, and cognitive learning. *Communication Education* 2001:50(1):59–68.

7. Kallison JM, Jr. Effects of lesson organization on achievement. *American Educational Research Journal* 1986:23(2):337–47.

8. Perry RP, Smart JC. *Effective teaching in higher education: Research and practice.* Bronx, NY: Agathon Press, 1997.

9. Bonner SE. Choosing teaching methods based on learning objectives: An integrative framework. *Issues in Accounting Education* 1999:14(1):11–38.

10. Van Driel JH, Beijaard D, Verloop N. Professional development and reform in science education: The role of teachers' practical knowledge. *Journal of Research in Science Teaching* 2001:38(2):137–58.

11. Spencer KJ, Schmelkin LP. Student perspectives on teaching and its evaluation. *Assessment & Evaluation in Higher Education* 2002:27(5):397–409.

12. Greimel-Fuhrmann B, Geyer A. Students' evaluation of teachers and instructional quality: Analysis of relevant factors based on empirical evaluation research. *Assessment & Evaluation in Higher Education* 2003:28(3):229–38.

13. Trigwell K, Shale S. Student learning and the scholarship of university teaching. *Studies in Higher Education* 2004:29(4):523–36.

14. Bloom BS. *Taxonomy of educational objectives, handbook I: Cognitive domain.* New York: David McKay, 1956.

15. Fink LD. *Creating significant learning experiences: An integrated approach to designing college courses.* San Francisco: Jossey-Bass, 2003.

16. Levine LE, Fallahi CR, Nicoll-Senft JM, Tessier JT, Watson CL, Wood RM. Creating significant learning experiences across disciplines. *College Teaching* 2008:56(4): 247–54.

17. Doutrich D, Hoeskel R, Wykoff L, Thiele J. Teaching teachers to teach with technology. *Journal of Continuing Education in Nursing* 2005:36(1):25–31.

18. Poldrack RA, Gabrieli JDE. Characterizing the neural mechanisms of skill learning and repetition priming: Evidence from mirror reading. *Brain* 2001:124(1):67.

19. Kiewra KA. Effects of repetition on recall and note-taking: Strategies for learning from lectures. *Journal of Educational Psychology* 1991:83(1):120–23.

20. Davis TM, Murrell PH. Turning teaching into learning. The role of student responsibility in the collegiate experience. ASHE-ERIC Higher Education Report No. 8. 1993.

21. David AP. Examining the relationship of personality and burnout in college students: The role of academic motivation. *Educational Measurement and Evaluation Review* 2010:1:90–104.

22. McDrury J, Alterio M. Achieving reflective learning using storytelling pathways. *Innovations in Education & Teaching International* 2001:38(1):63–73.

23. Rutledge PA, Mucciolo T, Bajaj G. *Special edition using Microsoft Office Power-Point 2007.* Indianapolis, IN: Que Publishing, 2007.

24. Rutledge PA, Mucciolo T, Grey J. *Special edition using Microsoft Office Power-Point 2003.* Indianapolis, IN: Que Publishing, 2003.

25. Bellamy K. Design standards for computer-generated teaching slides. *Journal of Visual Communication in Medicine* 1995:18(3):115–20.

26. Clark J. PowerPoint and pedagogy: Maintaining student interest in university lectures. *College Teaching* 2008:56(1):39–44.

27. Fry E. From lantern slides to image presentation systems: A discipline in transition. *Indiana Libraries* 2007:26(2):15–19.

28. Hillyard C, Thomas E. Students and teachers learning to see: Part 2—Using visual images in the college classroom to enhance the social context for learning. *College Teaching* 2008:56(2):74–77.

29. Niamtu Iii J. The power of PowerPoint. *Plastic and Reconstructive Surgery* 2001:108(2):466.

30. Rankin EL, Hoaas DJ. Teaching note: Does the use of computer-generated slide presentations in the classroom affect student performance and interest? *Eastern Economic Journal* 2001:27(3):355–66.

31. Thomas E, Place N, Hillyard C. Students and teachers learning to see: Part 1: Using visual images in the college classroom to promote students' capacities and skills. *College Teaching* 2008:56(1):23–27.

32. Webster J, Hackley P. Teaching effectiveness in technology-mediated distance learning. *Academy of Management Journal* 1997:40(6):1282–309.

33. Keller J. Killing me Microsoftly with PowerPoint. *Chicago Tribune*, January 5, 2003.

34. McDonald K. Points of view: PowerPoint in the classroom: Examining PowerPoint-lessness. *Life Sciences Education* 2004:3(3):160.

35. Brown AH, Benson B, Uhde AP. You're doing what with technology? An expose on "Jane Doe" college professor. *College Teaching* 2004:52(3):100–104.

36. DenBeste M. Power Point, technology and the web: More than just an overhead projector for the new century? *History Teacher* 2003:36(4):491–504.

37. Russell M, Bebell D, O'Dwyer L, O'Connor K. Examining teacher technology use. *Journal of Teacher Education* 2003:54(4):297–310.

38. Marcus A. The ten commandments of color: A tutorial. *Computer Graphics Today* 1986:3(11):7.

39. Valdez P, Mehrabian A. Effects of color on emotions. *Journal of Experimental Psychology* 1994:123(4):394.

40. Kaya N, Epps HH. Relationship between color and emotion: A study of college students. *College Student Journal* 2004:38(3):396–406.

41. Mucciolo T, Mucciolo R. *Purpose, movement, color: A strategy for effective presentations.* New York: MediaNet, Inc., 1999.

42. Yager D, Aquilante K, Plass R. High and low luminance letters, acuity reserve, and font effects on reading speed. *Vision Research* 1998:38(17):2527.

43. Hede A. An integrated model of multimedia effects on learning. *Journal of Educational Multimedia and Hypermedia* 2002:11(2):177–92.

44. Skiba DJ. Got large lecture hall classes? Use clickers. *Nursing Education Perspectives* 2006:27(5):278–80.

45. Astleitner H, Wiesner C. An integrated model of multimedia learning and motivation. *Journal of Educational Multimedia and Hypermedia* 2004:13(1):3–21.

46. Long PD, Ehrmann SC. Future of the learning space: Breaking out of the box. *EduCause Review* 2005:40(4):42.

47. Berliner DC. Learning about and learning from expert teachers. *International Journal of Educational Research* 2001:35(5):463–82.

48. Boice B. Classroom incivilities. *Research in Higher Education* 1996:453–86.

49. Rowland ML, Srisukho K. Dental students' and faculty members' perceptions of incivility in the classroom. *Journal of Dental Education* 2009:73(1):119.

50. Krueger AB. Economic considerations and class size. *The Economic Journal* 2003:113(485):34–63.

51. Hanushek EA. Assessing the effects of school resources on student achievement: An update. *Educational Evaluation and Policy Analysis* 1997:19(2):141–64.

52. Teven JJ. Teacher caring and classroom behavior: Relationships with student affect and perceptions of teacher competence and trustworthiness. *Communication Quarterly* 2007:55(4):433–50.

53. Meyers SA, Bender J, Hill EK, Thomas SY. How do faculty experience and respond to classroom conflict? *International Journal of Teaching and Learning in Higher Education* 2006:18(3):180–87.

54. Shelton JT, Elliott EM, Eaves SD, Exner AL. The distracting effects of a ringing cell phone: An investigation of the laboratory and the classroom setting. *Journal of Environmental Psychology* 2009:29(4):513–21.

CHAPTER 5

1. Mehrabian A. *Silent messages: Implicit communication of emotions and attitudes.* Belmont, CA: Wadsworth Publishing Company, 1971.

2. Jahangiri L, Mucciolo TW. Characteristics of effective classroom teachers as identified by students and professionals: A qualitative study. *Journal of Dental Education* 2008:72(4):484–93.

3. Trimboli A, Walker MB. Nonverbal dominance in the communication of affect: A myth? *Journal of Nonverbal Behavior* 1987:11(3):180–90.

4. Smith HA. Nonverbal communication in teaching. *Review of Educational Research* 1979:49(4):631–72.

5. Crumbley L, Henry B, Kratchman S. Students' perceptions of the teaching of college teaching. *Quality Assurance in Education* 2001:9(4):197–207.

6. Onwuegbuzie AJ, Witcher AE, Collins KMT, Filer JD, Weidmaier CD, Moore CW. Students' perceptions of characteristics of effective college teachers: A validity study of a teaching evaluation form using a mixed-methods analysis. *American Educational Research Journal* 2007:44(1):113.

7. De Gelder B. Towards the neurobiology of emotional body language. *Nature Reviews Neuroscience* 2006:7(3):242–49.

8. Meijer M. The contribution of general features of body movement to the attribution of emotions. *Journal of Nonverbal Behavior* 1989:13(4):247–68.

9. Coulson M. Attributing emotion to static body postures: Recognition accuracy, confusions, and viewpoint dependence. *Journal of Nonverbal Behavior* 2004:28(2):117–39.

10. Mehrabian A. Inference of attitudes from the posture, orientation, and distance of a communicator. *Journal of Consulting and Clinical Psychology* 1968:32(3):296–308.

11. Mehrabian A. Significance of posture and position in the communication of attitude and status relationships. *Psychological Bulletin* 1969:71(5):359.

12. Gorham J. The relationship between verbal teacher immediacy behaviors and student learning. *Communication Education* 1988:37(1):40–53.

13. Rutledge PA, Mucciolo T, Bajaj G. *Special edition using Microsoft Office Power-Point 2007.* Indianapolis, IN: Que Publishing, 2007.

14. Mucciolo T, Mucciolo R. *Purpose, movement, color: A strategy for effective presentations.* New York: MediaNet, Inc., 1999.

15. Khuwaileh AA. The role of chunks, phrases and body language in understanding co-ordinated academic lectures. *System* 1999:27(2):249–60.

16. Caso L, Maricchiolo F, Bonaiuto M, Vrij A, Mann S. The impact of deception and suspicion on different hand movements. *Journal of Nonverbal Behavior* 2006:30(1):1–19.

17. Rosip JC, Hall JA. Knowledge of nonverbal cues, gender, and nonverbal decoding accuracy. *Journal of Nonverbal Behavior* 2004:28(4):267–86.

18. Hulsmeyer BS, Bowling AK. Evaluating colleagues' classroom teaching effectiveness. *Nurse Educator* 1986:11(5):19–23.

19. Argyle M, Dean J. Eye-contact, distance and affiliation. *Sociometry* 1965:28(3):289–304.

20. Scherer KR, Banse R, Wallbott HG. Emotion inferences from vocal expression correlate across languages and cultures. *Journal of Cross-Cultural Psychology* 2001: 32(1):76–92.

21. Hammerschmidt K, Jürgens U. Acoustical correlates of affective prosody. *Journal of Voice* 2007:21(5):531–40.

22. Hanson HM, Chuang ES. Glottal characteristics of male speakers: Acoustic correlates and comparison with female data. *The Journal of the Acoustical Society of America* 1999:106:1064–77.

23. Titze IR. Physiologic and acoustic differences between male and female voices. *Journal of the Acoustical Society of America* 1989:85:1699–707.

24. Hanson HM. Glottal characteristics of female speakers: Acoustic correlates. *Journal of the Acoustical Society of America* 1997:101:466–81.

25. Mendoza E, Valencia N, Muñoz J, Trujillo H. Differences in voice quality between men and women: use of the long-term average spectrum (LTAS). *Journal of Voice* 1996:10(1):59–66.

26. Thorpe CW, Cala SJ, Chapman J, Davis PJ. Patterns of breath support in projection of the singing voice. *Journal of Voice* 2001:15(1):86.

27. Neal M. Academic register, hyperfluency, and the acquisition of academic discourse. Paper presented at the annual meeting of the 46th Conference on College Composition and Communication (23–25, March). Washington, DC, 1995.

28. Chesebro JL, McCroskey JC. The relationship of teacher clarity and immediacy with student state receiver apprehension, affect, and cognitive learning. *Communication Education* 2001:50(1):59–68.

29. Major RC, Fitzmaurice SF, Bunta F, Balasubramanian C. The effects of nonnative accents on listening comprehension: Implications for ESL assessment. *TESOL Quarterly* 2002:36(2):173–90.

30. Munro MJ, Derwing TM. Foreign accent, comprehensibility, and intelligibility in the speech of second language learners. *Language Learning* 1999:49(s1):285–310.

31. Lane H. Foreign accent and speech distortion. *Journal of the Acoustical Society of America* 1963:35:451–53.

32. Clark HH, Fox Tree JE. Using uh and um in spontaneous speaking. *Cognition* 2002:84(1):73–111.

33. Tree JEF. The effects of false starts and repetitions on the processing of subsequent words in spontaneous speech. *Journal of Memory and Language* 1995:34(6):709–38.

34. Arnold JE, Fagnano M, Tanenhaus MK. Disfluencies signal theee, um, new information. *Journal of Psycholinguistic Research* 2003:32:25–36.

35. Smith SM, Shaffer DR. Speed of speech and persuasion: Evidence for multiple effects. *Personality and Social Psychology Bulletin* 1995:21(10):1051.

36. Shuell TJ, Farber SL. Students perceptions of technology use in college courses. *Journal of Educational Computing Research* 2001:24(2):119–38.

37. Cassady JC. Student and instructor perceptions of the efficacy of computer-aided lectures in undergraduate university courses. *Journal of Educational Computing Research* 1998:19(2):175–89.

38. McDonald K. Points of view: PowerPoint in the classroom: Examining PowerPoint-lessness. *Life Sciences Education* 2004:3(3):160.

39. Keller J. Killing me Microsoftly with PowerPoint. *Chicago Tribune*, January 5, 2003.

40. Brown AH, Benson B, Uhde AP. You're doing what with technology? An expose on "Jane Doe" college professor. *College Teaching* 2004:52(3):100–104.

41. Russell M, Bebell D, O'Dwyer L, O'Connor K. Examining teacher technology use. *Journal of Teacher Education* 2003:54(4):297–310.

42. Rutledge PA, Mucciolo T, Grey J. *Special edition using Microsoft Office Power-Point 2003*. Indianapolis, IN: Que Publishing, 2003.

43. Bickford DJ, Wright DJ. Community: The hidden context for learning. In: Oblinger DG, ed. *Learning Spaces*. Boulder, CO: EduCause, 2006.

44. Webster J, Hackley P. Teaching effectiveness in technology-mediated distance learning. *Academy of Management Journal* 1997:40(6):1282–309.

45. Johnson SD, Aragon SR, Shaik N. Comparative analysis of learner satisfaction and learning outcomes in online and face-to-face learning environments. *Journal of Interactive Learning Research* 2000:11(1):29–49.

46. Perkins DN. What constructivism demands of the learner. *Educational Technology* 1991:31(9):19–21.

47. Savery JR, Duffy TM. Problem Based Learning: An instructional model and its constructivist framework. *Educational Technology* 1995:35:31–38.

48. Tynjälä PK. Towards expert knowledge? A comparison between a constructivist and a traditional learning environment in the university. *Educational Research* 1999:31:357–442.

49. Bonner SE. Choosing teaching methods based on learning objectives: An integrative framework. *Issues in Accounting Education* 1999:14(1):11–38.

50. Greimel-Fuhrmann B, Geyer A. Students' evaluation of teachers and instructional quality: Analysis of relevant factors based on empirical evaluation research. *Assessment & Evaluation in Higher Education* 2003:28(3):229–38.

51. Sheehan EP, Duprey T. Student evaluations of university teaching. *Journal of Instructional Psychology* 1999:26(3):1–7.

52. Weaver RR, Qi J. Classroom organization and participation: College students' perceptions. *Journal of Higher Education* 2005:76(5):570–601.

53. Flanders NA. *Basic teaching skills derived from a model of speaking and listening*. Teacher Education Division Publication Series. Report A72-19. San Francisco, CA: Far West Lab. for Educational Research and Development, 1972.

54. Flanders NA. Interaction analysis: A technique for quantifying teacher influence, 1970. Available at: http://www.eric.ed.gov/PDFS/ED088855.pdf

55. Murray HG. Teaching effectiveness in higher education. In: Smart JC, ed., *Higher education: Handbook of theory and research*. Vol. 7. New York: Agathon Press, 1991:135–72.

56. Skiba DJ. Got large lecture hall classes? Use Clickers. *Nursing Education Perspectives* 2006:27(5):278–80.

CHAPTER 6

1. Theall M, Abrami PC, Mets LA. *The student ratings debate: Are they valid? How can we best use them?* San Francisco: Jossey-Bass, 2001.

2. Glassick CE. Boyer's Expanded definitions of scholarship, the standards for assessing scholarship, and the elusiveness of the scholarship of teaching. *Academic Medicine* 2000:75:877–80.

3. Glassick CE, Huber MT, Maeroff GI. *Scholarship assessed: Evaluation of the professoriate*. Special Report. San Francisco, CA: Jossey Bass, 1997.

4. Boyer EL. Scholarship reconsidered: Priorities of the professoriate: Princeton, NJ: Princeton University Press, 1990.

5. Shulman L. The scholarship of teaching. *Change* 1999:31(5):11.

6. Shulman LS. Knowledge and teaching: Foundations of the new reform. *Harvard Educational Review* 1987:57(1):1–22.

7. Jahangiri L, Mucciolo TW. Presentation skills assessment tools. MedEdPORTAL (AAMC), 2010. Available at: https://www.mededportal.org/publication/7930.

8. Jahangiri L, Mucciolo TW. Characteristics of effective classroom teachers as identified by students and professionals: A qualitative study. *Journal of Dental Education* 2008:72(4):484–93.

9. Jahangiri L, Mucciolo TW, Choi M, Spielman AI. Assessment of teaching effectiveness in U.S. dental schools and the value of triangulation. *Journal of Dental Education* 2008:72(6):707–18.

10. The SPICE Model. Copyright 2010 by Leila Jahangiri and Tom Mucciolo. All Rights Reserved.

11. The SPICE Model Collector. Copyright 2010 by Leila Jahangiri and Tom Mucciolo. All Rights Reserved.

12. Berk RA. Survey of 12 strategies to measure teaching effectiveness. *International Journal of Teaching and Learning in Higher Education* 2005:17(1):48–62.

13. Bowen GA. Preparing a qualitative research-based dissertation: Lessons learned. *The Qualitative Report* 2005:10(2):208–22.

14. Drapeau M. Subjectivity in research: Why not? But. . . . *The Qualitative Report* 2002:7(3):1–14.

15. Felder R, Brent R. How to evaluate teaching. *Chem Eng Educ* 2004:38(3):202–4.

16. Golafshani N. Understanding reliability and validity in qualitative research. *The Qualitative Report* 2003:8(4):597–607.

17. Jick TD. Mixing qualitative and quantitative methods: Triangulation in action. *Administrative Science Quarterly* 1979:24(4):602–11.

Index

passion, 17, *18, 52, 112, 264, 270*; apologies and, 56–57; content and, 55–56, 57, *58*; credibility and, 54–55; definition of, 54; happiness and energy related to, 20; self-confidence and, *92–93*
PBL. *See* problem-based learning
peer assessment, 5, 7; method for, 13–14
performance, 105; definition of, 183; delivery in, 183–84; nonverbal, 183; process compared to, 115; Standard Evaluation of, *266*; of technology, 222; visible expressive behaviors for, 183, *184. See also* body language style; speaking style
performance skills, xvii, *184*; categorization of, 11, *11, 12*; learner preferences of, 185, *185*; strategies for, *255–57*; summary about, *255–57*
personal appearance, *19*, 26, *113, 264, 270*; affinity from, 105; attitude in, 105; BASIC principle for, 107; buttoned jackets in, 107–8; cameras and, 109; clothing in, 106–9; definition of, 104; distractions in, 107, 109–11; for environmental culture, 106–7; focusing on face in, 107–8; gender and, 106, 107–8; hair in, 108; inappropriate comments and, 110–11; learning environment and, 109–10; microphones in, 108–9; proximity for, 108; self-assessment of, 105; technology related to, 108–9
personality, 20, *264*
personality skills, xvii, *112–13*, 128; categorization of, 11, *11, 12*; key words about, 17, *18–19*
personality traits, 11–12, 20; across disciplines, 32. *See also specific traits*
perspectives, xvii; content and, 56–57
Peters, Tom, 259
philosophers, 3. *See also* constructivist philosophy
phonetics, 207
photographs, in visual design, 157
podcasts, *146*, 230; communication for, 231
podiums, 193

politically incorrect comments, 110–11
polleverywhere.com, 137
polling, 137, *146*, 245–46, *257*
positive reinforcement: caring from, 23–24; motivation and, *65*; rewards compared to, 24; as skill, 24; tardiness and, *25*
positivity, 45
power position, in body language style, 189
PowerPoint presentations, 151, 155, 163; benefits and limitations of, *144–45*; description of, 141; for interest, 141–42; motivation or, 62; polling program for, 137; quality of, *144–45*, 222–23
practical application: in content development, 125; in content organization, 122–23
preparation, *55*; against boredom, 62, *63*; intimidation or, *89*, 90; for lectures, 41–42
presence, *273*
presenters, 9
Presenter's Triangle: body language style and, *191*, 191–92, *201, 255*; technology and, *191*, 226–27
problem-based learning (PBL): benefits of, 238; description of, 237, *237*
problem solving: adaptive expertise for, 71–72; expertise and, *68*, 71; intellectual stimulation for, 82; logical connections and, 70–71; problem dissolving compared to, 71, 72
process: definition of, 115; of elimination, 134–35; opportunities for, 115–16; performance compared to, 115; Standard Evaluation of, *265*; of technology, 222. *See also* content
process skills, xvii, *181–82*; categorization of, 11, *11, 12*; feedback on, *116*, 117, *117*; priorities for, 117, *117*
professional learners, *277*; preferences of, 10, 12–13, *13*; self-confidence in, 86–87; in Standard Evaluation, *269*, 269–71, *270*
professionalism, 104; without happiness, 37–38; smiling and, 43–44

About the Authors

Dr. Leila Jahangiri completed her BDS at King's College, University of London, England; followed by her DMD, Certificate in Prosthodontics, and Masters of Medical Sciences (MMSc) degrees from Harvard School of Dental Medicine.

Since 1991, she has been an active clinician, researcher, and teacher with a continuing history of grants and peer-reviewed publications. She was on the original team that helped to convert Harvard School of Dental Medicine's curriculum to problem-based learning (PBL). Having taught undergraduates and residents at Harvard, the University of Medicine and Dentistry of New Jersey, and New York University College of Dentistry, her expertise has evolved into developing innovative curriculum and focusing on teaching effectiveness.

Currently, she is a Clinical Associate Professor, and since 2002 has been the Chair of the Department of Prosthodontics at New York University College of Dentistry. She is an active member of many professional organizations, serving on advisory boards and strategic education committees.

Tom Mucciolo is President of MediaNet, Inc., a Presentation Skills Company in New York City (www.medianet-ny.com). As a recognized industry expert regarding visual communications, he has served as a presentation skills consultant for major corporations since 1985, concentrating on the scripting, visual design, and delivery skills associated with presentations.

Tom is the co-author of five books: *Purpose, Movement, Color* (MediaNet, Inc.), and four *Special Edition Using Microsoft PowerPoint* editions: 2000, 2002, 2003, and 2007 (Macmillan/Pearson/MediaNet). Tom is the designer and featured speaker on two interactive CDs (*Mechanics-Basic Skills, Media-Design Skills*), covering delivery and design skills. He is chiefly responsible for the development of MediaNet's ShowSTARTER®, an artificial intelligence software program for designing business visuals.

In 2005, Tom joined the faculty of New York University, as an adjunct assistant professor, working with Dr. Leila Jahangiri, his co-author and colleague at NYU, to complete extensive research on teaching/presentation effectiveness. He has collaborated on several peer-reviewed journal articles on teaching effectiveness, evaluation, and scholarship.

CPSIA information can be obtained at www.ICGtesting.com
Printed in the USA
BVOW031250051111

275162BV00003BA/1/P